ESPAÑOL ESENCIAL 3

Fundamentals of Spanish

Stephen L. Levy

Former Head, Foreign Language Department
Roslyn (New York) Public Schools

AMSCO SCHOOL PUBLICATIONS, INC.,

a division of Perfection Learning®

**Para las familias Solórzano y De la Barreda,
con muchísimo afecto y agradecimiento**

Text and Cover Design by A Good Thing, Inc.
Illustrations by Felipe Galindo

Please visit our Web sites at:
www.amscopub.com and *www.perfectionlearning.com*

When ordering this book, please specify *either* **13486** *or*
ESPAÑOL ESENCIAL 3: FUNDAMENTALS OF SPANISH

ISBN 978-1-56765-493-6

Printed in the United States of America

11 12 13 14 15 16   18 17 16 15 14 13

Preface

Español Esencial 3 has been prepared for students who are in their third year of Spanish language study. It offers a comprehensive review and thorough understanding of the elements of the Spanish language generally covered in a third-year course. It is designed to be used as a complement or supplement to any basal textbook series, or solely for review and additional practice.

ORGANIZATION

Español Esencial 3 contains 20 chapters organized around related grammar topics. For ease of study and use, explanations of the grammatical concepts are presented concisely and clearly and are followed by examples that illustrate the concept. Care has been taken to avoid the use of complex structural elements and to present the practice exercises through contexts found in daily usage of the language.

EXERCISES

To maximize efficiency in learning, the exercises follow the grammatical explanations and examples. The exercises, which are set in functional and realistic contexts, provide meaningful practice of the concept and lead the student to use the language in a real-life communicative manner. Many of the exercises are also personalized to stimulate original student response and meaningful assimilation and internalization of the concepts under study. Based on linguistic or visual cues, the exercises lend themselves to both oral and written practice of the language. Each chapter contains an exercise designed for oral communication by the student working in pairs. This exercise is open-ended to provide students with the opportunity to express themselves and to voice their personal opinions in Spanish, within the scope of the concept under study. Many chapters also include a reading passage in which comprehension is checked through a multiple-choice exercise. The content of these readings is varied and challenging and includes use of the concepts under study in the chapter.

VOCABULARY

The vocabulary used in this book has been carefully controlled and is systematically recycled throughout subsequent chapters. The vocabulary topics are those most frequently found in a third-year Spanish course. Where more extended or broader vocabulary is used in an exercise, it is preceded by **Para Expresarse Mejor**, in which the vocabulary for the exercise is presented. A Spanish-English Vocabulary is included at the back of the book.

FLEXIBILITY AND OTHER FEATURES

The topical organization and the concise explanations followed by examples found in each chapter enable the teacher to follow any sequence suitable to the needs of the students and the objectives of the course. This flexibility is facilitated by the detailed table of contents at the front of the book. The Appendix features complete model verb tables and the principal parts of common irregular verbs that are covered in the book, as well as rules of Spanish punctuation, syllabication, and pronunciation.

Students and teachers will find the organization and layout of the book to be easy to follow and suitable and flexible to their individual needs. Its basic design is to facilitate and provide communicative use of the language while mastering the basic structures that are needed for meaningful communication to occur.

The Author

Contents

CHAPTER 1
The Present Tense

1.   Uses of the Present Tense

a. The present tense may have the following meanings in English:

El equipo *gana*.	*The team wins (is winning).*
Van al cine.	*They go (are going) to the movies.*
¿Hablas francés?	*Do you speak French?*
No, no *hablo* francés.	*No, I don't speak French.*

b. The present tense is often used instead of the future tense to ask for directions or to refer to an action that will take place in the immediate future.

Regreso después.	*I'll return afterwards.*
¿Lo compro ahora?	*Shall I buy it now?*
¿Dónde lo pongo?	*Where shall I put it?*
Hablamos más tarde.	*We'll speak later.*

c. The construction *hace* + time expression + *que* + present tense is used to express an action or event that began in the past and continues in the present. The question is expressed by *¿Cuánto tiempo hace que…* + present tense? or *¿Hace cuánto tiempo que …* + present tense?

Hace dos años que estudio el español.	*I have been studying Spanish for two years.*
Hace una hora que esperas noticias.	*You have been waiting for news for an hour.*
¿Cuánto tiempo hace que conduces?	*How long have you been driving?*

> NOTE: The present tense + *desde hace* + time expression is also used to express a past action or event that continues in the present. It's corresponding question is formed by *Desde cuándo…* + present tense.
>
> | | |
> |---|---|
> | **Espero noticias desde hace una hora.** | *I've been waiting for news for an hour.* |
> | **¿Desde cuándo conduces?** | *How long have you been driving?* |

2.   Forms of the Present Tense

a. Regular Verbs

1. The present tense of regular verbs is formed by dropping the infinitive ending (*-ar, -er, -ir*) and adding the following endings to the stem:

	comprar *to buy*	prometer *to promise*	abrir *to open*
yo	compro	prometo	abro
tú	compras	prometes	abres
él, ella, Ud.	compra	promete	abre
nosotros, -as	compramos	prometemos	abrimos
vosotros, -as	compráis	prometéis	abrís
ellos, ellas, Uds.	compran	prometen	abren

2. In a negative statement, *no* follows the subject and goes immediately before the verb.

    Yo *no* compro pan.   *I don't buy bread.*

3. In a question, the subject usually follows the verb.

    ¿Prometes (*tú*) decir la verdad?   *Do you promise to tell the truth?*

    No abren *ellos* la tienda a la una?   *Don't they open the store at one o'clock?*

NOTE: Subject pronouns are generally omitted, unless they are required for clarity or for emphasis.

    Compramos útiles.   *We are buying school supplies.*

    ¿Abre *ella* los regalos ahora?   *Is she opening the gifts now?*

Presente

EJERCICIO A   **Todos ayudan en casa.**   La señora Villarreal explica cómo su casa funciona como una compañía. Exprese la función de cada miembro de la familia.

EJEMPLO: Enrique / sacar la basura   Enrique **saca** la basura.

1. Estelita y Carmen / quitar la mesa   _Estila y carmen quitan la_

2. la abuela / confeccionar los postres   _la abula confecionalos postres nes_

3. el señor Villarreal / comprar la comida   El señor villareal compra la comi

4. la abuela y yo / preparar la comida   la abuela y _____

5. Alicia / lavar los platos   _____

    lava
6. Freddy / pasar la aspiradora   _____

    pasa
7. tú / sacudir los muebles   _____
    sacudepste

8. yo / barrer el piso   _____

EJERCICIO B   **El parque de atracciones**   Jorge habla con un primo y recuerda cómo ellos y unos amigos pasan un día en el parque de atracciones. Exprese lo que Jorge dice.

PARA EXPRESARSE MEJOR

el aparato *ride, apparatus*	**la raspadilla** *snow cone*
el carrusel *merry-go-round*	**el salón de espejos** *hall of mirrors*
la casa encantada *haunted house*	**las sillas voladoras** *flying swings*
la montaña rusa *rollercoaster*	

EJEMPLO: yo / subir en todos los aparatos   Yo **subo** en todos los aparatos.

1. Vicente / comer muchas raspadillas

   _____

2.. Sarita y Mirta / prometer subir en la montaña rusa

   _____

3. tú y Alfredo / recibir premios en los juegos de suerte

   _____

4. Clara / esperar en un banco

   _____

5. Lupe y yo / temer entrar en la casa encantada

   _____

6. tú / insistir en subir en el carrusel

   _____

7. yo / usar el boleto de Antonio para subir en las sillas voladoras

   _____

8. Uds. / pasar mucho tiempo en el salón de espejos

   _____

EJERCICIO C   **Necesitamos trabajar.**   Jenny y sus amigas solicitan trabajo para el verano. Complete el párrafo con la forma correcta de los verbos entre paréntesis.

Jenny y sus amigas ___desea___ ganar dinero durante las vacaciones de verano porque
                      1. (desear)

lo ___necesito___ para su primer año en la universidad. Ellas ___leen___ los
      2. (necesitar)   3. (leer)

anuncios en el periódico cada domingo y Jenny ___respondio___ a muchos anuncios.
                                                   4. (responder)

Ella ___espera___ recibir muchas ofertas de trabajo. Para prepararse para una entrevista,
        5. (esperar)

sus amigas le ___ayudan___ con muchas preguntas. Ella también ___deben___
                  6. (ayudar)   7. (deber)

aprender muchos programas en la computadora y ___toma___ un curso especial.
                                                    8. (tomar)

Cuando ella _____recibio_____ una contestación a su solicitud, _____abrio_____ el sobre
         9. (recibir)   10. (abrir)

con mucho miedo. Ahora ella _____busca_____ la ayuda de sus padres porque ella
                                     11. (buscar)

_____debe_____ presentarse a una entrevista el lunes próximo a las nueve y media.
  12. (deber)

EJERCICIO D   **Ahora no**   Daniel nunca hace las cosas cuando debe hacerlas. Diga cuándo él va a hacer estas cosas, usando una de las siguientes expresiones.

PARA EXPRESARSE MEJOR

después   *afterwards*

esta mañana (tarde)   *this morning (afternoon)*

esta noche   *tonight*

mañana   *tomorrow*

más tarde   *later*

EJEMPLO: sacar al perro   **Saco** al perro **más tarde.**

1. guardar la ropa

   Guardare las cosas despues

2. escribir una carta

   escribo la carta mañana

3. llamar a su primo

   llamo a mi primo mas tarde

4. terminar la tarea

   Terminare la tarea mañana

5. acompañar a su hermana

   acompano a mi hermana mas tarde

6. apagar la televisión

   apago la television mas tarde

EJERCICIO E   **Una entrevista**   Laura asiste a la inauguración de una exposición de pinturas en una galería de arte. Entrevistan al público para un programa de televisión. Exprese las preguntas que hace el reportero y las respuestas de las personas.

EJEMPLO: asistir a las exposiciones de arte   (*diez años*)

    ¿Cuánto tiempo hace que Ud. asiste a las exposiciones de arte?
    OR
    ¿Desde cuándo asiste Ud. a las exposiciones de arte?

    Hace diez años que asisto a las exposiciones de arte.
    OR
    Asisto a las exposiciones de arte **desde hace diez años.**

1. visitar las galerías de arte   (*cinco años*)

   _____

   _____

2. coleccionar obras de arte   (*tres años*)

   _____

   _____

3. estudiar las artes plásticas   (*seis meses*)

   _____

   _____

4. buscar pintores nuevos   (*un mes*)

   _____

   _____

5. leer las reseñas de las exposiciones en el periódico   (*dos años*)

   _____

   _____

6. descubrir nuevos estilos de pintar   (*cinco semanas*)

   _____

   _____

b. Irregular Verbs

1. The following verbs are irregular only in the *yo*-form of the present tense.

VERB	PRESENT TENSE
caber *to fit, to be room for*	*quepo*, cabes, cabe, cabemos, cabéis, caben
caer *to fall*	*caigo*, caes, cae, caemos, caéis, caen
conocer *to know, to be acquainted with*	*conozco*, conoces, conoce, conocemos, conocéis, conocen
dar *to give*	*doy*, das, da, damos, dais, dan
hacer *to make, to do*	*hago*, haces, hace, hacemos, hacéis, hacen
poner *to put, to place*	*pongo*, pones, pone, ponemos, ponéis, ponen
saber *to know*	*sé*, sabes, sabe, sabemos, sabéis, saben
salir *to go out, to leave*	*salgo*, sales, sale, salimos, salís, salen
traducir *to translate*	*traduzco*, traduces, traduce, traducimos, traducís, traducen
traer *to bring*	*traigo*, traes, trae, traemos, traéis, traen
valer *to be worth*	*valgo*, vales, vale, valemos, valéis, valen
ver *to see*	*veo*, ves, ve, vemos, veis, ven

NOTE: 1. Verbs like *conocer:*

agradecer *to thank*	**nacer** *to be born*
aparecer *to appear*	**obedecer** *to obey*
carecer *to lack*	**ofrecer** *to offer*
crecer *to grow*	**parecer** *to seem*
desaparecer *to disappear*	**permanecer** *to remain*
establecer *to establish*	**pertenecer** *to belong*
merecer *to deserve*	**reconocer** *to recognize*

2. Verbs like *poner:*

componer *to compose*	**imponer** *to impose*
disponer *to dispose*	**oponer(se)** *to oppose*
exponer *to expose*	**proponer** *to propose*

3. Verbs like *traducir:*

conducir *to conduct, lead; to drive*	**reducir** *to reduce*
producir *to produce*	

4. Other verbs like *traer:*

atraer *to attract*	**distraer** *to distract*
contraer *to catch, get*	

5. Most verbs ending in *-cer* or *-cir* that have a vowel directly before the *c*, change the *c* to *zc* in the *yo*-form, for example: *conocer* and *traducir.*

EJERCICIO F   **Diálogos breves** Complete los diálogos que Carlos oyó mientras esperaba un tren en el metro durante la hora pico. En cada grupo, use la forma correcta del verbo de la primera frase.

EJEMPLO: —¿Caben más personas en este tren?
            —Creo que **cabe** una persona más.
            —Yo lo dudo. Yo no **quepo** allí.

1. —¿Das dinero a los pobres?

    —Mi abuela siempre se lo _____ .

    —Yo se lo _____ de vez en cuando.

2. —¿Sales con Elvira esta noche?

    —Nosotros no _____ esta noche.

    —Yo no _____ tampoco esta noche.

3. —Empezó a llover. ¿Traes paraguas?

    —Sí, yo _____ uno en la bolsa.

    —¡Voy a mojarme; yo no _____ ninguno!

4. —¿Conocen los padres de Susie a su novio?

   —Sí, creo que lo _____ .

   —Yo aún no lo _____ .

5. —Dicen que mi ayudante trabaja bien y merece un aumento de sueldo.

   —Tú trabajas muchísimo. ¿No _____ tú un aumento también?

   —Claro, yo lo _____ más que ella.

6. —¿Qué haces el fin de semana?

   —Yo _____ todos los quehaceres de la casa.

   —¡Lástima! Yo no _____ nada. Mis hijos los _____ .

7. —¿Saben Uds. adónde vamos?

   —Sí, nosotros _____ la dirección de la tienda.

   —Me alegro porque yo no _____ nada.

8. —¿Ven Uds. con frecuencia a la familia de tu marido?

   —No, nosotros no los _____ a menudo. Viven en otro estado.

   —Tienes suerte. Yo _____ a mis suegros casi a diario.

9. —¿Traduces del francés al inglés mientras lees?

   —No, yo ya no _____ .

   —¡Qué bueno! Mi hermano _____ todo lo que lee.

10. —¿Te agradece José Luis todo lo que haces por él?

    —Sí, él siempre me lo _____ .

    —Yo te lo _____ también.

EJERCICIO G   **Preguntas** Jeremy asiste a una fiesta acompañado de la familia costarricense con que vive. Conteste las preguntas que le hacen otros invitados a la fiesta. Use la información dada en paréntesis en las respuestas.

1. ¿Conoces a muchas personas en esta fiesta? (*no*)

   _____

2. ¿Sabes hablar y escribir en español? (*un poco*)

   _____

3. ¿Careces de amistades en este país? (*no*)

   _____

4. ¿Sales mucho con los hijos de la familia? (*sí*)

   _____

5. ¿Permaneces en este país por mucho tiempo? (*3 meses*)

_____

6. ¿Conduces un carro en tu país? (*no*)

_____

7. ¿Obedeces las reglas de la familia? (*siempre*)

_____

8. ¿Propones invitar a la familia a visitar tu país? (*sí*)

_____

9. ¿Das lecciones de inglés a los hijos de la familia? (*a veces*)

_____

10. ¿Agradeces la amabilidad de la familia? (*sí*)

_____

2. Other verbs irregular in the present tense.

VERB	PRESENT TENSE
decir *to say, to tell*	*digo, dices, dice,* decimos, decís, *dicen*
estar *to be*	estoy, estás, está, estamos, estáis, están
haber *to have* (aux.)	he, *has, ha,* hemos, habéis, *han*
ir *to go*	voy, vas, va vamos, vais, *van*
oír *to hear*	*oigo, oyes, oye,* oímos, oís, *oyen*
ser *to be*	soy, eres, es, somos, sois, *son*
tener *to have*	*tengo, tienes, tiene,* tenemos, tenéis, *tienen*
venir *to come*	*vengo, vienes, viene,* venimos, venís, *vienen*

NOTE: 1. Verbs like *tener:*

      contener *to contain*   **mantener** *to maintain*

      detener *to detain*   **obtener** *to obtain*

      entretener *to entertain*   **sostener** *to sustain*

  2. Verbs like *venir:*

      convenir *to convene, to agree*

      prevenir *to prevent*

EJERCICIO H	**Dime lo que oyes y te diré dónde estás.** Silvia trata de entretener a un grupo de niños con un juego. Combine los sonidos de la primera columna con los lugares de la segunda columna y escriba qué oye cada persona y dónde está.

un avión
el tráfico
las olas
el canto de los pájaros
aplausos
el silbido del viento

la ciudad
el campo
el teatro
las montañas
la playa
cerca del aeropuerto

EJEMPLO: el mugido de las vacas   una granja
Miriam **oye** los mugidos de las vacas; **está** en una granja.

1. Nicolás _____ .

2. Tú _____ .

3. Emma y yo _____ .

4. Tony y Paco _____ .

5. Yo _____ .

6. Diana _____ .

EJERCICIO I   **Causa y efecto** Diga lo que tienen y lo que va a hacer cada una de las personas.

EJEMPLO: Lola / tener mucha sed / ir a tomar una limonada
Lola **tiene** mucha sed y **va** a tomar una limonada.

1. Gregorio / tener sueño / ir a acostarse

_____

2. yo / tener frío / ir a ponerme un suéter

_____

3. las chicas / tener antojo de algo dulce / ir a comer un helado

_____

4. tú / tener mucha prisa / ir a apresurarte

_____

5. Jeff y yo / tener ganas de ver una película / ir al cine

_____

6. Elsa / tener dolor de muela / ir a ver al dentista

_____

EJERCICIO J   **Fiestas en familia** Los miembros de la familia Orozco van a pasar las fiestas de fin de año juntos en la casa de los abuelos, pero no vienen juntos. Diga cuándo viene cada uno.

EjEMPLO: Patricia y su familia / el lunes   Patricia y su familia **vienen** el lunes.

1. Fernando y Luis / el sábado   _____

2. yo / el martes por la noche   _____

3. Aniluz / el miércoles   _____

4. los tíos / el martes por la mañana   _____

5. tú / el lunes por la tarde   _____

6. Javier y yo / el domingo   _____

EJERCICIO K   **Así son mis amigos.**   Paula describe a sus amigos y a sí misma. Exprese lo que ella dice.

EjEMPLO: Alma / alto y fuerte.   Alma **es alta** y fuerte.

1. Graciela / inteligente y serio   _____

2. Ralph y yo / cómico y divertido   _____

3. tú / creativo e inteligente   _____

4. yo / amigable y conservador   _____

5. Dalia / dulce y bondadoso   _____

6. José y Linda / sensitivo y bueno   _____

EJERCICIO L   **Una conferencia telefónica**   Complete la conferencia telefónica entre Víctor su amigo Pedro.

VÍCTOR: Diga. ¿Quién _____ ?
          (hablar)

PEDRO: _____ yo, Pedro. ¿Qué me _____ ?
          (ser)   (decir)

VÍCTOR: Todo _____ muy bien. ¿Y tú?
                 (estar)

PEDRO: Todo bien, también, gracias. ¿ _____ ocupado?
                                          (estar)

VÍCTOR: No, no _____ nada. Yo _____ el noticiero en la televisión.
                  (hacer)   (ver)

PEDRO: Yo _____ hacerte una pregunta. ¿ _____ (tú) al partido en
             (desear)   (ir)
          el estadio mañana?

VÍCTOR: Yo no _____ porque no _____ boleto y ellos _____
                  (saber)   (tener)   (decir)
          que todos los boletos _____ agotados.
                                  (estar)

PEDRO: Precisamente por eso te _____ ahora. Mi hermano no _____
(llamar) (tener)

ganas de ir al partido mañana y él me _____ a dar su boleto. Lo único
(ir)

_____ que yo no _____ transporte.
(ser) (tener)

VÍCTOR: Yo te _____ tu invitación. Mañana mi padre _____ que
(agradecer) (tener)

usar el tren y nosotros _____ su carro. Yo _____ .
(tener) (conducir)

PEDRO: Perfecto. Yo _____ a tu casa a eso de las once y media. Yo
(venir)

_____ una ruta rápida de tu casa para llegar al estadio.
(conocer)

VÍCTOR: Me _____ un plan ideal. Tú _____ el estacionamiento del
(parecer) (pagar)

carro y yo _____ los refrescos.
(pagar)

PEDRO: _____ bien. Nos _____ mañana.
(estar) (ver)

VÍCTOR: Adiós.

PEDRO: Hasta mañana.

EJERCICIO M   **Yo soy ...**   En su clase de español todos los alumnos tienen que presentarse a la clase. Para preparar esta tarea, la profesora dio las siguientes preguntas. Prepare las respuestas a las preguntas.

1. ¿Cómo te llamas?

_____

2. ¿Cuáles son algunas características de tu personalidad?

_____

3. ¿Cuáles son algunos de tus intereses?

_____

4. ¿Adónde vas con tus amigos los fines de semana?

_____

5. ¿Qué haces cuando no tienes planes con tus amigos?

_____

6. ¿Por qué estudias el español?

_____

7. ¿Qué esperas lograr este año?

_____

8. ¿Qué tienes que hacer para lograr tu meta?

_____

| EJERCICIO N |

La escuela como recuerdo   ¿Es la escuela sólo un edificio o simboliza algo más? ¿Por qué ocupa la escuela un lugar especial en el corazón de muchas personas? ¿Importa la arquitectura del edificio? ¿Recuerda Ud. los días felices (y/o tristes) de la escuela primaria, intermedia o secundaria? ¿Por qué? Cuando Ud. visita su antigua escuela, ¿corresponde ésta a los recuerdos que Ud. conserva en su memoria? ¿De qué cambios se da cuenta? ¿A qué o a quién(es) debe Ud. los recuerdos de su vida escolar?

Escriba un ensayo de unas cien palabras en el que reflexiona sobre su vida escolar. Incluya los datos y acontecimientos necesarios para explicar sus memorias de la vida escolar.

_____
_____
_____
_____
_____
_____
_____
_____
_____
_____
_____
_____
_____
_____
_____
_____

CHAPTER 2
Present Tense of Stem-Changing Verbs and Verbs with Spelling Changes

1. Stem-Changing Verbs*

a. Stem-changing verbs ending in *-ar* or *-er* change the stem vowel in the present tense as follows: *e* to *ie* and *o* to *ue* in all forms except those for *nosotros* and *vosotros*.

	cerrar to close	querer to want, to wish; to love	contar to count; to tell	mover to move
yo	cierro	quiero	cuento	muevo
tú	cierras	quieres	cuentas	mueves
él, ella, Ud.	cierra	quiere	cuenta	mueve
nosotros, -as	cerramos	queremos	contamos	movemos
vosotros, -as	cerráis	queréis	contáis	movéis
ellos, ellas, Uds.	cierran	quieren	cuentan	mueven

1. Verbs like *cerrar* and *querer*:

acertar *to be on target, to guess right* **encerrar** *to lock in, to contain*
apretar *to tighten, to squeeze* **entender** *to understand*
ascender *to ascend; to promote* **gobernar** *to govern*
atravesar *to cross* **helar** *to freeze*
comenzar *to begin* **nevar** *to snow*
confesar *to confess* **pensar** *to think*
defender *to defend* **perder** *to lose*
descender *to descend* **quebrar** *to break*
despertar(se) *to awaken; to wake up* **remendar** *to patch, to mend*
empezar *to begin* **sentar(se)** *to seat, to sit down*
encender *to light; to ignite*

2. Verbs like *contar* and *mover*:

acordarse (de) *to remember* **jugar (ue)** *to play (games, sports)*
acostar(se) *to put to bed; to go to bed* **llover** *to rain*
almorzar *to eat lunch* **morder** *to bite*
conmover *to move (emotionally)* **mostrar** *to show*
costar *to cost* **oler (hue)** *to smell*
devolver *to return, to give back* **poder** *to be able*
doler *to ache, to pain* **recordar** *to remember*
encontrar *to find, to meet* **renovar** *to remodel, to renew*

---

*All stem-changing verbs are identified in the vocabulary lists by the type of change (*ie, ue, i, y, í, ú*) after the verb. For example: *pedir (i)*.

resolver   *to solve; to resolve*   **volar**   *to fly*

soler   *to be in the habit of, to be accustomed to*   **volver**   *to return*

tronar   *to thunder*

EJERCICIO A   **Todos hacen algo.**   Exprese lo que hacen las siguientes personas.

EJEMPLO: la abuela / contar un cuento
La abuela **cuenta** un cuento.

1. Julián y Rosita / almorzar en un café al aire libre

_____

2. los comerciantes / cerrar las tiendas

_____

3. Felipe / acertar la respuesta a una adivinanza

_____

4. yo / atravesar el puente a pie

_____

5. los ancianos / jugar al dominó en el parque

_____

6. tú / volar en un helicóptero

_____

7. mi padre y yo / resolver un problema mecánico

_____

8. Alicia / devolver un videocasete

_____

EJERCICIO B   **¿Te fijas en eso?**   Exprese lo que Claudia dice cuando su amiga Linda le hace un comentario. Use la sugerencia dada en paréntesis.

EJEMPLO: LINDA: Hoy es el cumpleaños de Nilda.

   CLAUDIA: Su novio nunca **recuerda** la fecha.
                  (su novio / nunca recordar la fecha)

1. LINDA: La señora Valera prepara pasteles ricos.

   CLAUDIA: _____
                  (su cocina / siempre oler a canela)

2. LINDA: Yo nunca encuentro mis cosas cuando las necesito.

   CLAUDIA: _____
                  (tus hermanas / mover tus cosas de un lugar a otro)

3. LINDA: Gladys está muy triste y descontenta en el trabajo.

   CLAUDIA: _____
                  (su jefe / no recomendar un aumento de sueldo para ella)

4. LINDA: Ahora tu mamá sólo usa vasos desechables de plástico.

   CLAUDIA: _____
   (mis hermanos y yo / quebrar los vasos de vidrio)

5. LINDA: Yo tengo muchas ganas de tocar la guitarra.

   CLAUDIA: _____
   (cuándo / tú / comenzar la clase de guitarra)

6. LINDA: Otra vez se escapó el perrito de Lucy del jardín.

   CLAUDIA: _____
   (ellos / nunca cerrar la reja del jardín)

EJERCICIO C   **El horario** Ud. llama a la línea de información de los ferrocarriles de Madrid. Complete las frases con la forma correcta del verbo entre paréntesis.

OPERADOR: Buenos días, Ferrocarriles Nacionales. ¿En qué _____ servirle?
            (poder)

UD.:   Yo _____ información sobre el horario de los trenes que van de
            (querer)
            Madrid a Bilbao.

OPERADOR: ¿Cuándo _____ Ud. viajar?
            (pensar)

UD.:   Yo _____ salir pasado mañana muy temprano por la mañana y
            (pensar)
            _____ pasar tres días allí.
            (querer)

OPERADOR: El servicio _____ a las cinco de la mañana.
            (comenzar)

UD.:   ¿Y cuánto _____ los boletos de ida y vuelta?
            (costar)

OPERADOR: El boleto _____ setenta euros. ¿ _____ Ud. comprarlo
            (costar)   *(querer)*
            ahora mismo?

UD.:   Yo no _____ mi tarjeta de crédito en este momento.
            (encontrar)
            ¿ _____ Ud. esperar ahora o yo _____ a llamar más tarde?
            (poder)   *(volver)*

OPERADOR: Yo no _____ esperar ahora porque hay otras llamadas.
            (poder)
            Ud. _____ llamar después. Hay muchos asientos disponibles en el tren.
            (poder)

UD.:   Gracias. Yo _____ a llamar más tarde.
            (volver)

EJERCICIO D   **Una rutina** Conteste las preguntas que le hace un amigo. Use las sugerencias entre paréntesis.

1. ¿A qué hora te despiertas los fines de semana? *(8:00)*

_____

2. ¿Quién te despierta?   (*mi padre*)

    _____

3. ¿Sueles pasar los fines de semana en compañía de tus amigos?   (*sí*)

    _____

4. ¿Qué suelen Uds. hacer?   (*ver una película*)

    _____

5. ¿Dónde almuerzas cuando sales con tus amigos?   (*un café del centro comercial*)

    _____

6. ¿Atraviesas muchas calles para llegar al centro commercial?   (*sí*)

    _____

7. ¿Puedes llegar allí en transporte público?   (*no*)

    _____

8. ¿Te acuerdas de llamar a tus papás cuando vas a llegar tarde?   (*sí*)

    _____

9. ¿Comienzas a aprender a conducir?   (*sí*)

    _____

10. ¿A qué hora te acuestas los fines de semana?   (*medianoche*)

    _____

> **b.** Stem-changing verbs ending in *-ir* change the stem vowel in the present tense as follows: *e* to *ie*, *o* to *ue*, or *e* to *i* in all forms, except those for *nosotros* and *vosotros*.

	sentir to regret, to feel sorry	dormir to sleep	medir to measure
yo	siento	duermo	mido
tú	sientes	duermes	mides
él, ella, Ud.	siente	duerme	mide
nosotros, -as	sentimos	dormimos	medimos
vosotros, -as	sentís	dormís	medís
ellos, ellas, Uds.	sienten	duermen	miden

1. Verbs like *sentir*:

    advertir *to notify, to warn*   **mentir** *to lie*

    consentir *to consent*   **preferir** *to prefer*

    convertir *to convert*   **referir** *to recount; to refer*

    divertirse *to enjoy oneself, to have a good time*   **sentirse** *to feel (well, ill)*

    hervir *to boil*

2. Verbs like *dormir*:

    dormirse *to fall asleep*   **morir(se)** *to die*

3. Verbs like *medir:*

despedirse (de) *to take leave (of),*   **reñir** *to quarrel, to scold*
  to say goodbye (to)   **repetir** *to repeat*
gemir *to groan, to moan*   **servir** *to serve*
impedir *to prevent*   **sonreír(se)** *to smile*
pedir *to ask for, to request*   **vestir(se)** *to dress (oneself)*
reír(se) *to laugh*

EJERCICIO E   **Preferencias** Diga las preferencias de cada persona referente a la comida.

EJEMPLO: Elsa / una ensalada grande   Elsa **prefiere** una ensalada grande.

1. Esteban / la comida rápida   _____

2. yo / las sopas muy calientes   _____

3. Vicente e Irma / la comida española   _____

4. tú / los postres muy dulces   _____

5. Adela / las salsas picantes   _____

6. Emilio y yo / la comida japonesa   _____

EJERCICIO F   **Reacciones** Cada persona reacciona de manera distinta en la misma situación. Use la forma correcta del verbo entre paréntesis y exprese la reacción de cada persona en varias situaciones.

EJEMPLO: El señor está perdido y no encuentra la ruta.
          El señor **pide** instrucciones en una gasolinera.
          (pedir instrucciones en una gasolinera)

1. La madre pierde la paciencia porque su hijo no le hace caso.

   _____
   (reñir al hijo)

2. Los amigos pasan el día en la playa tomando el sol y nadando en el mar.

   _____
   (divertirse)

3. A la abuela no le interesa el programa en la televisión.

   _____
   (dormirse en el sofá)

4. A nosotros nos gustan mucho los cuentos de Fernando. Él es muy cómico.

   _____
   (reír a carcajadas)

5. Cuando hay invitados para cenar, Diana siempre le ayuda a su mamá.

   _____
   (servir la sopa)

6. Alberto sigue una dieta sana y goza de buena salud.

   _____
   (sentirse bien)

7. A mí me gustan muchísimo los camarones a la parrilla.

   _____
   (repetir el plato)

8. Tú quieres comprar un televisor nuevo con una pantalla muy grande.

   _____
   (medir la pared de la sala)

9. Tú piensas cenar en casa de un amigo.

   _____
   (advertirles a tus padres)

10. A los profesores les parece fastidioso que los estudiantes usen teléfonos celulares en la escuela.

    _____
    (impedir el uso de los teléfonos celulares en la escuela)

EJERCICIO G   **Un amigo divertido** Gerardo tuvo que escribir un párrafo sobre alguien que le cae muy bien. A Gerardo le faltan palabras para terminar el párrafo. Complete el párrafo con la forma correcta de uno de los verbos a continuación.

reír	**entender**	**sonreír**	**repetir**
divertirse	**mentir**	**gemir**	**divertir**

Mauricio _____ a sus amigos con sus cuentos y sus bromas. Todos los amigos
       1.

_____ mucho pero Marisol no _____ ; nunca _____ .
  2.   3.   4.

A veces Mauricio _____ un cuento varias veces porque cree que Marisol no lo
        5.

_____ . Cuando él hace eso los otros amigos _____ y le
  6.   7.

_____ otros cuentos. Nosotros _____ muchísimo en compañía de
  8.   9.

Mauricio. Yo no _____ cuando digo que un día él va a ser un cómico famoso.
       10.

c. Verbs that end in *-uir* (except *-guir*) have a *y* inserted after the *u* in all forms, except those for *nosotros* and *vosotros*.

concluir *to conclude, to end*			
yo	concluyo	nosotros, -as	concluimos
tú	concluyes	vosotros, -as	concluís
él, ella, Ud.	concluye	ellos, ellas, Uds.	concluyen

1. Verbs like *concluir*:

   construir *to construct*   **destruir** *to destroy*
   contribuir *to contribute*   **distribuir** *to distribute*

huir   *to flee*   **influir**   *to influence, to have influence*
incluir   *to include*   **sustituir**   *to substitute*

EJERCICIO H   **Una dieta sana**   Judy describe su dieta y la de varios amigos. Repita lo que ella dice, usando el verbo *sustituir*.

EJEMPLO: Rogelio / el pescado / la carne
Rogelio **sustituye** el pescado por la carne.

1. yo / la sacarina / el azúcar

   _____

2. Amelia / la pimienta / la sal

   _____

3. tú / el agua natural / los refrescos

   _____

4. Janet y yo / la fruta fresca / los dulces

   _____

5. Michael y Jane / la ensalada / las papas fritas

   _____

6. Rita / una galleta / el pan

   _____

EJERCICIO I   **Servicio comunitario**   Luis se siente muy orgulloso de organizar una campaña muy exitosa. Exprese los comentarios de Luis acerca de la campaña.

EJEMPLO: los comerciantes / contribuir mucho dinero
Los comerciantes **contribuyen** mucho dinero.

PARA EXPRESARSE MEJOR
la campaña   *campaign*   **el desafío**   *challenge*

---

1. todos mis amigos / contribuir muchas horas

   _____

2. yo / incluir a todos mis amigos

   _____

3. Milton e Iván / construir un quiosco para recibir las contribuciones

   _____

4. tú / distribuir comida caliente a los ancianos

   _____

5. nadie / huir del desafío

_____

6. la campaña / influir a todo el mundo

_____

>   **d.** Some verbs ending in *-iar* or *-uar* stress the *i* or the *u* (*í*, *ú*) in all forms except those for *nosotros* and *vosotros*. In the *vosotros* form, the *a* takes an accent mark.

	guiar to guide, to drive	**actuar** to act
yo	guío	actúo
tú	guías	actúas
él, ella, Ud.	guía	actúa
nosotros, -as	guiamos	actuamos
vosotros, -as	guiáis	actuáis
ellos, ellas, Uds.	guían	actúan

1. Verbs like *guiar:*

confiar (en) *to rely (on), confide (in)*   **fiarse (de)** *to trust*
enviar *to send*   **resfriarse** *to catch cold*
espiar *to spy*   **variar** *to vary*

2. Verbs like *actuar:*

continuar *to continue*   **graduarse** *to graduate*

EJERCICIO J   **¿En quién confía...?**   Todo el mundo confía en alguien. Diga en quiénes confían las siguientes personas.

EJEMPLO: el niño / los padres   El niño **confía** en los padres.

1. el enfermo / los médicos   _____

2. los criminales / el abogado y la corte   _____

3. los pasajeros de un avión / el piloto   _____

4. yo / mi mejor amigo   _____

5. tú / tus hermanos   _____

6. tú y yo / los buenos amigos   _____

EJERCICIO K   **Preguntas**   Conteste las preguntas que le hace un compañero de clase.

1. ¿Cuándo te gradúas?

_____

2. ¿Siempre actúan tú y tus amigos en las obras teatrales de la escuela?

_____

3. ¿A quién le envías esta tarjeta cómica?

_____

4. ¿Confías en los consejos de tus profesores?

_____

5. ¿Continúas tus estudios después de graduarte?

_____

6. ¿Varías los ejercicios físicos que haces?

_____

2. Verbs With Spelling Changes in the Present Tense

a. Verbs ending in *-cer* change the *c* to *z* before *o* or *a:*

convencer *to convince*			
yo	convenzo	nosotros, -as	convencemos
tú	convences	vosotros, -as	convencéis
él, ella, Ud.	convence	ellos, ellas, Uds.	convencen

1. Verbs like *convencer:*

    ejercer *to exert, to exercise or practice (a profession)*
    vencer *to conquer, overcome*

b. Verbs ending in *-ger* or *–gir* change *g* to *j* before *o* or *a:*

	escoger *to choose, to select*	afligir *to afflict, to grieve*
yo	escojo	aflijo
tú	escoges	afliges
él, ella, Ud.	escoge	aflige
nosotros, -as	escogemos	afligimos
vosotros, -as	escogéis	afligís
ellos, ellas, Uds.	escogen	afligen

1. Verbs like *escoger:*

    coger *to seize, to grasp, catch*   **recoger** *to gather, to pick up*
    proteger *to protect*

2. Verbs like *afligir*

    dirigir *to direct*   **fingir** *to pretend*
    exigir *to demand, require*

c. Verbs ending in *-guir* change *gu* to *g* before *o* or *a*.

distinguir *to distinguish*			
yo	distingo	nosotros, -as	distinguimos
tú	distingues	vosotros, -as	distinguís
él, ella, Ud.	distingue	ellos, ellas, Uds.	distinguen

1. Verbs like *distinguir:*

    extinguir *to extinguish*

    perseguir *to chase, to follow*

d. Some verbs with spelling changes also have stem changes.

	torcer *to twist*	elegir *to elect*	seguir *to follow, to continue*
yo	tuerzo	elijo	sigo
tú	tuerces	eliges	sigues
él, ella, Ud.	tuerce	elige	sigue
nosotros, -as	torcemos	elegimos	seguimos
vosotros, -as	torcéis	elegís	seguís
ellos, ellas, Uds.	tuercen	eligen	siguen

1. Verbs like *torcer:*

    cocer *to cook*   **mover** *to move*

2. Verbs like *elegir:*

    corregir *to correct*   **surgir** *to spurt up, to spring up*

3. Verbs like *seguir:*

    conseguir *to get, obtain, to succeed in*   **proseguir** *to continue, to proceed*

    perseguir *to pursue, to persecute*

NOTE: 1. Verbs ending in *-car, -gar,* and *-zar* have no spelling changes in the present tense. Changes occur only in the preterit tense (Chapter 3), in the present subjunctive (Chapter 10) and in commands (Chapter 13).

2. Verbs with spelling changes are identified in the vocabulary lists by the type of change in parentheses after the verb. For example: *convencer* (z), *escoger* (j).

EJERCICIO L   **¿Quién hace esto?**   Exprese a quién convence cada uno de los sujetos en las oraciones. Use las siguientes sugerencias.

a los ciudadanos   **a tus padres**   **a los nietos**   **a los senadores**

a mis hermanos   **a nuestros primos**   **al comprador**

EJEMPLO: el presidente   El presidente **convence** a los senadores.

1. El dependiente _____ .

2. La alcaldesa _____ .

3. Yo _____ .

4. Los abuelos _____ .

5. Tú _____ .

6. Nancy y yo _____ .

EJERCICIO M   **Despedida de soltera**   Cristina se casa pronto y sus amigas van a la tienda para comprarle unos regalos. Exprese lo que las amigas escogen.

EJEMPLO: Sonia / una licuadora.   Sonia **escoge** una licuadora.

1. Kim y yo / una cafetera eléctrica _____

2. yo / una tostadora _____

3. tú / un abrelatas eléctrico _____

4. Elena / un juego de cubiertos _____

5. Uds. / trapos de cocina _____

6. Alicia y Pilar / un juego de vasos _____

EJERCICIO N   **Así soy yo.**   Andy trata de analizar varias de sus cualidades. Exprese lo que él dice con la forma correcta del verbo entre paréntesis.

EJEMPLO: Cuando estoy encargado de la oficina, yo __exijo__ mucho a los empleados.
(exigir)

1. No puedo ir de compras solo porque no _____ bien los colores.
(distinguir)

2. Muchas veces no tengo qué ponerme porque no _____ la ropa de la tintorería.
(recoger)

3. Yo siempre _____ a mis hermanos menores.
(proteger)

4. Cuando mis padres me piden algo, nunca _____ estar ocupado.
(fingir)

5. Mis hermanos cuecen muy bien pero yo no _____ ni un huevo.
(cocer)

6. Cuando vamos a comer a un restaurante, yo _____ el plato más nutritivo.
(elegir)

7. Sarita corrige la gramática a todo el mundo. Yo no se la _____ a nadie.
(corregir)

8. Cuando tengo que armar algo, busco las instrucciones y las _____ a la letra.
(seguir)

9. Para lograr todos mis sueños para el futuro, yo me ——————— mucho.
   (exigir)

10. A veces me pongo furioso cuando no ——————— lo que quiero.
    (conseguir)

EJERCICIO O **Preguntas** Conteste las preguntas que le hace un amigo.

1. ¿Finges estar distraído cuando tus padres te piden algo?

   _____

2. ¿Te exigen mucho tus padres?

   _____

3. ¿Cueces la carne por mucho tiempo?

   _____

4. ¿Qué recoges de la lavandería los sábados?

   _____

5. ¿Sigues las instrucciones que te dan?

   _____

6. ¿Distingues entre lo bueno y lo malo?

   _____

7. ¿Corriges un error cuando lo cometes?

   _____

8. ¿Consigues todo lo que les pides a tus padres?

   _____

9. ¿Adónde te diriges ahora?

   _____

10. ¿Convences a tus padres fácilmente?

    _____

EJERCICIO P **Una encuesta oral y escrita** Ud. va a hacer una encuesta sobre algunas de las preferencias de varios de sus compañeros de clase.

1. Prepare preguntas para aprender cuáles programas de televisión, comidas y pasatiempos prefieren.

2. Hágales las preguntas oralmente a cinco de sus compañeros de clase.

3. Anote sus respuestas.

4. Organice la información en una tabla.

5. Finalmente, escriba un párrafo en que Ud. discuta las correlaciones y conclusiones que ha sacado de esta encuesta. Use tantos verbos de este capítulo como pueda.

CHAPTER 3
The Preterit Tense

The preterit tense is used to express an action or event that was completed at a specific time in the past.

1. The Preterit Tense of Regular Verbs

The preterit tense of regular verbs is formed by dropping the infinitive ending (*-ar, -er, -ir*) and adding the following:

	charlar *to chat*	comer *to eat*	abrir *to open*
yo	charlé	comí	abrí
tú	charlaste	comiste	abriste
él, ella, Ud.	charló	comió	abrió
nosotros, -as	charlamos	comimos	abrimos
vosotros, -as	charlasteis	comisteis	abristeis
ellos, ellas, Uds.	charlaron	comieron	abrieron

Charlé con Pablo ayer.   *I chatted with Pablo yesterday.*

Comimos en un restaurante anoche.   *We ate in a restaurant last night.*

Abrieron la taquilla a las cuatro.   *They opened the box office at 4:00.*

NOTE: 1.   All preterit forms are stressed on the endings rather than on the stem.

          2.   *-Ar* and *-er* verbs that have changes in the vowel of the stem (*o* to *ue* or *e* to *ie*) in the present tense, do not have these changes in any of the preterit forms: *cuento / conté, enciende / encendió.*

EJERCICIO A   **Un día en el centro**   Exprese lo que hizo la familia Ortiz cuando pasaron un día en el centro.

EJEMPLO: Armando / acompañar a José al centro
Armando **acompañó** a José al centro.

1. mamá / devolver un vestido
   devolvio un vestido

2. yo / comprar boletos para una obra de teatro
   yo compre boletos para una obra de teatro

3. papá y Sergio / pasar horas en una tienda de videojuegos
   pasaron horas en una tienda de

4. Jaime y yo / comer en un café al aire libre
   Jaime y yo comimos

5. tú / entrar en todas las zapaterías

Tu entraste

6. los niños / correr en el parque

los niñon corieron en

EJERCICIO B   **Mañana hay clases.**   Exprese lo que los alumnos hicieron en casa por la noche para prepararse para las clases del día siguiente.

EJEMPLO: Javier / terminar una investigación para la clase de ciencia
Javier **terminó** una investigación para la clase de ciencia.

1. yo / aprender de memoria un poema para la clase de inglés

yo aprendí

2. Vicente / escribir un artículo para la clase de periodismo

_V_

3. tú / rotular un cartel para las elecciones

tu rotulaste

4. Hilda y Berta / estudiar juntas para un examen en la clase de matemáticas

Hilda

5. Uds. / aprender unas fórmulas nuevas

uds aprendieron

6. yo / usar la computadora

yo huse ta computadora

7. mi hermano / diseñar un cohete

8. Magda y yo / mirar un documental en la televisión

EJERCICIO C   **Una explicación**   Complete el siguiente mensaje que Felipe les escribió a sus padres luego de llegar muy tarde a casa.

Yo _____ a casa tarde porque _____ por la casa de Eduardo cuando
   1. (regresar)   2. (pasar)

_____ de la escuela. Le _____ la calculadora que él me _____
3. (salir)   4. (devolver)   5. (prestar)

para terminar mi tarea de matemáticas. Él y yo _____ un rato y su mamá
6. (charlar)

nos _____ un refresco. Yo no me _____ en la hora. Cuando
7. (ofrecer)   8. (fijar)

_____ el reloj, yo me _____ . Y _____ a casa corriendo.
9. (mirar)   10. (sorprender)   11. (volver)

2.   The Preterit Tense of Stem-Changing Verbs

a. Stem-Changing Verbs Ending in -*IR*

Verbs ending in -*ir* that have a stem change in the present tense also have a stem change in the preterit tense. The stem vowel changes in the third-person singular and plural, from *o* to *u* and *e* to *i*, respectively.

	dormir *to sleep*	**servir** *to serve*	**medir** *to measure*
yo	dormí	serví	medí
tú	dormiste	serviste	mediste
él, ella, Ud.	durmió —	sirvió —	midió —
nosotros, -as	dormimos	servimos	medimos
~~vosotros, -as~~	~~dormisteis~~	~~servisteis~~	~~medisteis~~
ellos, ellas, Uds.	durmieron —	sirvieron —	midieron —

NOTE: 1.   In the preterit, *reír* (to laugh) and *sonreír* (to smile) are conjugated as follows:

	reír	**sonreír**
yo	reí	sonreí
tú	reíste	sonreíste
él, ella, Ud.	rió	sonrió
nosotros, -as	reímos	sonreímos
~~vosotros, -as~~	~~reísteis~~	~~sonreísteis~~
ellos, ellas, Uds.	rieron	sonrieron

2.   Verbs ending in -*ir* that have *ñ* directly before the ending (*gruñir, reñir*) drop the *i* of the ending in the third-person singular and plural (*gruñó, gruñeron*) because the *ñ* already contains the *i* sound.

EJERCICIO D   ¿Quién lo hizo?   Diga quién hizo las siguientes acciones.

pedirle permiso a la profesora   despedirse de sus anfitriones
sonreír al ver a su papá   medir el espacio
vestir la muñeca   dormirse en la silla
reñir a los trabajadores   servir la comida

EJEMPLO: El carpintero **midió el espacio.**

1. La anciana *se durmió en la silla* .

2. El jefe *riñó a los trabajadores.* .

3. Los meseros *sirvieron la comida* .

4. Los invitados *se despidieron de sus anfitriones* .

5. El bebé *sonrié al ver a su papá* .

6. Los alumnos _pidieron permiso a la profesora_.
7. La niña _vistió al muñeca_.

EJERCICIO E   **Padre e hijo**   Complete este fragmento de un artículo de la sección deportiva del periódico escolar. Dé las formas apropiadas de los verbos indicados.

Cuando José Luis _decidió_ (1. decidir) participar en un torneo de tenis, sus padres no le ✗ _impidieron_ (2. impedir) el paso. Al contrario, ellos _defendieron_ (3. defender) la decisión que él _tomó_ (4. tomar) y _decidió_ (5. decidir) ayudarlo totalmente. José Luis _compitió_ (6. competir) en varios torneos y su padre le _sirvió_ (7. servir) de entrenador. José Luis _decidió_ (8. decidir) aceptar la ayuda de su padre. _Particpó_ (9. participar) en muchas competencias, _repitió_ (10. repetir) muchas victorias y padre e hijo _se devirtieron_ (11. divertirse) mucho. Ellos nunca _reñieron_ (12. reñir). José Luis _sintió_ (13. sentir) mucho cuando _terminó_ (14. terminar) la última competencia y esta etapa de su vida _acabó_ (15. acabarse).

3.   The Preterit Tense of Spelling-Changing Verbs

a. Verbs ending in *-car*, *-gar*, and *-zar* change in the *yo*-form of the preterit, as follows: *c* to *qu*, *g* to *gu*, and *z* to *c*.

	explicar to explain	jugar to play (game)	alzar to lift
yo	expliqué	jugué	alcé
tú	explicaste	jugaste	alzaste
él, ella, Ud.	explicó	jugó	alzó
nosotros, -as	explicamos	jugamos	alzamos
vosotros, -as	explicasteis	jugasteis	alzasteis
ellos, ellas, Uds.	explicaron	jugaron	alzaron

1. Verbs like *explicar*:

acercarse *to approach*   **educar** *to educate*
aplicar *to apply*   **embarcar(se)** *to embark*
arrancar *to root out, to pull out*   **equivocarse** *to be mistaken*
atacar *to attack*   **fabricar** *to make, to manufacture*
buscar *to look for, to seek*   **indicar** *to indicate*
colocar *to place, to put*   **marcar** *to designate, to mark; to dial*
comunicar(se) *to communicate*   **masticar** *to chew*
dedicar *to dedicate, to devote*   **pescar** *to fish*

10 phrases Nosotros

publicar   *to publish*   significar   *to mean*
replicar   *to reply; to contradict (argue)* suplicar   *to beg, to implore*
sacar   *to take out*   tocar   *to touch, to play (music)*
sacrificar   *to sacrifice*

2. Verbs like *jugar:*

   agregar   *to add*   llegar   *to arrive*
   ahogar(se)   *to drown*   madrugar   *to rise early*
   apagar   *to put out, to extinguish*   negar   *to deny*
   cargar   *to load*   obligar   *to obligate, to compel*
   castigar   *to punish*   pagar   *to pay (for)*
   colgar   *to hang*   pegar   *to stick, to hit*
   encargar   *to put in charge; to entrust; to order* rogar   *to ask for, to beg*
   entregar   *to deliver, to hand over*

3. Verbs like *alzar:*

   abrazar   *to embrace, to hug*   empezar   *to begin*
   alcanzar   *to reach, to overtake*   gozar   *to enjoy*
   almorzar   *to eat lunch*   lanzar   *to throw*
   amenazar   *to threaten*   realizar   *to fulfill*
   avanzar   *to advance*   rezar   *to pray*
   comenzar   *to begin, to commence*   tropezar   *to stumble*
   deslizarse   *to slip, to glide*

fuerte | debile

	fuerte	debile
	CA	CE
	CO	CI
	CU	

ga -gue   ce -que -za

EJERCICIO F   **Todo está listo.** Ud. y un amigo pasaron un fin de semana acampando en las montañas. Ahora se preparan para volver a casa. Conteste las preguntas que su amigo le hace sobre los preparativos para volver a casa.

EJEMPLO: ¿Colgaste a secar la tienda de campaña?   Sí, **la colgué** a secar.

1. ¿Madrugaste hoy?

     Sí, yo madrugué hoy.

2. ¿Apagaste el fuego?

     Sí, apagué el fuego

3. ¿Buscaste la brújula? *= compass*

     Sí, busqué la brújula

4. ¿Colocaste todo el equipo en la mochila?

     Sí, coloqué todo el equipo en la mochila

5. ¿Cargaste el baúl del carro?

     Sí, cargué el baúl del carro

6. ¿Sacaste unos refrescos para el viaje?

     Sí, saqué unas refresco para el viaje

7. ¿Te comunicaste con los encargados del campamento?

   Si, me comuniqué con los encargados del campamento

8. ¿Pagaste la cuenta?

   Si, pagué la cuenta

9. ¿Almorzaste algo?

   Si, almorcé algo

10. ¿Realizaste tu deseo de acampar?

    Si, realizé mi deseo de acampar

EJERCICIO G   **Somos torpes.**   Cuando los jóvenes regresan a la escuela después de las vacaciones, siempre tienen una experiencia interesante que contarles a sus amigos. Exprese lo que contaron las siguientes personas, usando la forma apropiada de los verbos de la lista.

arrancar	deslizarse	lanzar	tocar
castigar	equivocarse	pegar	tropezar

EJEMPLO: Yo **me equivoqué** al marcar un número telefónico y contestó alguien en Chile.

1. Yo _____ cerca de la piscina y me rompí el tobillo.

2. Yo _____ las plantas favoritas de mi mamá por equivocación. Ella me

   _____ por una semana.

3. Yo _____ unas hojas en el jardín y me salió un salpullido horrible.

4. Yo _____ con una señora en el almacén. Era la mamá de Elena y no le dio gusto verme.

5. Yo le _____ a mi perro porque recogió el juguete de un niño en el parque.

6. Yo _____ una pelota y quebró la ventana de la casa vecina.

b. -*Er* and -*ir* verbs that contain a vowel immediately before the preterit ending change in the third-person singular and plural: -*ió* to -*yó*, and -*ieron* to -*yeron*, respectively. The *i* has an accent mark in all the other forms.

	creer to believe	oír to hear
yo	creí	oí
tú	creíste	oíste
él, ella, Ud.	creyó	oyó
nosotros, -as	creímos	oímos
vosotros, -as	creísteis	oísteis
ellos, ellas, Uds.	creyeron	oyeron

NOTE: *Traer* and *atraer* are exceptions to the above rule.

1. Verbs like *creer* and *oír*:

   caer *to fall*   **poseer** *to possess*
   leer *to read*

c. Verbs that end in *-uir* (*construir, contribuir, destruir, distribuir, huir, incluir*, etc.) also belong in this group, but no accent mark appears in the endings *-uiste, -uimos*, and *-uisteis*.

huir *to flee, to escape*			
yo	huí	nosotros, -as	huimos
tú	huiste	vosotros, -as	huisteis
él, ella, Ud.	huyó	ellos, ellas, Uds.	huyeron

NOTE: Verbs ending in *-guir* are the exception to the above rule.

EJERCICIO H **La fiesta de San Fermín** Cuando Rafael fue a España, decidió ir a Pamplona durante la célebre fiesta de San Fermín, cuando los toros se sueltan a correr por las calles. Exprese lo que Rafael presenció durante su estancia allí.

EJEMPLO: todo el mundo / madrugar ese día   Todo el mundo **madrugó** ese día.

1. unos niños / distribuir folletos anunciando la feria

   _____

2. los promotores de la feria / incluir las horas de la feria

   _____

3. los encargados de la feria / construir una barrera

   _____

4. Rafael / leer la historia de la feria

   _____

5. él / no creer la cantidad de personas que participaron

   _____

6. los toros / destruir muchas cosas

   _____

7. los médicos / contribuir sus servicios

   _____

8. todo el mundo / oír los gritos de la muchedumbre

   _____

9. los turistas / huir de las calles

   _____

10. Rafael / sacar muchas fotografías

   _____

EJERCICIO I   **¿Cómo estuvo tu día?**   Norma le cuenta a su mamá lo que pasó en la escuela hoy. Ella siempre compara lo que ella hace con lo que hacen otros alumnos. Cuente lo que dice.

EJEMPLO: Irma **leyó** un cuento original a la clase. Yo no **leí** nada.   (*leer*)

1. Yo _____ un dólar a una colección para los pobres. Elsa y Paula no

   _____ nada.   (*contribuir*)

2. Felipe _____ una torre en miniatura. Yo no _____ nada.   (*construir*)

3. Nuria no me _____ en su grupo. Yo no la _____ en el mío

   tampoco.   (*incluir*)

4. Jorge y Dolores se _____ durante el recreo. Yo no me _____ .   (*caer*)

5. Jenny no _____ los anuncios de la maestra. Yo sí los _____ .   (*oír*)

6. Yo _____ los marcadores a los alumnos. Las otras alumnas no les

   _____ nada.   (*distribuir*)

EJERCICIO J   **Reacciones**   Todo el mundo responde o reacciona de manera distinta a diferentes circunstancias o noticias. Exprese cómo reaccionaron estas personas.

EJEMPLO: El perro **gruñó** cuando ellos le **quitaron** el hueso.
          (gruñir)   (quitar)

1. La señora _____ a llorar cuando _____ la noticia.
            (empezar)   (oír)

2. Las niñas _____ cuando los niños las _____ .
            (sonreír)   (saludar)

3. Mamá me _____ cuando yo _____ la calle solo.
          (reñir)   (cruzar)

4. Yo _____ mucho cuando José me _____ un chiste.
     (reír)   (contar)

5. Los jugadores _____ jugando cuando _____ una tormenta.
                (seguir)   (caer)

6. A Fernando le _____ tanto el postre que él lo _____ tres veces.
                (gustar)   (repetir)

7. Tú _____ mucha tristeza cuando nadie _____ a tiempo a la fiesta.
     (sentir)   (llegar)

8. Al abuelo le _____ el programa en la televisión y se _____ .
               (aburrir)   (dormir)

9. Uds. se _____ cuando el químico _____ en el laboratorio.
          (asustar)   (hervir)

10. Lina se _____ mareada cuando ella _____ de las sillas volantes.
           (sentir)   (bajar)

EJERCICIO K   **Muchas preguntas** Ud. acaba de regresar de su primer viaje al extranjero. Conteste las preguntas que le hicieron los miembros de su familia.

1. ¿Qué sentiste cuando despegó el avión? (*miedo*)

   _____

2. ¿Pasaste muchas horas en los cafés al aire libre? (*sí*)

   _____

3. ¿Cuántas ciudades visitaste en este viaje? (*3*)

   _____

4. ¿A cuántos conciertos asististe? (*varios*)

   _____

5. ¿Dónde jugaste al voleibol? (*en la playa*)

   _____

6. ¿Dónde pescaste? (*en el mar*)

   _____

7. ¿Con qué frecuencia practicaste el español? (*todos los días*)

   _____

8. ¿Gozaste de tu visita a los museos? (*muchísimo*)

   _____

9. ¿Alcanzaste a conocer muchos lugares turísticos? (*demasiados*)

   _____

10. ¿Se divirtió el grupo? (*mucho*)

   _____

4. Verbs Irregular in the Preterit

a. The following verbs have an irregular stem in the preterit. The endings for these verbs are: *-e, -iste, -o, –imos, -isteis* and *–ieron* (*-eron* if *j* precedes the ending).

andar to walk	anduve anduviste anduvo	anduvimos anduvisteis anduvieron
caber to fit	cupe cupiste cupo	cupimos cupisteis cupieron
estar to be	estuve estuviste estuvo	estuvimos estuvisteis estuvieron

haber *to have (aux.)*	*hube* *hubiste* *hubo*	*hubimos* *hubisteis* *hubieron*
hacer *to do, to make*	*hice* *hiciste* *hizo*	*hicimos* *hicisteis* *hicieron*
poder *to be able, can*	*pude* *pudiste* *pudo*	*pudimos* *pudisteis* *pudieron*
poner *to put*	*puse* *pusiste* *puso*	*pusimos* *pusisteis* *pusieron*
querer *to want*	*quise* *quisiste* *quiso*	*quisimos* *quisisteis* *quisieron*
saber *to know*	*supe* *supiste* *supo*	*supimos* *supisteis* *supieron*
tener *to have*	*tuve* *tuviste* *tuvo*	*tuvimos* *tuvisteis* *tuvieron*
venir *to come*	*vine* *viniste* *vino*	*vinimos* *vinisteis* *vinieron*
decir *to say, to tell*	*dije* *dijiste* *dijo*	*dijimos* *dijisteis* *dijeron*
producir *to produce*	*produje* *produjiste* *produjo*	*produjimos* *produjisteis* *produjeron*
traer *to bring*	*traje* *trajiste* *trajo*	*trajimos* *trajisteis* *trajeron*

NOTE:
1. The third-person singular form of *hacer* is *hizo*. The *c* changes to *z* to retain the original sound of the infinitive.

2. All compounds of *poner* (*componer, proponer,* etc.), *tener* (*mantener,* etc.), *hacer* (*satisfacer,* etc.), *venir* (*convenir,* etc.), and *traer* (*atraer,* etc.) are conjugated in the same manner as the basic verb.

3. All verbs ending in *-ducir,* such as *conducir* and *traducir,* are conjugated like *producir.*

b. *Dar, ser,* and *ir* are also irregular in the preterit. *Dar* takes the endings of regular *-er* / *-ir* verbs; *ser* and *ir* have the same forms in the preterit.

	dar *to give*	ser *to be* ir *to go*
yo	di	fui
tú	diste	fuiste
él, ella, Ud.	dio	fue
nosotros, -as	dimos	fuimos
vosotros, -as	disteis	fuisteis
ellos, ellas, Uds.	dieron	fueron

NOTE: The accent mark is omitted in the preterit forms of *dar, ver, ser,* and *ir.*

EJERCICIO L   **Un día productivo** La señora Santos le cuenta a su esposo lo que todos pudieron hacer hoy. Exprese lo que ella dice.

EJEMPLO: Grisel / ir de compras   Grisel **pudo** ir de compras.

1. yo / buscar un vestido para la boda   _____

2. mi mamá / hablar con el dentista   _____

3. tú / cambiar la llanta ponchada del carro   _____

4. Tony y yo / hacer la lista de los invitados   _____

5. la vecina / cortar el césped   _____

6. Uds. / divertirse por la tarde   _____

EJERCICIO M   **Huelga de transporte público** Cuente lo que las personas tuvieron que hacer cuando los choferes de transporte público se declararon en huelga.

EJEMPLO: yo / andar al centro   Yo **tuve** que andar al centro.

1. Mercedes / sacar su bicicleta   _____

2. los señores / compartir un taxi   _____

3. tú / quedarte en casa   _____

4. mis amigos / levantarse más temprano   _____

5. yo / pedirles favores a todas mis amigas   _____

6. nosotros / posponer nuestra visita al museo _____

EJERCICIO N   **Unas vacaciones desastrosas** Complete la entrada que Marcy escribió en su diario sobre las vacaciones que ella y su familia pasaron en la playa. Exprese la forma correcta de los verbos entre paréntesis.

Mi familia y yo apenas _____ al hotel cuando el cielo _____ tan
1. (llegar)   2. (ponerse)
negro como de noche. Nosotros _____ muchos truenos y _____
3. (oír)   4. (ver)
muchos relámpagos. _____ a llover a cántaros y las calles _____
5. (empezar)   6. (inundarse)
pronto. Cuando _____ del carro nosotros _____ mucho porque mi
7. (bajar)   8. (mojarse)
mamá no _____ paraguas. Mi papá _____ a la administración
9. (traer)   10. (ir)
y _____ las llaves de los cuartos. Ellos nos _____ cuartos en un
11. (conseguir)   12. (dar)
piso alto del hotel. Nosotros _____ a los cuartos en el ascensor y yo
13. (subir)
_____ la maleta, _____ la ropa en el armario y _____
14. (deshacer)   15. (poner)   16. (ponerse)
un traje de baño. Mi hermano _____ lo mismo. Mi hermano y yo _____
17. (hacer)   18. (bajar)
en el ascensor. _____ a la piscina pero no _____ usarla porque la
19. (ir)   20. (poder)
habían cerrado. Las luces del hotel _____ varias veces. Por fin mis padres
21. (apagarse)
_____ y _____ con nosotros cerca de la piscina. Ellos _____
22. (bajar)   23. (dar)   24. (tener)
que bajar por la escalera. Mi padre _____ a la administración. Él _____
25. (dirigirse)   26. (pedir)
un cambio de cuarto a un piso inferior. El gerente del hotel no _____ acceder
27. (poder)
a su solicitud. Mi hermano _____ al salón de juegos pero ningún juego
28. (ir)
_____ porque la electricidad _____ por completo. Nosotros
29. (funcionar)   30. (irse)
_____ comer en el restaurante del hotel. _____ cola para entrar y
31. (decidir)   32. (hacer)
_____ más de una hora. Por fin un mesero nos _____ en una mesa
33. (esperar)   34. (sentar)
y _____ varias velas en la mesa. El mesero _____ las velas y
35. (poner)   36. (encender)
_____ de leernos el menú. Yo _____ una hamburguesa con papas
37. (tratar)   38. (pedir)
fritas. Mi familia _____ lo mismo. No _____ luz hasta la mañana
39. (pedir)   40. (haber)
siguiente, cuando _____ el sol. ¡ _____ unas vacaciones desastrosas!
41. (salir)   42. (ser)

EJERCICIO O   **Noticias sociales**   Complete las siguientes noticias que aparecieron en el
periódico ayer. Use la forma apropiada del verbo entre paréntesis.

1. El Primer Ministro y su esposa _____ a la isla de Menorca para pasar quince
    (ir)
    días de vacaciones.

2. Se _____ una gran fiesta anoche en honor de la quinceañera Luz Gallardo y
   (dar)

   Fermín. Más de 150 amigas y compañeros _____ de buena comida y música.
   (gozar)

   La celebración _____ lugar en el «Gran Salón» del Club de España.
   (tener)

3. Los padres de la señorita Virginia López y Díaz _____ el compromiso de su
   (anunciar)

   hija con el señor Javier Mateos y Aragón. Los comprometidos se _____ en
   (conocer)

   una excursión de alpinismo.

4. El cantante Enrique Catedrales _____ a la capital para dar un concierto en
   (venir)

   beneficio de las organizaciones de obras humanitarias. Sus aficionados no _____
   (caber)

   en el auditorio.

5. Antes de salir de vacaciones, el Primer Ministro _____ en el aeropuerto para
   (estar)

   recibir a un grupo de estudiantes de intercambio de varias partes del mundo. Él les

   _____ la bienvenida a nuestro país y les _____ mucho éxito en
   (dar)   (desear)

   sus estudios.

EJERCICIO P   **Preguntas y más preguntas**   Por fin una amiga pudo ponerse en contacto
con Ud. Responda a las preguntas y los comentarios que ella le hace.

1. ¿Adónde fuiste ayer?   (*el centro*)

   _____

2. ¿Con quiénes fuiste?   (*unos primos*)

   _____

3. ¿Qué hicieron allí?   (*ir al cine*)

   _____

4. ¿A qué función fueron?   (*5:30*)

   _____

5. ¿Qué película vieron Uds.?   (*una película extranjera*)

   _____

6. ¿Qué te pareció la película?   (*bastante buena*)

   _____

7. Mi hermana estuvo en ese cine, ¿diste con ella?   (*no*)

   _____

8. ¿A qué hora llegaste a casa?   (*10:00*)

   _____

9. ¿Por qué no me llamaste anoche?   (*acostarme*)

_____

10. Te dejé varios recados en la máquina de contestar.   (*no recibirlos*)

_____

EJERCICIO Q   **Actividad oral y escrita**   (En este ejercicio Ud. trabajará con un compañero de clase.) Su pariente favorito trató de comunicarse con Ud. por teléfono todo el día de ayer, pero no pudo. Conteste sus preguntas (¿adónde fue, con quién estuvo, cuándo, por cuánto tiempo?, etc.) Luego escriba un resumen detallado de cómo Ud. pasó el día.

_____

_____

_____

_____

_____

_____

_____

_____

_____

7. ¿Cómo era Rico?

   _____

8. ¿Qué hacía Rico cuando la familia estaba en casa?

   _____

9. ¿Qué temía la mamá?

   _____

10. ¿Qué oía Rico?

    _____

11. ¿Adónde iba la familia los viernes?

    _____

12. ¿Qué efecto tenía eso?

    _____

13. ¿Qué le hacían los hijos a la mamá?

    _____

14. ¿Cómo reaccionaba ella?

    _____

b. Uses of the Imperfect Tense

1. The imperfect tense is used to describe what was happening, used to happen, or happened repeatedly in the past. Expressions such as _todos los días, siempre,_ and _a menudo_ are often clues for using the imperfect.

Carl _jugaba_ al fútbol.	_Carl played (used to play) football._
Ana siempre _cosía_ su propia ropa.	_Ana always sewed (used to sew) her own clothing._

2. The imperfect is used to describe persons or things in the past.

Donna _era_ bonita y tímida.	_Donna was pretty and shy._
Los cuartos del hotel _eran_ grandes.	_The hotel rooms were large._

3. With the verbs _creer, pensar, querer,_ and _saber,_ the imperfect expresses a state of mind in the past.

El maestro _creía_ (pensaba, sabía) que yo estaba ausente.	_The teacher believed (thought, knew) that I was absent._
Queríamos ir a la playa.	_We wanted to go to the beach._

4. The imperfect expresses the time of day in the past.

Eran las once.	_It was eleven o'clock._

5. The imperfect is used to describe what was going on in the past when another action or event expressed in the preterit occurred.

Tú _dormías_ cuando yo _llegué._	_You were sleeping when I arrived._

6. The construction *hacía* + time expression + *que* + imperfect tense is used to describe an action or event that began and continued in the past. In such situations the question is expressed by *¿Cuánto tiempo hacía que...* + imperfect tense? or *¿Hacía cuánto tiempo que...* + imperfect tense?.

Hacía tres años que tocaba la trompeta.	*He had been playing the trumpet for three years.*
¿Cuánto tiempo hacía que no los veías?	*How long hadn't you seen them?*

7. The imperfect tense + *desde hacía* + time expression is also used to describe an action or event that began in the past and continued in the past. In such situations, the question is expressed by *¿Desde cuándo* + imperfect tense?.

***Tocaba* la trompeta *desde hacía* tres años.**	*He had been playing the trumpet for three years.*
¿*Desde cuándo* no los *veías*?	*How long hadn't you seen them?*

EJERCICIO G **¡Cuéntamelo todo!**   Gloria acaba de conocer a una joven de Buenos Aires. Conteste las preguntas que Gloria le hace acerca de su vida en Buenos Aires.

1. ¿Con quién salías?

    _____

2. ¿Dónde vivían ellos?

    _____

3. ¿Adónde iban Uds.?

    _____

4. ¿Con qué frecuencia los veías?

    _____

5. ¿Cómo eran ellos?

    _____

6. ¿Por qué te gustaba pasar el tiempo con ellos?

    _____

7. ¿Tenían intereses similares?

    _____

8. ¿Quién decidía lo que iban a hacer?

    _____

9. ¿A qué deportes jugaban?

    _____

10. ¿Se portaban bien contigo?

    _____

EJERCICIO H   **Todo cambia.**   La abuela de Janet le explica como se hacían las cosas en su pueblo cuando ella tenía la edad de su nieta. Exprese lo que ella dice.

EJEMPLO: nosotros / ordenar la ropa de un catálogo
Nosotros **ordenábamos** la ropa de un catálogo.

1. las señoritas / no poder salir solas

    _____

2. el novio / tener que recoger a la chica en su casa

    _____

3. yo / no viajar sola

    _____

4. tus amigos / escribirte cartas

    _____

5. todo el mundo / ir al cine los sábados

    _____

6. mi hermano menor / acompañarme cuando yo / salir con un muchacho

    _____

7. los padres / castigar a los hijos

    _____

8. nosotros / respetar a los mayores

    _____

EJERCICIO I   **Dos acciones a la vez**   Exprese quién hacía estas acciones al mismo tiempo.

EJEMPLO: Roger / leer / comer   Roger **leía** mientras **comía.**

1. yo / cantar / bañarse

    _____

2. Elsa y María / oír discos compactos / estudiar

    _____

3. mi tía / maquillarse / conducir el carro

    _____

4. tú / roncar / dormir

    _____

5. Ud. / mirar a las personas / hacer cola

    _____

6. Fernando / jugar un videojuego / caminar a la escuela

    _____

EJERCICIO J   **Una interrupción**   Exprese en una sola frase lo que interrumpió la acción de estas personas.

EJEMPLO: Jaime / bostezar / el maestro / hacerle una pregunta
Jaime **bostezaba** cuando el maestro **le hizo** una pregunta.

1. mi papá / regar el jardín / caer una tormenta

mi papa riega el jardin mientra caia una tormenta

2. los exploradores / poner una tienda de campo / una serpiente / aparecer

los exploradores ponian una tienda de campo mientras una

3. yo / esperar mi vuelo / la aerolínea / anunciar una demora

Yo esperaba mi vuelo de arolina pero anuncian una demora

4. tú / atravesar una calle ancha / el semáforo / cambiar

Tu atrabiasas una calle ancha pero el semaforo se cambia

5. Linda / conducir el carro / el policía / detenerla

Lind conducia el carro cuando el policia a detenia

6. nosotros / dormir la siesta / las campanas de la iglesia / sonar

Nosotros dormiamos la siesta cuando las campanas de la iglesias sonaban

EJERCICIO K   **Los años pasan.**   Ud. va a una reunión de su clase graduada de la escuela secundaria y quiere saber de los acontecimientos de sus compañeros de clase. Prepare la pregunta y contéstela usando la información entre paréntesis.

EJEMPLO: Virginia / trabajar en la oficina del alcalde   (dos años)
¿Cuánto tiempo hacía que Virginia **trabajaba** en la oficina del alcalde?
Hacía dos años que Virginia **trabajaba** en la oficina del alcalde.

1. tú / ser el comandante del avión   (un año)

Hace un año que era comandante de avion

2. Luisa y Alicia / correr en los maratones   (tres años)

ce 3 años
Luisa y alicia corian en los maratones

3. Miguel / vivir en el extranjero   (cinco años)

Miguel hace 5 años vivia en el extranjero

4. la señora Ortiz / enseñar   (seis meses)

la señora ortiz hace 6 años

enseñaba

5. ellos / construir casas *(cinco años)*

Ellos hace 5 años contruian casas

6. nosotros / no vernos *(diez años)*

nosotros hace 10 años no nos veíamos

EJERCICIO L **¿Desde cuándo…?** A Ud. le gustaría saber desde cuándo sus amigos hacían varias actividades. Exprese las preguntas que Ud. hace y las respuestas que ellos dan usando las expresiones *¿Desde cuándo…?* y *desde hacía…*

EJEMPLO: Marta / conducir un carro
¿Desde cuándo conducía Marta un carro?
Marta **conducía** un carro **desde hacía seis meses.**

1. Alejando / reparar motocicletas

2. tú / estudiar italiano

3. Rafael y Luis / trabajar de cocineros

4. nosotros / ir al mismo gimnasio

5. Guadalupe / tocar la guitarra

6. Uds. / asistir juntos a los conciertos

2.   The Preterit and Imperfect Tenses Compared

The preterit and imperfect tenses are used to describe actions or events that occurred in the past. However, their use is very different and depends on the context and the meaning the speaker wishes to convey.

a. The preterit is used to express the beginning or end of an action or event occurring in the past. It may also indicate the complete event (both beginning and end).

El bebé *comenzó* a llorar.	*The baby began to cry.*
Dejó de nevar.	*It stopped snowing.*
Yo te *llamé* ayer.	*I called you yesterday.*

b. The imperfect is used to indicate the continuance of a situation or event in the past. Neither the beginning nor the end is indicated. It is used:

1.   To express what was happening, used to happen, or happened repeatedly in the past.

Ellos *hablaban* mientras *miraban* la película.	*They were talking while they watched (were watching) the film.*
Nos *veíamos* todos los días.	*We used to see each other every day.*
Ella *trabajaba* en un banco.	*She was working (used to work) in a bank.*

2.   To describe persons, things, or situations in the past.

Yo *tenía* el pelo largo.	*I had long hair.*
La fábrica *era* grande.	*The factory was large.*

3.   To express the time of day in the past.

Eran las seis y media.	*It was six thirty.*

4.   To describe an action or event that began in the past and continued in the past (*hacía* + time expression + *que* + imperfect) and to express *how long had...?* (*¿cuánto tiempo hacía que...* + pluperfect?).

Hacía dos horas que hablaban por teléfono.	*They had been talking on the telephone for two hours.*
¿Cuánto tiempo hacía que tu abuelo se había jubilado?	*How long had your grandfather been retired?*

5.   To describe what was going on in the past (imperfect) when another action or event occurred, that is, began or ended (preterit).

Yo *estudiaba* cuando se *apagó* la luz.	*I was studying when the light went out.*

EJERCICIO M   ¿Sueño o pesadilla?   Escoja la forma apropiada del verbo y complete la descripción que Alberto da a sus padres de lo que le pasó anoche.

_____ las dos de la mañana y todo _____ tranquilo en la casa. Todo
1. (Eran / Fueron)   2. (estaba / estuvo)

el mundo _____ profundamente. Todos, menos yo. Yo _____ los
            3. (dormía / durmió)   4. (oía / oí)

ronquidos dulces de los otros miembros de mi familia. Me _____ temprano y
5. (acostaba / acosté)

no _____ ninguna dificultad en dormirme.
6. (tenía / tuve)

Mi cabeza apenas _____ la almohada y me _____ . Pero de
7. (tocaba / tocó)   8. (dormía / dormí)

repente, algo me _____ y me _____ en la cama. Yo no
9. (despertaba / despertó)   10. (sentaba / senté)

_____ soñando. La luz de la luna _____ por la ventana. Yo me
11. (estaba / estuve)   12. (entraba / entró)

_____ de la y me _____ por la ventana. _____ la
13. (bajaba / bajé)   14. (asomaba / asomé)   15. (Caía / Cayó)

primera nevada del invierno y todos los árboles _____ cubiertos de una capa
16. (estaban / estuvieron)

de nieve fresca. Todo _____ a la luz de la luna llena.
17. (brillaba / brilló)

EJERCICIO N **Una excursión especial** Complete la descripción que Susan escribió de una
excursión especial que ella hizo con sus compañeros de clase. Complete su
relato con la forma apropiada del verbo entre paréntesis.

Cuando el avión _____ en el aeropuerto de Barajas, España, todos mis
1. (aterrizaba / aterrizó)

compañeros _____ mirar por las ventanillas del avión. _____ el
2. (querían / quisieron)   3. (Era / Fue)

primer viaje que nosotros _____ al extranjero. Nuestra maestra de español nos
4. (hacíamos /hicimos)

_____ . El piloto _____ la señal de «abrocharse los cintur-
5. (acompañaba / acompañó)   6. (apagaba / apagó)

ones», y nosotros _____ de los asientos, _____ nuestras
7. (brincábamos / brincamos)   8. (recogíamos / recogimos)

cosas y nos _____ a pisar el suelo español por primera vez.
9. (preparábamos / preparamos)

Cuando _____ la inmigración y la aduana, todos _____
10. (pasábamos / pasamos)   11. (teníamos / tuvimos)

el pasaporte en la mano. Un autobús de turismo nos _____ en la puerta del
12. (esperaba / esperó)

aeropuerto. Nosotros le _____ las maletas al chofer y _____ al
13. (dábamos / dimos)   14. (subíamos / subimos)

autobús. El viaje al hotel no _____ mucho aunque _____ a
15. (tardaba / tardó)   16. (llegábamos / llegamos)

Madrid en la hora punta, cuando los madrileños _____ a trabajar.
17. (iban / fueron)

_____ al hotel y _____ sus maletas en sus cuartos.
18. (llegábamos / llegamos)   19. (dejaban / dejaron)

_____ un hotel pequeño pero limpio y céntrico. Nosotros _____
20. (Era / Fue)   21. (teníamos / tuvimos)

que apurarnos porque en menos de media hora _____ en una excursión de
22. (salíamos / salimos)

orientación por toda la ciudad. En el autobús, un guía nos _____ mucho de la
23. (contaba / contó)

historia de la ciudad y nos ＿＿＿＿＿＿＿ los sitios de mayor interés. El autobús
                            24. (indicaba / indicó)

＿＿＿＿＿＿＿ una parada de cuarenta minutos en el Parque del Buen Retiro y por
25. (hacía / hizo)

fin ＿＿＿＿＿＿＿ estirar las piernas después de muchas horas sentados en el avión y
   26. (podíamos / pudimos)

en el autobús. Todos ＿＿＿＿＿＿＿ alborotados porque ＿＿＿＿＿＿＿ muchas
                     27. (estábamos / estuvimos)   28. (teníamos / tuvimos)

ganas de conocer personalmente muchos de los lugares que sólo ＿＿＿＿＿＿＿ por
                                                              29. (conocíamos / conocimos)

medio de fotografías en su libro de texto.

EJERCICIO O   **Un problema**   Complete las oraciones del siguiente pasaje con la forma
apropiada del pretérito o del imperfecto, según el caso.

Yo ＿＿＿＿＿＿＿ corriendo a la casa porque ＿＿＿＿＿＿＿ a cántaros y ＿＿＿＿＿＿＿
   1. (llegar)   2. (llover)   3. (querer)

refugiarme del aguacero, que me ＿＿＿＿＿＿＿ de pies a cabeza. ＿＿＿＿＿＿＿
                                4. (mojar)   5. (sacar)

las llaves del bolsillo y ＿＿＿＿＿＿＿ de abrir la puerta con una de ellas. La llave
                         6. (tratar)

＿＿＿＿＿＿＿ en la cerradura, pero no ＿＿＿＿＿＿＿ vuelta. ＿＿＿＿＿＿＿ de
7. (entrar)   8. (dar)   9. (tratar)

abrir la puerta con todas las llaves en el llavero, pero ninguna ＿＿＿＿＿＿＿ . Por fin,
                                                                10. (funcionar)

yo ＿＿＿＿＿＿＿ a la puerta y mamá me la ＿＿＿＿＿＿＿ .
   11. (tocar)   12. (abrir)

EJERCICIO P   **Un día emocionante**   Complete el siguiente pasaje, en el cual María recuerda
un día emocionante para ella y varios amigos. Use la forma apropiada del
pretérito o del imperfecto, según el caso.

Ayer varios amigos y yo ＿＿＿＿＿＿＿ un día muy emocionante. ＿＿＿＿＿＿＿ el
                        1. (pasar)   2. (ser)

día en que ＿＿＿＿＿＿＿ las cartas de las universidades a las cuales ＿＿＿＿＿＿＿
           3. (llegar)   4. (solicitar)

admisión. Nadie ＿＿＿＿＿＿＿ ir a la escuela ni salir de la casa ese día. Lo único que
                5. (querer)

nosotros ＿＿＿＿＿＿＿ hacer ＿＿＿＿＿＿＿ esperar la llegada del correo. Mis
         6. (querer)   7. (ser)

padres no me ＿＿＿＿＿＿＿ faltar a la escuela.
             8. (dejar)

Después de las clases yo ＿＿＿＿＿＿＿ corriendo a la casa y ＿＿＿＿＿＿＿ el
                         9. (volver)   10. (buscar)

correo en el buzón, pero no ＿＿＿＿＿＿＿ nada. Yo ＿＿＿＿＿＿＿ nerviosísima
                            11. (haber)   12. (estar)

cuando ＿＿＿＿＿＿＿ en la casa. La carta ＿＿＿＿＿＿＿ en la mesa del comedor. Yo
       13. (entrar)   14. (estar)

la ___15. (recoger)___ y ___16. (querer)___ abrirla, pero ___17. (temblar)___ de miedo. Poco a

poco ___18. (abrir)___ el sobre y ___19. (sacar)___ la carta. Pero yo no ___20. (poder)___

leerla. Yo se la ___21. (dar)___ a mi mamá y cuando ella ___22. (comenzar)___ a leerla, ella

___23. (gritar)___ y me ___24. (abrazar)___ . ___25. (ser)___ una carta llena de buenas

noticias. Mi mamá y yo ___26. (ponerse)___ felices.

EJERCICIO Q   **El recital**   Anoche Ud. asistió al recital de un primo. Conteste las preguntas que le hace un amigo que no pudo asistir al recital.

1. ¿Cuántas personas había en el teatro?

___

2. ¿Estaba nervioso Andrés?

___

3. ¿Cuántas piezas tocó?

___

4. ¿Cómo las tocó?

___

5. ¿Lo aplaudió mucho el público?

___

6. ¿A quién dedicó el recital?

___

7. ¿Sabías que él iba a hacer eso?

___

8. ¿Qué dijeron sus maestros?

___

9. ¿Cómo estaba él después del recital?

___

10. ¿Adónde fueron Uds. después del recital?

___

EJERCICIO R   **Lectura**   Lea este anuncio que apareció en el diario del domingo pasado. Luego conteste las preguntas.

> **Necesitamos su ayuda...**
>
> Por más de veinte años, El Asilo de Animales recoge animales domésticos abandonados y los ofrece a personas responsables que buscan la compañía de una mascota cariñosa, leal y fiel. Estos animales merecen tener un hogar protector y sano. Si a Ud. le interesa adoptar una mascota, visítenos para conocer a su «mejor amigo». Con un pequeño donativo, puede llevárselo a casa el mismo día.
>
> **HORARIO: 0800 – 2000 HORAS TODOS LOS DÍAS.**
> **TELÉFONO: 567-08-09**
> **CALLE PROVIDENCIA 100, COLONIA ROMA**

1. ¿Quién puso este anuncio?

   _____

2. ¿Cuánto tiempo hacía que se ofrecía este servicio?

   _____

3. ¿A quiénes se dirigía el anuncio?

   _____

4. ¿Qué requisitos les pidieron a los interesados?

   _____

5. ¿Cuánto cobraban por este servicio?

   _____

CHAPTER 5
The Future and Conditional Tenses

1. The Future Tense

a. Forms of the Future Tense

1. The future tense of regular verbs is formed by adding the following endings to the infinitive:

	descansar *to rest*	defender *to defend*	recibir *to receive*
yo	descansaré	defenderé	recibiré
tú	descansarás	defenderás	recibirás
él, ella, Ud.	descansará	defenderá	recibirá
nosotros, -as	descansaremos	defenderemos	recibiremos
vosotros, -as	descansaréis	defenderéis	recibiréis
ellos, ellas, Uds.	descansarán	defenderán	recibirán

NOTE: 1. Future-tense endings are the same for *-ar*, *-er*, and *-ir* verbs.

2. All future endings, except *-emos*, have an accent mark.

2. The future tense of irregular verbs is formed as follows:

(a) The following verbs drop the *e* of the infinitive before adding the future endings:

caber *to fit*	cabré cabrás cabrá	cabremos cabréis cabrán
haber *to have (aux.)*	habré habrás habrá	habremos habréis habrán
poder *to be able*	podré podrás podrá	podremos podréis podrán
querer *to want,* *to wish*	querré querrás querrá	querremos querréis querrán
saber *to know*	sabré sabrás sabrá	sabremos sabréis sabrán

(b) The following verbs replace the *e* or *i* of the infinitive ending with *d*, before adding the future-tense endings:

poner *to put*	pondré	pondremos
	pondrás	pondréis
	pondrá	pondrán
salir *to leave, to go out*	saldré	saldremos
	saldrás	saldréis
	saldrá	saldrán
tener *to have*	tendré	tendremos
	tendrás	tendréis
	tendrá	tendrán
valer *to be worth*	valdré	valdremos
	valdrás	valdréis
	valdrá	valdrán
venir *to come*	vendré	vendremos
	vendrás	vendréis
	vendrá	vendrán

(c)   The following verbs drop the *e* and *c* of the infinitive stem before adding the future-tense endings:

decir *to say, to tell*	diré	diremos
	dirás	diréis
	dirá	dirán
hacer *to do, to make*	haré	haremos
	harás	haréis
	hará	harán

b. Uses of the Future Tense

The future tense is used:

1.   To express future time.

| **Te *veré* mañana.** | *I will see you tomorrow.* |
| **¿A qué hora *llamarán* ellos?** | *At what time will they call?* |

2.   To express wonderment or probability in the present time.

¿Qué hora *será*?	*I wonder what time it is?*
***Serán* las cinco.**	*It's probably five o'clock.*
***Tendrán* hambre.**	*They must be (probably are) hungry.*

EJERCICIO A   **Mañana**   Todo el mundo tiene planes para mañana. Exprese lo que las siguientes personas van a hacer.

EJEMPLO: Luisa / ir de compras   Luisa **irá** de compras.

1. Gerardo y Luis / asistir a un partido de fútbol

2. mi mamá / visitar a una amiga

_____

3. yo / nadar en la piscina del club deportivo

_____

4. tú / escribir un ensayo para la clase de inglés

_____

5. Nancy y yo / aprender a montar en caballo

_____

6. mi abuelo / jugar al dominó

_____

7. Uds. / dormir una siesta larga

_____

8. Juan / leer una novela

_____

| **EJERCICIO B** | **En quince años...**   Ud. y varios amigos hablan del futuro. Exprese la reacción sugerida entre paréntesis a lo que ellos dicen. |

PARA EXPRESARSE MEJOR

coser _to sew_   **diseñar** _to design_   **la moda** _fashion_

EJEMPLO: A Norma le fascina trabajar en el teatro. (_ser famoso_)
            Norma **será** famosa.

1. Lisa piensa estudiar medicina. (_curar a muchos enfermos_)

_____

2. Tú no puedes dejar la computadora por un minuto. (_crear programas nuevos_)

_____

3. Víctor es muy competidor. (_ganar muchas competencias_)

_____

4. Yo diseño y coso muy bien y me gustan las revistas de moda. (_tener mi propia compañía_)

_____

5. A Uds. les gusta conocer otras culturas. (_hacer muchos viajes a países exóticos_)

_____

6. Enrique y Felipe trabajan muy bien juntos. (_abrir un negocio juntos_)

_____

7. Nosotros somos buenos amigos. (*ser amigos siempre*)

_____

EJERCICIO C   **¡Ahora no; más tarde!**   Exprese lo que responden las siguientes personas cuando alguien les dice lo que deben hacer ahora.

EJEMPLO: ¡Juan, saca la basura ahora!   **La sacaré más tarde.**

1. Niños, ¡vengan a comer!

_____

2. Estela, ¡haz la tarea ahora!

_____

3. Sarita debe decirte quién llamó.

_____

4. ¡Pongan los libros en el librero!

_____

5. Héctor debe buscar un estacionamiento más cerca.

_____

6. Ricky, ¡cambia el canal de televisión!

_____

7. ¡No vayan Uds. de compras ahora!

_____

8. Tú no puedes salir ahora.

_____

EJERCICIO D   **Circunstancias**   Exprese lo que las siguientes personas harán en estas circunstancias.

EJEMPLO: yo / tener hambre / comer   **Si tengo** hambre, **comeré.**

1. ellos / estar aburrido / salir con los amigos

_____

2. Ud. / tener frío / ponerse un suéter

_____

3. yo / estar cansado / descansar

_____

4. Miguel / querer entretenerse / ver una película

_____

5. nosotros / sentirse solo / llamar a un amigo

_____

6. Jenny y Ana / desear hacer ejercicio / ir al gimnasio

_____

7. tú / oír un chiste / reírse a carcajadas

_____

| EJERCICIO E | **Oral y escrito**   Ud. habla del futuro con un amigo. Usando las sugerencias, prepare una serie de preguntas sobre el tema. Luego, escriba las respuestas que dio a sus preguntas. |

SUGERENCIAS:

asistir a la universidad	**mudarse a**	**trabajar en**
estudiar	**tener éxito**	**viajar**
llegar a ser		

PREGUNTAS:

_____

_____

_____

_____

_____

_____

_____

RESUMEN:

_____

_____

_____

_____

_____

_____

_____

_____

| EJERCICIO F | **Lectura**   Lea el siguiente artículo sobre un evento especial y conteste las preguntas. |

Competencia y exposición culinarias

¿Le interesa la gastronomía? ¿Le gusta viajar?... Pues, le ofrecemos una oportunidad de aprender más acerca de las artes culinarias mientras disfruta de viajar. Muchos estudiantes de artes culinarias en España participarán en una competencia gastronómica que reunirá además a destacados profesionales de la cocina internacional y a decenas de compañías de vinos, uten-silios de cocina y productos alimenticios, entre otros.

La «Tercera Exposición y Reunión de Expertos Culinarios», que se llevará a cabo del 2 al 4 de octubre en la Sala de Exposiciones de Madrid, contará con competencias en las que los equipos de las principales escuelas de artes culinarias del país medirán sus habilidades y destrezas en varias categorías. Los estudiantes ganadores de estas competencias podrán recibir becas de estudio y premios en metálico.

Durante estos tres días, prestigiosos profesionales de España y del exterior ofrecerán interesantes seminarios sobre vinos y diversos temas gastronómicos, en los cuales, al igual que la exhibición de productos, podrán participar tanto los estudiantes de artes culinarias como el público en general.

Para recibir información sobre este evento estelar, llame a los teléfonos 53-88-09-78 o 53-88-09-80; o mande un mensaje electrónico a *gastronomia@eventos.es*. No se olvide de visitar nuestro sitio Web: *www.gastronomia.es*, para inscribirse.

1. ¿Qué anuncia este artículo?

   (a) Una reunión para los dueños de restaurantes

   (b) Una venta de artículos para la cocina

   (c) Un intercambio de recetas culinarias

   (d) Una oportunidad de aprender más sobre las artes culinarias

2. ¿Quiénes competirán en las competencias?

   (a) Los expertos culinarios más conocidos del mundo

   (b) Equipos de los institutos culinarios españoles

   (c) Los proveedores de productos alimenticios

   (d) Los profesores de las escuelas de gastronomía

3. ¿Qué recibirán los ganadores de las competencias?

   (a) Premios en forma de becas o dinero

   (b) Productos de las compañías que patrocinan el evento

   (c) Suscripciones a revistas sobre la gastronomía

   (d) Trabajo en restaurantes de cinco estrellas

4. ¿Qué otras actividades habrá durante los tres días?

   (a) Seminarios especiales

(b) Tómbolas

(c) Una cena preparada por los ganadores

(d) Informes sobre las dietas sanas

5. Para inscribirse, las personas interesadas deben

(a) mandar su solicitud de inscripción y cheque por correo.

(b) usar la solicitud de inscripción en forma electrónica.

(c) acudir a una escuela culinaria española.

(d) llamar por teléfono al patrocinador del evento.

2.   The Conditional Tense

a. Forms of the Conditional

1. The conditional tense of regular verbs is formed in the same way as the future tense. The following endings are added to the infinitive:

	descansar *to rest*	defender *to defend*	recibir *to receive*
yo	descansaría	defendería	recibiría
tú	descansarías	defenderías	recibirías
él, ella, Ud.	descansaría	defendería	recibiría
nosotros, -as	descansaríamos	defenderíamos	recibiríamos
vosotros, -as	descansaríais	defenderíais	recibiríais
ellos, ellas, Uds.	descansarían	defenderían	recibirían

NOTE: 1. The endings for the conditional are the same for *-ar, -er,* and *-ir* verbs.

2. All conditional endings have an accent mark.

2. The conditional of irregular verbs is formed as follows:

(a) The following verbs drop the *e* of the infinitive ending before adding the conditional endings:

caber *to fit*	cabría	cabríamos
	cabrías	cabríais
	cabría	cabrían
haber *to have* (*aux.*)	habría	habríamos
	habrías	habríais
	habría	habrían

poder *to be able*	podría podrías podría	podríamos podríais podrían
querer *to want,* *to wish*	querría querrías querría	querríamos querríais querrían
saber *to know*	sabría sabrías sabría	sabríamos sabríais sabrían

(b) The following verbs replace the *e* or *i* of the infinitive ending with *d*, before adding the conditional endings.

poner *to put*	pondría pondrías pondría	pondríamos pondríais pondrían
salir *to leave,* *to go out*	saldría saldrías saldría	saldríamos saldríais saldrían
tener *to have*	tendría tendrías tendría	tendríamos tendríais tendrían
valer *to be worth*	valdría valdrías valdría	valdríamos valdríais valdrían
venir *to come*	vendría vendrías vendría	vendríamos vendríais vendrían

(c) The following verbs drop the *e* and *c* of the infinitive stem, before adding the conditional endings.

decir *to say, to tell*	diría dirías diría	diríamos diríais dirían
hacer *to do, to make*	haría harías haría	haríamos haríais harían

b. Uses of the Conditional

The conditional is used:

1. To express what would or could happen in the future or to make a polite request.

    Mi mamá no lo *prepararía* así.   *My mother wouldn't prepare it that way.*

Me *gustaría* **hablar con el gerente.**   *I would like to speak to the manager*

2. To express wonderment or probability in the past.

    ¿Qué hora *sería*?   *I wonder what time it was.*
    Serían **las cinco.**   *It was probably five o'clock.*

    NOTE: 1. The expression *deber de* in the imperfect, followed by an infinitive, may also be used to express probability in the past.

        Debían de ser **las cinco.**   *It was probably (It must have been) five o'clock.*

        Ella *debía de tener* **diez años.**   *She must have been ten years old.*

    2. The future tense is commonly used in combination with the present or future tenses; the conditional tense, with a past tense.

        Cree **que** *irá*.   *He believes he will go.*
        Creía **que** *iría*.   *He believed he would go*

EJERCICIO G   **Según el tiempo** Exprese lo que Ud. y sus amigos harían o no harían, según las condiciones del tiempo. Use las siguientes actividades.

SUGERENCIAS:

andar en el parque	**jugar al tenis**
arreglar su casa	**leer una novela**
descansar todo el día	**(no) quedarse en casa**
esquiar en las montañas	**oír discos compactos**
ir a la playa	**patinar en el lago**
ir al centro comercial	**ver una película**
jugar a los videojuegos	**visitar un museo**

EJEMPLO: **Nosotros iríamos a la playa.**
             No nos quedaríamos en casa.

1. _____

    _____ .

2. _____

    _____ .

3. _____   4. _____

   _____ .   _____ .

EJERCICIO H   **Consejo legal**   Bárbara tiene un problema y piensa consultar a un abogado. Complete las frases con la forma apropiada de los verbos para expresar lo que pasaría.

EJEMPLO: El abogado me **escucharía.**
     (escuchar)

1. Yo le _____ lo que pasó y le _____ el reporte policial del accidente.
        (explicar)   (dar)

2. El abogado me _____ más preguntas y él _____ el asunto.
              (hacer)   (investigar)

3. Yo _____ a los testigos al accidente.
      (identificar)

4. Él los _____ en su oficina y _____ su declaración.
         (entrevistar)   (tomar)

5. Luego él me _____ si _____ demandar al chofer del camión.
             (decir)   (valer)

6. Él me _____ y yo no _____ que hacer nada.
        (aconsejar)   (tener)

7. El abogado lo _____ todo.
                (hacer)

8. Él _____ los documentos necesarios y los _____ .
      (preparar)   (tramitar)

9. Nosotros _____ la respuesta del demandado.
            (esperar)

10. La consulta no me _____ nada; _____ gratuita.
                     (costar)   (ser)

11. Si no ganamos, yo no _____ que pagarle nada al abogado.
                        (tener)

EJERCICIO I   **Causa y efecto**   Exprese qué pasaría luego de hacer las siguientes cosas.

EJEMPLO: oír música   Yo **me pondría** de buen humor.

1. leer un periódico _____

2. tomar vitaminas _____

3. escuchar un noticiero _____

4. dar dinero a una caridad _____

5. visitar un museo _____

6. reciclar las cosas en la basura _____

7. hacerme socio de un gimnasio _____

| EJERCICIO J | **Reacciones distintas**   Exprese cómo Ud. y sus amigos reaccionan de manera distinta en las siguientes circunstancias. |

EJEMPLO: Los alumnos están en el aula de clase y el profesor no llega.
            yo / esperar su llegada   Yo **esperaría** su llegada.
            Rafael / irse después de diez minutos   Rafael **se iría** después de diez minutos.

1. Uds. pidieron un videojuego de una tienda y llegó roto.

   yo / devolverlo a la tienda

   _____

   tú / llamar primero por teléfono

   _____

2. Uds. están en un restaurante y el mesero les sirvió platos equivocados.

   Jane y yo / comer el plato que nos sirvieron

   _____

   Jimmy / pedir el plato que ordenó

   _____

3. Uds. están en la playa y, de repente, un niño que nadaba cerca de Uds. pidió auxilio.

   yo / tratar de ayudarlo

   _____

   Celia / buscar al salvavidas

   _____

4. Ud. choca con un carro que estaba estacionado en la calle. El dueño del carro no está presente.

   yo / dejar una nota en el parabrisas del carro

   _____

   Linda y Federico / irse sin decir nada

   _____

5. Ud. acompaña a una amiga al centro comercial. Mientras ella se prueba varios vestidos, le pide su opinión.

   yo / ayudarle a encontrar otros vestidos

Virginia / decirle que todos le quedan bien

EJERCICIO K **Preguntas** Anoche Ud. asistió a una función en la escuela, cuyo propósito era recaudar fondos para el equipo de fútbol. Conteste las preguntas que le hizo un amigo que no pudo asistir a la función. Responda usando el condicional y las sugerencias entre paréntesis.

1. ¿Cuántas personas asistieron a la función? (*100*)

2. ¿A qué hora terminó la función? (*10:00*)

3. ¿Qué hora era cuando regresaste a casa? (*10:30*)

4. ¿Adónde fueron los otros amigos después de la función? (*a casa también*)

5. ¿Cuánto dinero procuraron para el equipo? (*$2,000*)

6. ¿Cuándo tenían planeados otros eventos semejantes? (*yo / no saber*)

EJERCICIO L **Un viaje a España** La profesora de español ha anunciado un viaje a España durante las vacaciones de primavera. A Ud. le gustaría participar en esta excursión, pero primero tendría que convencer a sus padres.

• Prepare una lista de los beneficios que Ud. sacaría de esta experiencia y de los sacrificios que Ud. haría para llevarla a cabo.

• Luego, escríbales una carta a sus padres, en la cual Ud. les presenta sus ideas y les pide permiso de hacer el viaje.

SUGERENCIAS: ahorrar el dinero que Ud. gana   hacer nuevas amistades
aprender otras costumbres   no comprar muchos recuerdos
conocer lugares de interés   practicar el español

CHAPTER 6
Reflexive Verbs; Commands With Reflexive Verbs

1. **Reflexive Verbs**

    a. Reflexive verbs require a reflexive pronoun (*me, te, se nos, os, se*) that refers the action of the verb back to the subject. In the simple tenses, reflexive pronouns generally precede the verb.

	PRESENT TENSE	PRETERIT TENSE	IMPERFECT TENSE
yo	*me* peino	*me* peiné	*me* peinaba
tú	*te* peinas	*te* peinaste	*te* peinabas
él, ella, Ud.	*se* peina	*se* peinó	*se* peinaba
nosotros, -as	*nos* peinamos	*nos* peinamos	*nos* peinábamos
vosotros, -as	*os* peináis	*os* peinasteis	*os* peinabais
ellos, ellas, Uds.	*se* peinan	*se* peinaron	*se* peinaban

	FUTURE TENSE	CONDITIONAL TENSE
yo	*me* peinaré	*me* peinaría
tú	*te* peinarás	*te* peinarías
él, ella, Ud.	*se* peinará	*se* peinaría
nosotros, -as	*nos* peinaremos	*nos* peinaríamos
vosotros, -as	*os* peinaréis	*os* peinaríais
ellos, ellas, Uds.	*se* peinarán	*se* peinarían

    NOTE: When the statement is negative, *no* comes before the reflexive pronoun.

        Ella *no* se peinó.   *She didn't comb her hair.*

    b. In compound tenses like the present perfect and pluperfect, for example, reflexive pronouns come before the form of the helping (auxiliary) verb *haber*.

	PRESENT PERFECT	PLUPERFECT
yo	*me* he peinado	*me* había peinado
tú	*te* has peinado	tú *te* habías peinado
él, ella, Ud.	*se* ha peinado	*se* había peinado
nosotros, -as	*nos* hemos peinado	*nos* habíamos peinados
vosotros, -as	*os* habéis peinado	*os* habíais peinado
ellos, ellas, Uds.	*se* han peinado	*se* habían peinado

    NOTE: If the statement is negative, *no* is placed before the reflexive pronoun.

        Ella *no* se había peinado.   *She hadn't combed her hair.*

    c. When a reflexive verb is used as an infinitive, the reflexive pronoun is attached to the end of the infinitive or placed before the conjugated verb. Both forms are acceptable.

Quiero peinar*me*.
Me quiero peinar. } *I want to comb my hair.*

Voy a peinar*me*.
Me voy a peinar. } *I'm going to comb my hair.*

d. When a reflexive verb is used in a progressive tense, the reflexive pronoun is attached to the end of the present participle (gerund) or placed before the conjugated verb. When the reflexive pronoun is attached to the gerund, an accent mark is required. Both forms are accepted.

Estoy peinándo*me*.
Me estoy peinando. } *I'm going to comb my hair.*

COMMON REFLEXIVE VERBS

acostarse (ue) *to go to bed*

afeitarse *to shave*

asustarse *to be frightened*

bañarse *to take a bath, to bathe*

callarse *to be silent, quiet*

cepillarse *to brush (one's hair, teeth, clothes)*

desayunarse *to have breakfast*

desmayarse *to faint*

despedirse (i) *to say goodbye, to take leave of*

despertarse (ie) *to wake up*

divertirse (ie) *to enjoy oneself, to have a good time*

dormirse (ue) *to fall asleep*

ducharse *to take a shower*

enfadarse *to get angry*

enojarse *to get angry*

equivocarse *to be mistaken*

esconderse *to hide*

irse *to leave, to go away*

lavarse *to wash oneself*

levantarse *to get up*

llamarse *to be named, to be called*

maquillarse *to put on makeup*

marcharse *to leave, to go away*

pasearse *to take a walk*

peinarse *to comb one's hair*

ponerse *to put on (clothing), to become*

quedarse *to stay, to remain*

quejarse *to complain*

quitarse *to take off (clothing)*

secarse *to dry oneself*

sentarse (ie) *to sit down*

vestirse (i) *to get dressed*

EJERCICIO A   **Actividades rutinarias.** Según los dibujos, exprese quién hace estas actividades rutinarias.

EJEMPLO: Mi papá **se afeita.**

1. La señora _____
   _____ .

4. Tú _____
   _____ .

2. Paco y Luis _____
   _____ .

5. Marisa _____
   _____ .

3. Ali y yo _____
   _____ .

6. La familia _____
   _____ .

EJERCICIO B   ¿Qué hicieron?   Use las sugerencias entre paréntesis para expresar lo que hicieron las siguientes personas.

EJEMPLO: Nilda oyó truenos y vio muchos relámpagos.   (*esconderse debajo de la cama*)
   Nilda **se escondió** debajo de la cama.

1. Arturo llegó cansadísimo a la casa.   (*sentarse en el sofá y dormirse*)

   _____

2. Tú recibiste una invitación a última hora para ir al teatro.   (*vestirse rápidamente*)

   _____

3. No me gustó la manera en que un dependiente me atendió en el almacén.   (*quejarse al gerente*)

   _____

4. Los niños trabajaron en el jardín toda la mañana. (*lavarse las manos*)

   _____

5. La cantante recibió muchos aplausos del público. (*ponerse contenta*)

   _____

6. Roger usó la computadora de su hermano sin pedirle permiso. (*enojarse*)

   _____

7. Yo regresé a casa de una fiesta de disfraces. (*quitarse el disfraz*)

   _____

EJERCICIO C   **Unas preguntas**   Al regresar de un intercambio escolar, su familia le hace preguntas sobre su rutina diaria allá. Conteste las preguntas usando las sugerencias entre paréntesis.

1. ¿Te acostabas tarde todos los días? (*sí*)

   _____

2. ¿Podías despertarte solo por la mañana? (*sí*)

   _____

3. ¿Cuántas veces a la semana te lavabas el pelo? (*7*)

   _____

4. ¿Cómo se llamaba la familia con quien vivías? (*Ayala*)

   _____

5. ¿Se paseaban a menudo tú y los otros jóvenes de tu escuela? (*sí*)

   _____

6. ¿De qué te quejabas? (*nada*)

   _____

7. ¿Te duchabas por la mañana o por la noche? (*P.M.*)

   _____

8. ¿Te callabas cuando no tenías nada que decir? (*sí*)

   _____

9. ¿Qué te ponías cuando hacía frío? (*una malla*)

   _____

10. ¿Con quiénes te desayunabas generalmente? (*la familia*)

    _____

EJERCICIO D   **Primero hacemos esto.**   Exprese lo que estas personas quieren (piensan o van a) hacer antes de hacer otra cosa.

Ejemplo: la señora / maquillarse / vestirse

   La señora **quiere maquillarse antes de** vestirse.

1. Jorge / desayunarse / bañarse

2. yo / ponerse el traje de baño / tomar el sol

3. ellos / lavarse las manos / comer

4. tú / despedirse de tus padres / salir de la casa

5. mi papá y yo / pasearse / ver la televisión

EJERCICIO E **¿Qué hacían cuando …?** Exprese lo que estas personas estaban haciendo cuando otra cosa pasó.

EJEMPLO: Chris / ducharse / sonó el teléfono
Chris **estaba duchándose** cuando sonó el teléfono.

1. los niños / divertirse / llegó la policía

2. yo / desayunarse / oí la noticia

3. Ud. / marcharse / otros invitados llegaron

4. tú / dormirse / oíste un ruido extraño

5. Anita y yo / sentarse en el cine / se fue la luz

EJERCICIO F **Actividades** Exprese lo que habían hecho las siguientes personas.

EJEMPLO: Rafael / escaparse de su cuarto   Rafael **se había escapado** de su cuarto.

1. tú / caerse en la calle

2. Evan y Sara / enojarse con sus compañeros

3. Jeremy / encerrarse en su cuarto

4. Rebecca y Amanda / esconderse detrás del sofá

5. yo / ponerse nervioso

_____

| EJERCICIO G | **Amigas desde la niñez**   Exprese lo que la mamá de Marisol cuenta de la amistad entre Linda y Marisol. Use el tiempo indicado entre paréntesis en su respuesta.

EJEMPLO: Marisol y Linda / conocer en la guardería infantil   (_pretérito_)
            Marisol y Linda **se conocieron** en la guardería infantil.

1. ellas / ver todos los días   (_imperfecto_)

_____

2. las dos niñas / buscar siempre   (_imperfecto_)

_____

3. ellas / poner a jugar juntas   (_imperfecto_)

_____

4. Linda y Marisol / no enojar nunca   (_pretérito_)

_____

5. ellas / extrañar durante los fines de semana   (_imperfecto_)

_____

6. las dos familias / hacer buenos amigos   (_pretérito_)

_____

e. Some verbs have special meanings when used reflexively:

BASIC MEANING	REFLEXIVE MEANING
aburrir _to bore_	**aburrirse** _to become bored (to bore oneself)_
acostar _to put to bed_	**acostarse** _to go to bed (to put oneself to bed)_
bañar _to bathe (someone)_	**bañarse** _to take a bath (to bathe oneself)_
cansar _to tire_	**cansarse** _to become tired (to tire oneself)_
colocar _to place (something)_	**colocarse** _to place oneself; to get a job_
engañar _to deceive_	**engañarse** _to deceive oneself; to be mistaken_
esconder _to hide (something)_	**esconderse** _to hide (oneself)_
parar _to stop (something)_	**pararse** _to stop oneself, to stop_
poner _to put (something)_	**ponerse** _to place oneself; to put (something) on; to become_
sentar _to seat_	**sentarse** _to sit down (to seat oneself)_

f. Some verbs are always used reflexively in Spanish, but not usually in English.

acordarse [ue] (de) _to remember_

apoderarse (de) _to take possession of_

apresurarse (a) _to hurry_

aprovecharse (de) _to avail oneself (of); to profit (by); to take unfair advantage (of)_

arrepentirse [ie] (de) _to repent, to regret_

atreverse (a) *to dare (to)*	**fijarse (en)** *to stare (at), to notice*
burlarse (de) *to make fun (of)*	**irse** *to go away*
desayunarse *to have breakfast*	**negarse [ie] (a)** *to refuse (to)*
desmayarse *to faint*	**olvidarse (de)** *to forget*
empeñarse (en) *to insist (on)*	**parecerse [zc] (a)** *to resemble*
enterarse (de) *to find out (about)*	**pasearse** *to stroll*
escaparse (de) *to escape (from)*	**quejarse (de)** *to complain*
fiarse (de) *to trust*	**reírse [í] (de)** *to laugh (at), to make fun (of)*
figurarse *to imagine*	**tratarse (de)** *to concern, to be a question (of)*

g. Reflexive verbs express reciprocal action corresponding to English *each other* and *one another.*

Nos llamamos **por teléfono.**	*We call each other by telephone.*
Ellos *se respetan.*	*They respect each other.*

NOTE: *Uno a otro (Una a otra)* or *el uno al otro (la una a la otra)* may be added to clarify or reinforce the meaning of the reflexive pronoun.

Ellos se respetan *uno al otro* **(***el uno al otro***).**	*They respect each other.*

h. Reflexive verbs are often used to express a passive action when the subject is a thing (not a person) and when the doer of the action is not indicated.

Las tiendas *se abren* **a las diez.**	*The stores are opened at ten o'clock.*
Esta ganga *se terminará* **mañana.**	*This sale will end tomorrow.*

2.   Commands With Reflexive Verbs

a. In affirmative commands, reflexives pronouns follow the reflexive verb and are attached to it. Affirmative commands with more than two syllables have a written accent mark over the stressed vowel. In a negative command, the reflexive pronoun precedes the verb.

	AFFIRMATIVE COMMANDS	NEGATIVE COMMANDS
tú	¡Levántate!	¡No *te* levantes!
Ud.	¡Levántese!	¡No *se* levante!
Uds.	¡Levántense!	¡No *se* levanten!

EJERCICIO H   **Haz lo que te digo.**   Patti va a pasar la noche en casa de una amiga. Exprese lo que su madre le dice antes de irse.

EJEMPLO: portarse bien   **¡Pórtate** bien!

1. cepillarse los dientes antes de acostarse _____

2. no acostarse tarde _____

3. no enfadarse _____

4. despertarse temprano _____

5. bañarse y luego vestirse _____

6. cambiarse de ropa _____

7. no ponerse ropa sucia _____

8. peinarse bien _____

9. no quejarse de la comida _____

10. no irse sin decir «gracias». _____

EJERCICIO I   ¡Escúchenme bien!   Exprese los mandatos que la madre les da a sus hijos.

EJEMPLO: ponerse serio   **¡Pónganse** serios!

1. ponerse los zapatos _____

2. cuidarse mucho _____

3. no ensuciarse la ropa _____

4. no caerse en el jardín _____

5. desayunarse bien _____

6. lavarse la cara y las manos _____

7. no secarse las manos en la ropa _____

8. no enojarse conmigo _____

9. divertirse mucho _____

10. no irse de la casa _____

EJERCICIO J   **Un mal rato**   Esteban y José están en una reunión. Complete su diálogo en que los dos no están de acuerdo.

ESTEBAN: Yo ya no quiero _____ en esta reunión. Yo estoy _____ .
                                    (quedarse)   (aburrirse)

JOSÉ: ¡No _____ tan pronto! Tú siempre _____ de algo o
                     (aburrirse)   (quejarse)
           _____ rápidamente.
              (cansarse)

ESTEBAN: ¡No _____ tan serio conmigo! ¿Por qué _____ en
                      (ponerse)   (empeñarse)
           _____ aquí más tiempo?
              (quedarse)

JOSÉ: Yo no _____ en _____ aquí. Sólo que estoy _____ .
                  (empeñarse)   (quedarse)   (divertirse)
           ¡ _____ con esos chicos y _____ a hablar con ellos!
                (sentarse)   (ponerse)
           ¡ _____ de la oportunidad de conocer a otras personas!
                (aprovecharse)

ESTEBAN: Ya ves, otra vez tú estás _____ de mí.
                                        (burlarse)

JOSÉ: Yo no _____ de ti, pero yo _____ a _____ en
                  (burlarse)   (negarse)   (irse)

este momento, cuando yo estoy _____ .
                                    (divertirse)

ESTEBAN: Bueno, amigo, yo _____ de ti y _____ . Adiós.
                              (despedirse)   (irse)

EJERCICIO K

Los buenos amigos   Usando los verbos indicados, exprese lo que Luz dice sobre la amistad y lo que caracteriza una verdadera amistad.

EJEMPLO: querer   Los buenos amigos **se quieren.**

1. respetar   _____

2. comunicar   _____

3. defender   _____

4. apoyar   _____

5. ayudar   _____

6. escribir   _____

7. no enojar   _____

8. consolar   _____

EJERCICIO L

¿Qué debo hacer?   Complete las frases con lo que Ud. debe hacer en estas circunstancias.

EJEMPLO: Mi reloj no funciona, pero conozco un lugar donde se **reparan** relojes.
                                                                  (reparar)

1. Tengo ganas de un helado. ¡Qué bien! Aquí hay un lugar donde _____ helado.
                                                                      (vender)

2. Necesito una foto de tamaño pasaporte. ¿Aquí _____ fotos?
                                                     (sacar)

3. Quiero comprar este videojuego, ¿en esta tienda _____ tarjetas de débito?
                                                         (aceptar)

4. Debo echar esta carta al correo pero primero debo buscar un lugar

   donde _____ estampillas.
              (comprar)

5. Quiero aprender una lengua extranjera. Mi papá me dijo que en esta escuela

   _____ italiano.
      (enseñar)

EJERCICIO M

Lectura   Lea este artículo que se publicó en el periódico y conteste las preguntas.

PARA EXPRESARSE MEJOR

el nivel *level*   **la empanada** *meat pie*   **la quitación** *horsemanship*
elogiado *praised*   **el volantín** *kite*

Las novedades de septiembre

El próximo miércoles circulará la revista «El Boletín», correspondiente a septiembre, en la cual se estrenará una serie de interesantes novedades y funciones. Nuevamente se incluirá un sensacional ciclo de teatro, organizado por varios grupos culturales, con obras de muy buen nivel y que han sido elogiadas por la crítica.

Y por tratarse del mes de la patria, también habrá promociones de empanadas, conservas y mermeladas naturales típicas chilenas, un curso de volantines que promete ser muy entretenido y clases de equitación.

En materia de libros, la oferta estará mejor que nunca, incluyendo una venta especial que se realizará en el Centro de Exposiciones y en la cual participarán algunas de las más importantes editoriales presentes en el país. También habrá muy buena música, con colecciones sorprendentes de artistas famosos en discos compactos.

1. ¿Qué circulará el próximo miércoles?

    (a) La última edición de una revista

    (b) Un nuevo diario

    (c) Una serie de reseñas sobre varias películas

    (d) Una nueva publicación en forma electrónica

2. La gente podrá enterarse de

    (a) las actividades de la alta sociedad.

    (b) las últimas noticias mundiales.

    (c) los ganadores de varios certámenes.

    (d) los eventos planeados para el mes.

3. ¿Por qué habrá promociones especiales?

    (a) Porque desean lanzar unos productos nuevos

    (b) Porque es el mes en que se celebran las fiestas patrias

    (c) Porque responden a los deseos del público

    (d) Porque desean limitar la participación del público

4. ¿Qué se podrá comprar en el Centro de Exposiciones?

   (a) Volantines de alta calidad

   (b) Libros y discos compactos

   (c) Comida típica chilena

   (d) Juegos para entretenerse

EJERCICIO N **Ejercicio oral y escrito** Seguir una rutina es parte de la vida diaria. Con un(a) compañero(a) de clase, discuta su rutina diaria y exprese lo que hace, y cuándo. Trate de usar tantos verbos reflexivos como pueda. Luego, escriba un párrafo en que anote tanto las semejanzas como las diferencias en su rutina.

CHAPTER 7
The Past Participle; the Perfect (Compound) Tenses

1.   Past Participles

a. Past Participles of Regular Verbs

The past participle of regular verbs is formed by dropping the infinitive ending and adding *-ado* or *-ido*.

INFINITIVE	PAST PARTICIPLE	MEANING
traba**jar**	traba**jado**	*worked*
compren**der**	comprend**ido**	*understood*
reci**bir**	recib**ido**	*received*

NOTE: The past participle of *-er* and *-ir* verbs with stems ending in a vowel have an accent mark.

INFINITIVE	PAST PARTICIPLE	MEANING
caer	caído	*fallen*
creer	creído	*believed*
leer	leído	*read*
oír	oído	*heard*
reír	reído	*laughed*
traer	traído	*brought*

b. Irregular Past Participles

1. The following verbs have irregular past participles ending in *-to*.

INFINITIVE	PAST PARTICIPLE	MEANING
ab**rir**	abier**to**	*opened*
cub**rir**	cubier**to**	*covered*
escri**bir**	escri**to**	*written*
mo**rir**	muer**to**	*died*
poner	pues**to**	*put*
resolver	resuel**to**	*resolved*
romper	ro**to**	*broken*
ver	vis**to**	*seen*
volver	vuel**to**	*returned*

2. The following verbs have irregular past participles ending in *-cho*.

INFINITIVE	PAST PARTICIPLE	MEANING
decir	di**cho**	*said*
hacer	he**cho**	*done, made*

EJERCICIO A	**Un mensaje electrónico incompleto** Use los participios pasados de los verbos en paréntesis para completar este mensaje electrónico que Inés le mandó a su amigo Carlos.

Querido Carlos:

Han _____ 1. (pasar) varios días y no he _____ 2. (tener) noticias tuyas ni te he _____ 3. (encontrar) en el Internet. Siempre hemos _____ 4. (tratar) de comunicarnos cuando estamos en el Internet al mismo tiempo. Me imagino que has _____ 5. (estar) muy ocupado desde que has _____ 6. (tomar) el nuevo puesto en la compañía.

De todos modos, quiero decirte que nuestras charlitas en el Internet me han _____ 7. (hacer) mucha falta. Esas pláticas, aunque breves, han _____ 8. (ser) muy placenteras y hemos _____ 9. (poder) estar en contacto, a pesar de los horarios pesados que nos han _____ 10. (poner) en el trabajo. Durante la semana pasada, me he _____ 11. (reunir) con otros amigos mutuos y todos han _____ 12. (preguntar) por ti porque ellos tampoco han _____ 13. (recibir) noticias tuyas. Gloria ha _____ 14. (planear) una reunión en su casa para el último fin de semana del mes. Ella ya ha _____ 15. (volver) de su viaje y ha _____ 16. (escribir) las invitaciones. Yo ya he _____ 17. (oír) algunas de sus experiencias en ese viaje y me he _____ 18. (reír) muchísimo. Como siempre, ella ha _____ 19. (disfrutar) del viaje y ha _____ 20. (aprender) mucho. Espero verte pronto.

Tu amiga, Inés

2.   The Perfect (Compound) Tenses

a. The present perfect tense is used to describe an action that began in the past and continues up to the present or an action that took place in the past but is connected with the present. It is formed by the present tense of *haber* and a past participle.

	AUXILIARY VERB	PAST PARTICIPLE
yo	he	
tú	has	
él, ella, Ud.	ha	trabajado / comprendido / recibido
nosotros, -as	hemos	
vosotros, -as	habéis	
ellos, ellas, Uds.	han	

NOTE: 1. To make a verb in the perfect tenses negative, *no* is placed before *haber*. To make a verb interrogative, the subject is placed after the past participle.

> *No* **he recibido la carta.**   *I haven't received the letter.*
> **¿Ha leído** *ella* **ese libro?**   *Has she read that book?*

2. Nothing comes between *haber* and the past participle. Pronouns (reflexive and object) come before *haber*.

> **Ellos** *se* **han lavado las manos.**   *They have washed their hands.*

b. The pluperfect tense is used to describe an action that was completed in the past before another action took place. It is formed by the imperfect tense of *haber* and a past participle.

	AUXILIARY VERB	PAST PARTICIPLE
yo	había	
tú	habías	
él, ella, Ud.	había	trabajado / comprendido / recibido
nosotros, -as	habíamos	
vosotros, -as	habíais	
ellos, ellas, Uds.	habían	

Ella me *había* **conocido antes.**   *She had met me before.*
Yo no la *había* **visto nunca.**   *I had never seen her.*

c. The future perfect tense is used to describe an action or event that will have been completed in the past. It is formed by the future tense of haber and a past participle.

	AUXILIARY VERB	PAST PARTICIPLE
yo	habré	
tú	habrás	
él, ella, Ud.	habrá	trabajado / comprendido / recibido
nosotros, -as	habremos	
vosotros, -as	habréis	
ellos, ellas, Uds.	habrán	

NOTE: 1. The future perfect may be used to express probability in the past.

> **¿Habrán comido?**   *I wonder if they have eaten.*
> **Habrá tomado otro autobús.**   *He has probably taken another bus.*

2. The expression *deber de* followed by the perfect infinitive may be substituted for the future perfect in expressing probability in the past.

> **Deben de haber comido temprano.**   *They must have eaten early.*
> **Debe de haber tomado otro autobús.**   *He must have taken another bus.*

d. The conditional perfect is used to describe an action or event that would have been completed in the past. It is formed by the conditional tense of *haber* and a past participle.

	AUXILIARY VERB	PAST PARTICIPLE
yo	habría	
tú	habrías	
él, ella, Ud.	habría	trabajado / comprendido / recibido
nosotros, -as	habríamos	
vosotros, -as	habríais	
ellos, ellas, Uds.	habrían	

NOTE: The conditional perfect is used to express probability in past time.

¿*Habrían comido*?   *I wonder if they had eaten.*

Habría tomado **otro autobús.**   *He had probably taken another bus.*

e. The perfect infinitive is used after prepositions. It is formed with the infinitive of *haber* and a past participle.

AUXILIARY VERB	PAST PARTICIPLE
haber	trabajado / comprendido / recibido

Ella recibió cien dólares por *haber*   *She received one hundred dollars for having*
trabajar **ocho horas.**   *worked eight hours.*

EJERCICIO B   **Muchas hazañas** Exprese qué actividades ha hecho cada uno de los siguientes sujetos.

EJEMPLO: Jorge / ganar muchas medallas   Jorge **ha ganado** muchas medallas.

1. los detectives / resolver muchos crímenes _____

2. yo / participar en muchos concursos _____

3. Roberto / escribir muchos poemas _____

4. tú / organizar una campaña de reciclaje _____

5. Jane y yo / hacer experimentos _____

6. Mercedes / aprender tres idiomas _____

7. los bomberos / salvar a muchas personas _____

EJERCICIO C   **Todo está listo.** Fernando es el encargado de un restaurante. Exprese lo que él y sus compañeros han hecho antes de abrir el restaurante.

EJEMPLO: los meseros / limpiar las mesas   Los meseros **han limpiado** las mesas.

1. Jaime / barrer el piso   _____

2. yo / revisar las reservaciones _____

3. el cocinero / preparar los especiales _____

4. tú / escribir el menú del día   _____

5. los meseros / poner las mesas   _____

6. Silvia / arreglar las flores   _____

7. nosotros / abrir la puerta   _____

EJERCICIO D   **¿Qué han hecho?**   Exprese lo que han hecho cada uno de los sujetos.

EJEMPLO: Nick **ha pagado la cuenta.**

1. Selene _____
   _____.

3. Mamá _____
   _____.

2. El mesero _____
   _____.

4. Yo _____
   _____.

5. Tú _____

_____ .

6. Papá _____

_____ .

EJERCICIO E   **Preguntas**   Conteste las preguntas que le hace un nuevo amigo.

1. ¿Han montado tú y tus amigos a caballo en la playa?

_____

2. ¿Has entrado en una casa encantada?

_____

3. ¿Has conducido un carro alguna vez?

_____

4. ¿Han comido Uds. en un restaurante japonés?

_____

5. ¿Les ha gustado esa comida?

_____

6. ¿Has asistido a algún estreno de una película?

_____

7. ¿Has ganado algún sorteo?

_____

EJERCICIO F   **¡Imagínense!**   Exprese lo que los niños habían hecho antes de que volvieran sus padres.

EJEMPLO: Miguel / limpiar el garaje   Miguel **había limpiado** el garaje.

1. Emilio y Víctor / recoger los juguetes _____

2. Aniluz / doblar la ropa _____

3. yo / terminar la tarea _____

4. Nancy / leer un cuento corto _____

5. Emilio y yo / apagar la computadora _____

6. tú / ponerse la pijama _____

EJERCICIO G   **Ya había pasado.**   Exprese lo que ya había pasado cuando ocurrieron los siguientes eventos.

EJEMPLO: Danny / volver a casa / sus sobrinos / irse
Cuando Danny **volvió a casa,** sus sobrinos ya **se habían ido.**

1. Gina / llegar a la oficina / su jefe / buscarla

   _____

2. tú / juntar el dinero para comprar el carro / el vendedor / venderlo a otra persona

   _____

3. yo / recibir la invitación / la fiesta / tener lugar

   _____

4. Lisa y yo / ver a Victoria / ella / recibir el premio

   _____

5. Alfredo y Nina / llegar al restaurante / terminarse los precios especiales

   _____

6. la ambulancia / llegar al hospital / el bebé / nacer

   _____

EJERCICIO H   **Las elecciones**   Exprese lo que ya había pasado cuando Blanca decidió servir de voluntaria durante la campaña electoral.

EJEMPLO: un voluntario / diseñar un folleto
Un voluntario ya **había diseñado** un folleto.

1. un grupo de voluntarios / distribuir folletos de casa en casa

   _____

2. los hijos del candidato / hacer llamadas telefónicas a su favor

   _____

3. Elena / enviar mensajes electrónicos

   _____

4. Pedro / concertar una entrevista con los periodistas

   _____

5. Kim y Jason / acompañar al candidato a los centros comerciales

   _____

EJERCICIO I   **Actividades nuevas**   Exprese lo que Raúl dice que él y sus amigos no habían hecho antes de acampar en las montañas.

EJEMPLO: yo / acampar en las montañas   Yo nunca **había acampado** en las montañas.

1. yo / dormir en una tienda de campaña

   _____

2. mis amigos y yo / nadar en un lago

   _____

3. Jaime / practicar el alpinismo

   _____

4. tú / ver un oso de cerca

   _____

5. ninguno de nosotros / hacer una hoguera de campamento

   _____

6. Luke y Oscar / pescar en el lago

   _____

7. yo / ir en canoa

   _____

EJERCICIO J   **Después de un año** Exprese lo que las siguientes personas dicen que habrá pasado después de un año en la universidad.

EJEMPLO: Rosa / aprender mucho   Rosa **habrá aprendido** mucho.

1. yo / escribir muchos ensayos

   _____

2. Tim / hacer muchos experimentos en el laboratorio

   _____

3. tú / leer muchas novelas

   _____

4. Alice / escoger su área de especialización

   _____

5. nosotros / conocer a muchos jóvenes

   _____

6. Nick / ponerse más serio

   _____

EJERCICIO K   **¿Qué habrá pasado?** Exprese lo que habrá pasado en las siguientes circunstancias.

EJEMPLO: Los señores discuten con el gerente del restaurante. (_No gustarles la comida_)
           A los señores **no les habrá gustado** la comida.

PARA EXPRESARSE MEJOR

la cola   *line* **estrenar**   *to open (a film, play)* **chocar**   *to crash*
la muleta   *crutch*   **la bandera**   *flag*   **el desfile**   *parade*

1. Había mucha cola para entrar en el cine.   (*estrenar una nueva película*)

   _____

2. Vemos a varios policías en la carretera.   (*chocar dos carros*)

   _____

3. Un joven sale del consultorio médico usando muletas.   (*romperse la pierna*)

   _____

4. Muchas personas llevan banderas pequeñas en la mano.   (*asistir a un desfile*)

   _____

5. Oímos las sirenas de los bomberos.   (*haber un edificio*)

   _____

6. Todo el mundo llevaba impermeable y trae paraguas.   (*llover mucho*)

   _____

EJERCICIO L   **Acciones diferentes**   Exprese lo que las siguientes personas habrían hecho en varias circunstancias.

EJEMPLO: Ana se puso muy frustrada porque la computadora no respondía a sus órdenes.
           José **habría apagado** la computadora.
           (*José / apagar la computadora*)

1. Mirta fue al centro a pie porque los autobuses estaban en huelga.

   _____
   (*yo / volver a casa*)

2. Tú llamaste a tu novio ocho veces ayer y nunca pudiste hablar con él.

   _____
   (*Susan / llamarle una sola vez*)

3. Javier y Laura no pudieron entrar al cine porque se agotaron los boletos.

   _____
   (*nosotros / comprar los boletos de antemano*)

4. Yo hice muchas compras y las cargué a mi tarjeta de crédito.

   _____
   (*Daniel / pagar al contado*)

5. Uds. tuvieron que abrir todos los regalos al pasar por la seguridad del aeropuerto.

   _____
   (*yo / enviarlos por correo*)

6. A Karen le faltaba un ingrediente para la receta que iba a preparar.

   _____
   (*tú / ir al supermercado a comprarlo*)

EJERCICIO M   **¿Qué habría hecho?**   Exprese lo que Ud. habría hecho en varias situaciones.

EJEMPLO: A un niño se le cayó el helado al suelo.
Yo le **habría comprado** otro helado.
(comprarle otro helado)

1. Ud. encontró una cartera llena de dinero y tarjetas de crédito.

   _____
(devolverla al dueño)

2. Sus amigos salieron anoche para celebrar el fin del año escolar.

   _____
(acompañarlos)

3. Ayer unos amigos fueron al aeropuerto en taxi.

   _____
(llevarlos al aeropuerto en mi carro)

4. Sus padres castigaron a su hermano porque les dijo una mentira.

   _____
(decirles la verdad)

5. Su padre no le dejó una propina al mesero en el restaurante porque no le gustó el servicio que recibió.

   _____
(dejarle al mesero una propina pequeña)

6. Por el pronóstico de mal tiempo, poca gente asistió a una reunión en la escuela por la noche.

   _____
(cancelar la reunión)

EJERCICIO N   **Muy merecido**   Exprese lo que las siguientes personas han recibido por haber hecho algo especial.

EJEMPLO: ganar el maratón / ella / una medalla
Por **haber ganado** el maratón, ella **ha recibido** una medalla.

1. participar en un concurso / los alumnos / un certificado de honor

   _____

2. vender muchos carros / el señor / un aumento de sueldo

   _____

3. escribir una novela / el autor / un premio literario

   _____

4. trabajar en una compañía por 30 años / la secretaria / un reloj de oro

   _____

5. salvar a muchas personas / los bomberos / el agradecimiento del pueblo

   _____

6. ser muy gracioso / el niño / un nuevo juguete

   _____

EJERCICIO O   **Reflexiones**   Cuando llegamos al final de algo, por ejemplo, unas vacaciones largas, solemos reflexionar sobre lo que hemos hecho durante esa temporada y también sobre lo que habríamos hecho. Trabaje con un compañero y reflexione sobre lo que Ud. ha hecho y lo que Ud. habría hecho durante ese período. Luego, escriba un resumen de sus reflexiones.

_____

_____

_____

_____

_____

_____

_____

_____

_____

EJERCICIO P   **Lectura**   Lea este artículo y luego conteste las preguntas.

PARA EXPRESARSE MEJOR

la golosina *sweet*	**beneficiado** *beneficiary*
el ordenador *computer*	**saborear** *to savor*
rechazar *to reject*	**quizá(s)** *perhaps*
de hecho *in fact*	**azotar** *to beat; lash; whip*

Golosinas para olvidar la crisis

Argentina celebra hoy el Día del Niño, un día en el que tradicionalmente los niños de la casa reciben regalos. Pero la crisis económica que sufre su país también les ha afectado a ellos. Un estudio ha revelado que se ha vendido un 52% menos de juguetes que el año pasado. Sólo las golosinas han aumentado sus ventas.

Según ese estudio, conducido en unos 300 comercios de todo el país, las ventas de las jugueterías descendieron este día un 52%, se vendieron un 78% menos de ordenadores, un 62% menos de artículos deportivos, un 48% menos de discos compactos y casetes y un 12% menos de libros, entre otras cosas. El problema es que la mayoría de los juguetes eran de importación, de países asiáticos, y su precio ha subido entre un 100 y un 150% desde que empezó la crisis. Además, han desaparecido las tiendas de «todo a dos pesos» que eran un lugar habitual de compra de cosas para niños.

Pero ningún niño rechaza un dulce, y probablemente muchos niños argentinos hayan disfrutado comiendo las golosinas que sus familias les han regalado este año. De hecho, el negocio de las dulcerías es el único que ha salido beneficiado en el Día del Niño. Las ventas de golosinas han subido un 8%.

Saboreando sus dulces, los niños quizá olviden la crisis que azota a su país y de la que son más conscientes de lo que deberían. Un periódico argentino realizó una encuesta entre más de 10.000 chicos entre los 11 y 17 años. Los resultados de esa encuesta indican que el 74% cree que la crisis afectó el desarrollo normal de sus clases, un 17% dice que han tenido que dejar de comprar ropa y un 15% que ha reducido las salidas con sus amigos. Por el momento, parece que es una época poco dulce para los chicos.

1. ¿Cómo celebraban El Día del Niño?

    (a) Cancelaban las clases en toda la república.

    (b) Les daban regalos a los niños.

    (c) Había eventos especiales para los niños.

    (d) Pasaban películas apropiadas para los niños en los cines.

2. La disminución en la venta de juguetes se debe

    (a) a los cambios de interés de los niños.

    (b) al aumento de los precios.

    (c) a las nuevas leyes de importación.

    (d) a la falta de existencia en las jugueterías.

3. Según este artículo, ¿qué comercio ha beneficiado más este año?

    (a) Los elaboradores de dulces

    (b) Los discos compactos

    (c) Las tiendas de todo a un precio

    (d) Las tiendas de libros

4. ¿Qué revela la encuesta realizada entre los chicos?

    (a) Los chicos no han escapado los efectos de la crisis económica.

    (b) Muchos chicos no están enterados de la crisis.

    (c) Hay una falta de comprensión de la crisis entre los niños.

    (d) Los niños buscan otros modos de olvidar la crisis.

CHAPTER 8

SER and *ESTAR*; Adjectives Used With *SER* and *ESTAR*

1. *SER* and *ESTAR*

Spanish has two different verbs, *ser* and *estar*, that both correspond to the English verb *to be. Ser* and *estar* are not interchangeable and their use depends on the context.

a. Forms of *SER**

	PRESENT TENSE	PRETERIT TENSE	IMPERFECT TENSE	FUTURE TENSE	CONDITIONAL TENSE
yo	soy	fui	era	seré	sería
tú	eres	fuiste	eras	serás	serías
él, ella, Ud.	es	fui	era	será	sería
nosotros, -as	somos	fuimos	éramos	seremos	seríamos
vosotros, -as	sois	fuisteis	erais	seréis	seríais
ellos, ellas, Uds.	son	fueron	eran	serán	serían

b. Uses of *SER*

1. To express an inherent characteristic, a description, or an identification:

Este café *es* bueno.	*This coffee is good.*
La mujer *es* bondadosa.	*The woman is kind.*
María *es* responsable.	*María is responsible.*
Felipe *es* fuerte.	*Felipe is strong.*
¿Quién *es*? — Es Linda.	*Who is it? — It's Linda.*

2. To express occupation or nationality:

Silvia *es* dentista.	*Silvia is a dentist.*
Mi papá *es* ingeniero.	*My father is an engineer.*
Pedro *es* peruano.	*Pedro is Peruvian.*
Elsa *es* puertorriqueña.	*Elsa is Puerto Rican.*

3. To express time, dates, and where an event takes place:

¿Qué hora *es*? — *Son* las seis.	*What time is it? It's six o'clock.*
Es el veinte de septiembre.	*It's September 20.*
¿Dónde *es* la fiesta?	*Where is the party?*
La fiesta *es* en casa de Miguel.	*The party is in Miguel's house.*

4. With *de*, to express origin, possession, or material:

Sus padres *son* de Puerto Rico.	*Her parents are from Puerto Rico.*

---

*For the compound and subjunctive forms of *ser*, see the Appendix on page 273.

Este café *es* de Colombia.	*This coffee is from Colombia.*
Es la mochila de Nick.	*It's Nick's backpack.*
Esta corbata *es* de seda.	*This tie is made of silk.*
La escultura *es* de bronce.	*The sculpture is made of bronze.*

5. With impersonal expressions:

Es necesario comer bien.	*It is necessary to eat well.*
Es importante cumplir con la palabra.	*It is important to keep one's word.*

6. To express a passive action with a past participle (see Chapter 9).

La carta *fue* escrita por el alcalde.	*The letter was written by the mayor.*
Los edificios *fueron* destruidos por el temblor.	*The buildings were destroyed by the earthquake.*

NOTE: Adjectives used with *ser* must agree with the subject in gender and number.

El monument*o* es alt*o*.	*The monument is tall.*
Las empanad*as* son delicios*as*.	*The meatpies are delicious.*

EJERCICIO A **Características positivas y negativas** Sally y unos amigos hablan de otros compañeros de escuela. Exprese lo que ellos dicen.

EJEMPLO: Caterina / simpático / tímido   Caterina **es simpática** pero **es tímida** también.

1. Arturo / fuerte / sensitivo   _Arturo es fuerte y sensitivo_

2. Nancy y Elsa / divertido / envidioso _Nancy y elsa son divertidy pero también envidios_

3. José / independiente / perezoso _Jose es independiente pero envidioso Perrezozo_

4. Luisa / bonito / aburrido   _____

5. Carlos y Lola / cómico / antipático _carlos y lola son sinpaticos perro antipatica tambien_

6. Nosotros / bondadoso / crítico   _____

EJERCICIO B **Origen, nacionalidad y ascendencia** Tom habla del origen, nacionalidad y ascendencia de los miembros del Círculo Internacional de la escuela. Exprese lo que él dice.

EJEMPLO: Kim / los Estados Unidos / norteamericano / coreano
Kim **es de** los Estados Unidos. **Es norteamericana de ascendencia coreana.**

1. Patrick / Chile / chileno / irlandés
Patrick es de chile. Es chileno de ascendencia irlandes

2. Pierre y Francine / Francia / francés / francés
Pierre y francine son de francia. Es frances y acendencia francesa

3. Pilar / Cuba / cubano / español

Pilar es de cuba. Es cubana de hacendencia española

4. Vito y María / la Argentina / argentino / italiano

vito y maria so de la argentina. Es Argentino de hacendencia italiano

5. Ivan / México / mexicano / ruso

Ivan es de mexico. Es mexicano de hacendencia rusa

| EJERCICIO C | **Amigo por correspondencia**   Alfredo recibió una carta electrónica de un amigo nuevo. Complete las frases con la forma apropiada del verbo *ser*. |

Querido amigo:

Ésta _es_ una carta de introducción. Mi nombre _es_ Oscar Ramírez y _soy_
     1.   2.   3.

de Puebla, México. Mi familia _es_ grande: tengo dos hermanos y dos hermanas. Mis
                      4.

hermanos _son_ mayores que yo y mis hermanas _son_ menores. Ellas _son_ gemelas.
        5.   6.   7.

Nosotros _somos_ una familia muy unida. Mi padre _es_ profesor en la universidad y
        8.   9.

mi mamá _es_ ama de casa. Antes de casarse mi mamá _era_ maestra de
      10.   11.

primaria. _Es_ bonito tener cuatro hermanos porque siempre tienes con quien hablar y
     12.

jugar. Yo _soy_ muy atlético; me gustan el fútbol, el tenis y la natación.
      13.

También _soy_ un estudiante aplicado. Mi gran deseo _es_ conocer el mundo y
      14.   15.

tener amistades en otros países. Creo que _es_ posible hacerlo por medio de la correspon-
                      16.

dencia electrónica. ¿Te gustaría _ser_ mi amigo? Si tu respuesta _es_ afirmativa,
                       17.   18.

contéstame y cuéntame cómo tú _eres_ . _Es_ la hora de mi programa favorito.
                      19.   20.

Hasta pronto.

c. Forms of *ESTAR**

	PRESENT TENSE	PRETERIT TENSE	IMPERFECT TENSE	FUTURE TENSE	CONDITIONAL TENSE
yo	estoy	estuve	estaba	estaré	estaría
tú	estás	estuviste	estabas	estarás	estarías
él, ella, Ud.	está	estuvo	estaba	estará	estaría
nosotros, -as	estamos	estuvimos	estábamos	estaremos	estaríamos
vosotros, -as	estáis	estuvisteis	estabais	estaréis	estaríais
ellos, ellas, Uds.	están	estuvieron	estaban	estarán	estarían

*For the compound and subjunctive forms of *estar*, see the Appendix on page 270.

d. Uses of ESTAR

1. To express location or position:

Bogotá *está* en Colombia. — *Bogota is in Colombia.*

¿Dónde *están* los niños? — *Where are the children?*

Luisa *está* cerca de la puerta. — *Luisa is near the door.*

2. To indicate a state or condition:

Yo *estoy* sentado (cansado). — *I am seated (tired).*

La bicicleta *está* sucia (rota). — *The bicycle is dirty (broken).*

Nosotros *estamos* contentos (tristes). — *We are happy (sad).*

El maestro *está* bien (enfermo). — *The teacher is well (ill).*

Las ventanas *están* cerradas (abiertas). — *The windows are closed (open).*

El pájaro *está* muerto (vivo). — *The bird is dead (alive).*

> NOTE: 1. A condition does not identify, describe, or express a characteristic. It may be a phase: *Ella está enferma (contenta)*; a temporary state: *Yo estoy sentado (ocupado)*; or the result of an action: *Las luces están encendidas.*
>
> 2. Adjectives used with *estar* agree with the subject in gender and number.

3. To form the progressive tenses with the present participle (gerund):

Están charlando. — *They are chatting.*

Estarán llegando en este momento. — *They are probable arriving at this moment.*

4. In the following common expressions:

estar a punto de + infinitive   *to be just about to*

Estamos a punto de terminar la comida. — *We are just about to finish the meal.*

estar para + infinitive   *to be about to*

Estoy para acostarme. — *I'm about to go to bed.*

estar por   *to be in favor of*

Ella *está por* los derechos humanos. — *She's in favor of human rights.*

estar por + infinitive   *to be ready (disposed) to*

Están por jugar al tenis. — *They are ready to play tennis.*

estar conforme, estar de acuerdo (con)   *to be in agreement (with), to agree*

Ellos *están conformes* con las reglas. ⎱
Ellos *están de acuerdo* con las reglas. ⎰ — *They are in agreement with the rules.*

estar de vuelta   *to be back*

Norma, ¿cuándo *estarás de vuelta*? — *Norma, when will you be back?*

EJERCICIO D   **¿Dónde está...?**   Luke nunca recuerda dónde pone las cosas. Exprese las preguntas que él hace y las respuestas que le da su mamá.

EJEMPLO: mi chaqueta negra / en el armario

¿Dónde **está** mi chaqueta negra? Tu chaqueta negra **está** en el armario.

1. mis llaves de la casa / sobre la mesa

_____

2. la pelota de béisbol / debajo del sofá

_____

3. el boleto al concierto / en tu cartera

_____

4. las revistas deportivas / al lado de la cama

_____

5. mi cámara / en la mochila

_____

6. mi impermeable / cerca de la puerta

_____

EJERCICIO E   **El momento de la verdad**   Acaban de poner los resultados de las elecciones del consejo de estudiantes en el tablero de anuncios y todos los estudiantes observan con interés. Complete la siguiente descripción de la escena con la forma apropiada de *estar*.

Muchos estudiantes _____ delante del tablero de anuncios que _____ en el patio
                          1.   2.

de la escuela. Ellos _____ esperando los resultados de las elecciones del gobierno escolar.
                          3.

Los candidatos _____ en la parte delantera de la muchedumbre. Se nota que uno de los
                     4.

candidatos a presidente _____ nervioso, mientras el otro parece _____ preocupado.
                              5.   6.

Yo _____ en la parte trasera del grupo. Todos los alumnos _____ ansiosos de saber
       7.   8.

los resultados.

Los candidatos _____ hablando con sus partidarios y les _____ dando las gracias
                     9.   10.

por su ayuda durante la campaña. Por fin colocan los nombres de los ganadores de las

elecciones y todo el mundo _____ aplaudiendo a los ganadores, quienes _____ alegres.
                                11.   12.

EJERCICIO F   **Una noche de gala**   Complete los comentarios que hace el locutor de un evento especial. Use la forma apropiada de *ser* o *estar*.

Muy buenas tardes a todos. _____ 1. Bernal Díaz y voy a _____ 2. el locutor de esta feria cinematográfica. Yo _____ 3. de Colombia, pero ahora _____ 4. en la Costa del Sol, donde muchos de los artistas famosos de cine _____ 5. en este momento. Marisol Peñales _____ 6. a mi lado durante toda la transmisión. Ella _____ 7. de la famosa emisora madrileña que _____ 8. transmitiendo este programa. Nosotros _____ 9. seguros de que _____ 10. una noche inolvidable, tanto para las personas que _____ 11. en este auditorio como para Uds. que _____ 12. en sus casas.

Ya _____ 13. las cinco de la tarde aquí y los artistas _____ 14. entrando en el auditorio. Las sonrisas que llevan en las caras indican que _____ 15. muy contentos de _____ 16. aquí esta noche pero notamos que algunos artistas _____ 17. nerviosos también. Ya _____ 18. abiertas las puertas del auditorio y muchas personas ya _____ 19. sentadas. _____ 20. una noche de elegancia, talento y nervios. Las mujeres _____ 21. vestidas en los últimos diseños de la moda. Y los hombres _____ 22. muy elegantes en sus smokings. La ceremonia _____ 23. para comenzar. La orquesta _____ 24. lista; los músicos sólo _____ 25. esperando la señal del conductor para llenar el auditorio de música. El _____ 26. saludando al público desde el foro. Ahora Marisol _____ 27. aquí conmigo y nosotros _____ 28. de vuelta en un minuto después de un mensaje del patrocinador de este evento.

EJERCICIO G **Servicio voluntario** Ud. y unos compañeros de su escuela están participando en un proyecto de servicio voluntario en Costa Rica. Complete, con la forma apropiada de *ser* o *estar*, la descripción del proyecto que Uds. van a mandar a un periódico local.

Nosotros _____ 1. estudiantes de una escuela secundaria. _____ 2. en Costa Rica porque _____ 3. participando en un programa de servicio voluntario. _____ 4. construyendo una nueva escuela. La otra escuela _____ 5. cerrada porque _____ 6. destruida en una tormenta. El trabajo _____ 7. muy duro y nosotros _____ 8. cansadísimos cuando llegamos a casa. Nosotros _____ 9. muy entusiasmados porque sabemos que nuestro trabajo _____ 10. muy importante. _____ 11. en una parte rural de Costa Rica donde la vegetación _____ 12. muy densa y el sol brilla durante la mayor parte del día.

Cada voluntario —————— viviendo con una familia diferente. Todas las familias
                        13.
—————— muy cariñosas y generosas. La familia con que yo —————— viviendo
   14.   15.
—————— grande: hay cuatro hijos. El padre —————— carpintero y la madre ——————
   16.   17.   18.
enfermera y trabaja en una clínica. El padre —————— costarricense pero la madre ——————
                                                 19.   20.
de Nicaragua. Los hijos —————— buenos y divertidos y —————— listos para ayudarnos.
                           21.   22.
Ellos —————— aprendiendo el inglés. Nosotros vamos a —————— aquí hasta el primero
         23.   24.
de agosto. —————— una experiencia inolvidable. —————— importante ayudar a otras
              25.   26.
personas y conocer sus costumbres.

EJERCICIO H   Mi mejor amiga Cristina describe a su mejor amiga. Complete las frases con
la forma correcta de *ser* o *estar*.

Gisela —————— mi mejor amiga. Ella —————— de Alemania, pero ella y su familia
          1.   2.
—————— en los Estados Unidos ahora. Ella tiene dos hermanas pero Gisela —————— la
   3   4.
mayor. Su casa —————— en la misma cuadra en que yo vivo. —————— una casa grande
                  5.   6.
con un jardín amplio.

Su mamá —————— una jardinera buena y ella siempre —————— en el jardín. Su
            7.   8.
casa —————— llena de flores del jardín. A Gisela le gusta ir de compras y compra lo que
        9.
—————— de moda. Ella prefiere la ropa de fibras naturales como el algodón, la lana y la
   10.
seda. Según ella, —————— más fácil mantener la ropa en buenas condiciones. Su padre
                     11.
—————— un hombre de negocios y viaja mucho. Ahora él —————— en el Japón. Cuando
   12.   13.
su padre —————— de vuelta de un viaje, él nos cuenta de sus experiencias. Gisela
            14.
—————— una chica simpática y buena y nosotras siempre —————— juntas. ——————
   15.   16.   17.
bonito tener una amiga como Gisela.

2.   Adjectives Used with *SER* and *ESTAR*

Some adjectives may be used with either *ser* or *estar*, but the meaning of an adjective
used with *ser* will differ from its meaning when used with *estar*. In all cases, adjectives
used with *ser* and *estar* agree with the subject in gender and number.

El niño es bueno.	*The boy is good.*	(characteristic)
La comida está buena.	*The food is good.*	(condition)

Ella es lista.	*She's clever/smart.* (characteristic)
Ella está lista.	*She's ready.* (condition)
El señor es pálido.	*The man is pale-complexioned.* (characteristic)
El señor está pálido.	*The man is pale.* (condition)
Es seguro.	*He is safe/reliable. (description/characteristic)*
Está seguro.	*He is sure.* (condition/state of mind)
La niña es viva.	*The girl is sharp/quick.* (characteristic)
La niña está viva.	*The girl is alive.* (state-phase)
Es joven.	*He is young.* (description)
Está joven.	*He looks young.* (condition)
Ella es aburrida.	*She is boring.* (characteristic)
Ella está aburrida.	*She is bored.* (condition/state)

EJERCICIO 1   **Comentarios**   Unas vecinas están haciendo comentarios sobre las personas que viven en su vecindario. Complete sus comentarios con la forma correcta de *ser* o *estar*.

1. Los hijos de la familia Domínguez _____ muy vivos pero no _____ bien educados.

2. La paella que prepara la señora Durango siempre _____ muy sabrosa pero hoy

   _____ más sabrosa que nunca.

3. Últimamente Felipe _____ muy pálido. ¿ _____ enfermo?

4. ¿Oyeron los gritos anoche? Los señores Camacho _____ peleando otra vez y sus

   ventanas siempre _____ abiertas.

5. Yo no sé por qué los jóvenes siempre _____ jugando al fútbol en la

   calle. _____ muy peligroso.

6. La ropa que lleva la señora Pérez _____ muy sencilla. Ella siempre

   _____ bien maquillada.

7. Los hermanos Soto _____ muy listos pero nunca _____ listos cuando mis

   hijos pasan por ellos.

8. La señora Tamayo _____ abogada y su oficina _____ cerca de aquí.

9. Migdalia y yo queremos ver la película que estrenó ayer pero todos dicen que la película

   _____ aburrida.

10. Ayer visité a la señora Leal. _____ una persona limpia pero todos los muebles

    _____ cubiertos de polvo.

EJERCICIO J | **Actividad oral y escrita** Ud. y su clase de español van a hacer un viaje de intercambio a México. Los alumnos de la escuela de intercambio les han pedido a Uds. un párrafo autobiográfico que publicarán en el periódico de la escuela. Trabajando con un compañero, haga una serie de preguntas para enterarse de la información que necesitan para hacer esta tarea (nacionalidad, personalidad, familia, etc.). Luego, escriba un párrafo autobiográfico en el cual Ud. se describe a sí mismo.

EJERCICIO K | **Lectura** Lea el siguiente aviso y luego conteste las preguntas.

PARA EXPRESARSE MEJOR

conforme a *according to, in accordance with*   **prever** *to foresee*

el diseño *design*   **solicitar** *to request*

Solicitamos su comprensión

Estamos inaugurando la nueva versión de El Diario Digital con una nueva batería de servidores, nuevo hosting, nuevo diseño, nueva ingeniería y nueva arquitectura.

Nuestro objetivo es mejorar nuestro servicio conforme a sus recomendaciones.

La experiencia indica que estos procesos están acompañados de inestabilidad y dificultades que no pueden preverse con anticipación.

Las corregiremos tan rápido como sea posible.

Gracias.

---

1. ¿Qué piden en este anuncio?

   (a) Que los lectores tengan paciencia

   (b) Que los lectores manden sugerencias

   (c) Que la inauguración tenga éxito

   (d) Que el público no los abandone

2. ¿Qué están haciendo?

   (a) Están inventando un nuevo producto.

   (b) Están solicitando recomendaciones.

   (c) Están reparando su sistema básico.

   (d) Están ofreciéndoles ayuda a sus lectores.

3. Los cambios que están haciendo están basados en

   (a) unas experiencias malas.

   (b) los experimentos que han llevado a cabo.

   (c) las sugerencias de sus clientes.

   (d) unas recomendaciones de los ingenieros.

4. ¿Qué dicen de las inestabilidades y dificultades que habrá?

   (a) Buscan un sistema para mejorarlas.

   (b) Es imposible saberlas de antemano.

   (c) Pueden durar por mucho tiempo.

   (d) Será difícil corregirlas.

CHAPTER 9
The Passive Voice

In the active voice, the subject generally performs an action. In the passive voice, the subject is acted upon.

ACTIVE	El hombre *vendió* muebles.	*The man sold furniture.*
PASSIVE	*Los muebles fueron vendidos* por el hombre.	*The furniture was sold by the man.*
	Se venden muebles aquí.	*Furniture is sold here.*

1.   Formation and Use of the Passive Voice

a. If the agent (doer) is mentioned or implied, the passive construction in Spanish is similar to English: subject + form of *ser* + past participle + *por* + agent (doer).

La carta *fue escrita por* **ella.**	*The letter was written by her.*
La noticia *será anunciada por* **el presidente.**	*The news will be announced by the president.*
Los alumnos *son castigados por* **el maestro.**	*The students are punished by their teacher.*

NOTE: 1.   In the passive voice, the past participle is used as an adjective and agrees with the subject in gender and number.

2.   The agent is preceded by *por*. However, if the past participle expresses feeling or emotion, rather than action, *por* may be replaced by *de*.

El alcalde es respetado/admirado *de* **los ciudadanos.**	*The mayor is respected/admired by the citizens.*

EJERCICIO A   **Listos para la Navidad**   Usando la voz pasiva, exprese quién hizo las siguientes cosas en preparación para la Navidad.

EJEMPLO: La abuela preparó el pavo.   El pavo **fue preparado por** la abuela.

1. La tía envolvió todos los regalos.   _____

2. El padre compró el árbol.   _____

3. Todo el mundo puso los adornos en el árbol.   _____

4. Enrique y Pablo colgaron las luces.   _____

5. El abuelo dio el brindis.   _____

6. Los invitados llevaron los postres.   _____

7. La madre encendió las velas.   _____

EJERCICIO B   **Una tormenta**   Usando la voz pasiva, exprese lo que pasó durante una
tormenta.

EJEMPLO: El viento desarraigó muchos árboles.
            Muchos árboles **fueron desarraigados por** el viento.

1. Las lluvias inundaron las calles.

   _____

2. La policía cerró la carretera.

   _____

3. Muchas personas abandonaron sus carros.

   _____

4. Un relámpago cortó el servicio de teléfonos.

   _____

5. El alcalde anunció un estado de emergencia.

   _____

6. Las autoridades cancelaron todos los eventos públicos.

   _____

2.   Other Passive-Voice Constructions

a. If the agent (doer) is not mentioned or implied and the subject is a thing, the reflexive
construction is preferred in Spanish. The subject usually follows the verb in such
constructions.

Aquí *se habla* **japonés.**	*Japanese is spoken here.*
Aquí *se hablan* **todas las lenguas modernas.**	*All modern languages are spoken here.*
Se *vende* **esta casa.**	*This house is for sale.*
Se *apagaron* **las luces.**	*The lights went out.*

b. The pronoun *se* may also be used as an indefinite subject. In such constructions, *se*
is not reflexive and is used only with the third-person singular form of the verb.

se dice:	*it is said, one says, people say, they say, you say*
se cree:	*it is believed, one believes, people believe, they believe, you believe*
se sabe:	*it is known, one knows, people know, they know, you know*

NOTE: 1.   The forms *dicen* (they say), *creen* (they believe), and *saben* (they know)
are used without *se*.

Se dice	}	*It is said*	}
Dicen	**que ella es talentosa.**	*It is said*	*that she is talented.*

---

2. The indefinite *se* may be used to express the passive when the doer is indefinite (not mentioned or implied) and a person is acted upon. Although the person acted upon is a direct object, the forms *le* and *les* (instead of *lo* and *los*) are used for the masculine.

Se aplaudió **al actor.**	*The actor was applauded.*
Se le **aplaudió.**	*He was applauded.*
Se aplaudió **a los actores.**	*The actors were applauded.*
Se les **aplaudió.**	*They were applauded.*
Se felicitó **a la niña.**	*The girl was congratulated.*
Se la **felicitó.**	*She was congratulated.*
Se felicitó **a las niñas.**	*The girls were congratulated.*
Se las **felicitó.**	*They were congratulated.*

3. The active third-person plural is often preferred instead of the indefinite *se* construction.

Aplaudieron **al actor (a los actores).**	*They applauded the actor (actors).*
Lo (Los) *aplaudieron.*	*They applauded him (them).*
Felicitaron **a la niña (a las niñas).**	*They congratulated the girl (girls).*
La (Las) *felicitaron.*	*They congratulated her (them).*

EJERCICIO C   **¿Dónde se compra...?**   Exprese dónde se compran los siguientes artículos.

PARA EXPRESARSE MEJOR

la papelería *stationery store*   **la perfumería** *perfumery*   **el quiosco** *kiosk*

EJEMPLO: pan   **Se compra** pan en la panadería.

1. leche _____

2. periódicos y revistas _____

3. zapatos _____

4. útiles _____

5. jabón elegante _____

6. aspirinas _____

7. carne _____

EJERCICIO D   **El primer día de clases**   Exprese lo que la maestra les dice a los alumnos el primer día de clases.

EJEMPLO: responder en voz alta   **Se responde** en voz alta.

1. preparar la tarea cada día   _____

2. traer los libros a la clase   _____

3. prestar atención   _____

4. prohibir mascar chicle   _____

5. pedir permiso para salir del salón   _____

6. levantar la mano antes de hablar   _____

7. decir todo en español   _____

8. respetar a los compañeros   _____

EJERCICIO E   **El plan del día**   Exprese los siguientes planes usando la forma reflexiva de los verbos.

EJEMPLO: Saldré con unas amigas.
             Se saldrá con unas amigas.

1. Mis amigas y yo nos reuniremos en la estación del metro.

_____

2. Viajaremos en tren.

_____

3. Bajaremos del tren en la Plaza Mayor.

_____

4. Comeremos en un restaurante de servicio rápido.

_____

5. Luego visitaremos las tiendas.

_____

6. Buscaremos adornos para el quinceañero de Norma.

_____

7. Tomaremos refrescos en un café.

_____

8. Volveremos a casa temprano.

_____

EJERCICIO F   **Así se hace.**   Los invitados a una cena quieren saber cómo preparar el exquisito plato de pescado que acaban de comer. Exprese la explicación que les da la anfitriona.

PARA EXPRESARSE MEJOR

acomodar *to place*	**papel de celofán** *waxed paper*
agregar *to add*	**retirar** *to remove*
deshacer *to melt, mash*	**rociar** *to sprinkle*
engrasar *to grease*	**sazonar** *to season*
la fécula de maíz *corn starch*	**tapar** *to cover*
marinar *to marinade*	**verter** *to pour*
el molde *baking dish*	

EJEMPLO: Sazone los filetes de pescado con sal, rocíelos con jugo de limón y déjelos marinar en la heladera una hora.

Se sazonan los filetes de pescado con sal, **se los rocían** con jugo de limón y **se los dejan** marinar en la heladera una hora.

1. Engrase un molde que se pueda usar tanto en el horno como en la mesa. Acomode los filetes de pescado codo a codo.

2. Coloque sobre cada filete un trocito de manteca y tápelos con papel de celofán.

3. Cocínelos en el horno durante 15 minutos.

4. Deshaga el roquefort con un tenedor junto con 50 gramos de manteca y una cucharadita de fécula de maíz.

5. Agréguele poco a poco la crema de leche hasta incorporarla toda.

6. Retire el molde del horno y quítele el papel y vierta la crema de roquefort sobre los filetes.

7. Ponga el molde en el horno bien caliente hasta gratinar la superficie.

8. Sirva, rodeando el molde con papitas hervidas.

EJERCICIO G **Consejos al viajero** Ricardo viaja al extranjero por primera vez. Exprese los consejos que le dan sus amigos, usando los verbos *aceptar, agregar, cambiar, comer, dar, guardar, incluir, llevar.*

EJEMPLO: **Se cambia** dinero en los bancos. OR **Cambian** dinero en los bancos.

1. _____ una propina al portero del hotel.

2. _____ un cinco por ciento sobre el importe total en los taxis.

3. _____ el servicio en la cuenta en los restaurantes.

4. _____ la documentación y el dinero en un lugar seguro.

5. _____ las tarjetas de crédito en muchos lugares.

6. _____ las cosas valiosas en la caja del hotel.

7. _____ la comida principal por la tarde.

EJERCICIO H **Un niño precoz** Luisito siempre comparte con otras personas lo que ha aprendido. Exprese lo que él dice.

EJEMPLO: **Se dice** «por favor» cuando uno pide algo.

1. _____ «salud» cuando alguien estornuda.

2. _____ que no existe vida en los otros planetas.

3. _____ que hay cincuenta y dos semanas en un año.

4. _____ lluvia para el fin de semana.

5. _____ que la práctica hace al maestro.

6. _____ que si hoy es domingo, mañana será lunes.

EJERCICIO I **Actividad oral y escrita** Trabajando con un compañero, identifique una celebración que tuvo lugar en su pueblo y discuta por qué y por quiénes fue organizada, cómo se llevó a cabo, cómo afectó la rutina del pueblo, etc. Luego, escriba un resumen de estos datos, usando la voz pasiva donde sea posible.

_____

_____

_____

_____

_____

_____

_____

_____

_____

EJERCICIO J **Lectura** Lea el siguiente párrafo y luego conteste las preguntas.

El metro

Madrid cuenta con una completa red de diez líneas que se distinguen por sus colores. Se sabe que es la forma más sencilla, rápida y barata de desplazarse por la ciudad. El servicio permanece abierto de 6:00 A.M. 1:30 A.M., en las 127 estaciones que posee. Se calcula que su frecuencia de paso oscila desde los 3-5 minutos durante el día hasta los 10-15 minutos durante la noche. Se venden billetes sencillos pero si van a realizar más de un viaje, se recomienda adquirir el Metrobús (billete de 10 viajes) y que también es válido para el autobús. Se adquieren los billetes en las taquillas y en las máquinas automáticas de las estaciones, en los quioscos de periódicos, estancos y casetas de la EMT. Se puede también solicitar un mapa de la red de metro en las taquillas. Es gratuito.

1. ¿Cómo se reconocen las líneas del metro madrileño?

   (a) Por los nombres

   (b) Por los números

   (c) Por los colores

   (d) Por los billetes

2. ¿Qué se sabe del metro?

   (a) Es la manera más eficaz de viajar en la ciudad.

   (b) El servicio es muy informal.

   (c) Los trenes son antiguos.

   (d) Hay muchas interrupciones de servicio.

3. El metro está abierto

   (a) las veinticuatro horas del día.

   (b) durante las horas pico.

   (c) los días festivos.

   (d) desde muy temprano hasta muy tarde.

4. ¿Qué se sabe de los billetes?

   (a) Son válidos por un día.

   (b) Se venden en muchas partes.

   (c) El precio incluye un mapa.

   (d) Son intransferibles.

CHAPTER 10
The Subjunctive Mood;
Present and Present-Perfect Subjunctive;
the Subjunctive in Noun Clauses

1.   The Subjunctive Mood

The term *mood* describes the form of the verb showing the subject's attitude. There are two moods in Spanish: the indicative and the subjunctive. The indicative mood states facts and expresses certainty or reality. The subjunctive mood expresses uncertainty, doubt, wishes, desires, conjecture, supposition, and conditions that are unreal or contrary to fact. The subjunctive mood occurs more frequently in Spanish than in English.

In Spanish, the subjunctive normally occurs in dependent clauses introduced by a conjunction or a relative pronoun.

INDICATIVE	SUBJUNCTIVE
Yo sé que hoy *es* día de fiesta. *I know that today is a holiday.*	**Yo dudo que hoy *sea* día de fiesta.** *I doubt that today is a holiday.*
Creo que ella me *llamará* más tarde. *I believe that she will call me later.*	**Espero que ella me *llame* más tarde.** *I hope that she will call me later.*
He oído que el viaje *es* difícil. *I heard that the trip is difficult.*	**No creo que el viaje *sea* difícil.** *I don't believe the trip to be difficult.*

2.   The Present and Present-Perfect Subjunctive

a. The Present Subjunctive

1. The present subjunctive of regular verbs is formed by dropping the ending *-o* of the first person singular (*yo*-form) of the present indicative and adding the following endings:

INFINITIVE	PRESENT INDICATIVE YO-FORM	PRESENT SUBJUNCTIVE	
andar *to walk*	**ando**	ande andes ande	andemos andéis anden
vender *to sell*	**vendo**	venda vendas venda	vendamos vendáis vendan
recibir *to receive*	**recibo**	reciba recibas reciba	recibamos recibáis reciban

2. In the present subjunctive, spelling-changing verbs ending in *-car, -gar,* and *-zar,* change *c* to *qu, g* to *gu,* and *z* to *c,* respectively. These spelling changes are the same as those occuring in the *yo*-form of the preterit.

INFINITIVE	PRESENT INDICATIVE YO-FORM	PRESENT SUBJUNCTIVE	
bus*car* *to search*	**busqué**	busque	busquemos
		busques	busquéis
		busque	busquen
pa*gar* *to pay*	**pagué**	pague	paguemos
		pagues	paguéis
		pague	paguen
go*zar* *to enjoy*	**gocé**	goce	gocemos
		goces	gocéis
		goce	gocen

NOTE: In the case of *averiguar, u* changes to *ü* before *e* to keep the *u*-sound, which otherwise would be silent.

Preterit: *averigüé*   Present Subjunctive: *averigüe*

3. Stem-changing *-ar* and *-er* verbs have the same stem changes in the present subjunctive as in the present indicative (*e* to *ie, o* to *ue*):

INFINITIVE	PRESENT INDICATIVE YO-FORM	PRESENT SUBJUNCTIVE	
pen*sar* *to think*	**pienso**	piense	pensemos
		pienses	penséis
		piense	piensen
po*der* *to be able*	**puedo**	pueda	podamos
		puedas	podáis
		pueda	puedan

Stem-changing *-ir* verbs have the same stem changes in the present subjunctive as in the present indicative (*e* to *ie, o* to *ue, e* to *i*). In the *nosotros* and *vosotros* forms, the stem vowel *e* changes to *i* and *o* changes to *u:*

INFINITIVE	PRESENT INDICATIVE YO-FORM	PRESENT SUBJUNCTIVE	
sen*tir* *to feel*	**siento**	sienta	sintamos
		sientas	sintáis
		sienta	sientan
dor*mir* *to sleep*	**duermo**	duerma	durmamos
		duermas	durmáis
		duerma	duerman
ser*vir* *to serve*	**sirvo**	sirva	sirvamos
		sirvas	sirváis
		sirva	sirvan

4. Some verbs ending in *-iar* or *-uar* have an accent mark on the *i* or the *u* (*í, ú*) in all forms except those for *nosotros* and *vosotros*.

INFINITIVE	PRESENT INDICATIVE YO-FORM	PRESENT SUBJUNCTIVE	
enviar *to send*	**envío**	envíe	enviemos
		envíes	enviéis
		envíe	envíen
continuar *to continue*	**continúo**	continúe	continuemos
		continúes	continuéis
		continúe	continúen

5. The following verbs have irregular forms in the present subjunctive:

INFINITIVE	PRESENT SUBJUNCTIVE	
caber *to fit*	quepa	quepamos
	quepas	quepáis
	quepa	quepan
dar *to give*	dé	demos
	des	deis
	dé	den
estar *to be*	esté	estemos
	estés	estéis
	esté	estén
haber *to have*	haya	hayamos
	hayas	hayáis
	haya	hayan
ir *to go*	vaya	vayamos
	vayas	vayáis
	vaya	vayan
saber *to know*	sepa	sepamos
	sepas	sepáis
	sepa	sepan
ser *to be*	sea	seamos
	seas	seáis
	sea	sean
tener *to have*	tenga	tengamos
	tengas	tengáis
	tenga	tengan

b. The Present-Perfect Subjunctive

The present-perfect subjunctive consists of the present subjunctive of *haber* plus a past participle.

haya			hayamos		
hayas	}	llamado	hayáis	}	llamado
haya			hayan		

The present-perfect subjunctive is used in the same way the present subjunctive is used. However, it is used to indicate that the action of the dependent clause happened before the action of the main clause.

Espero que *hayas entendido.*   *I hope that you understood.*

3. The Subjunctive in Noun Clauses

A noun clause is a clause that functions as a noun —it can serve as either the subject or the object of the verb. Noun clauses incorporated into a longer sentence are called dependent or subordinate clauses and are introduced by the conjunction *que* in Spanish.

a. The subjunctive is used after verbs and expressions of advice, command, demand, desire, hope, permission, preference, prohibition, request, or suggestion.

aconsejar   *to advise*

Te *aconsejo* **que** *viajes* **en avión.**   *I advise you to travel by plane.*

decir   *to tell (to order)*

Le *dicen* **que** *llegue* **a tiempo.**   *They tell her to arrive on time.*

dejar   *to let, to allow*

La maestra *deja* **(*permite*) que los**   *The teacher allows the children*
niños *jueguen* **en el patio.**   *to play in the patio.*

desear   *to wish, to want*

Deseo **que tú me** *acompañes.*   *I want you to accompany me.*

esperar   *to hope*

Espero **que nos** *veamos* **pronto.**   *I hope that we see each other soon.*

exigir   *to require, to demand*

El gobierno *exige* **que los**   *The government requires that*
ciudadanos *paguen* **impuestos.**   *the citizens pay taxes.*

hacer   *to make, to cause*

El padre *hace* **que su hijo** *pida*   *The father makes his son apologize.*
una disculpa.

insistir (en)   *to insist (on)*

Mis amigos *insisten* **en que yo**   *My friends prefer (insist) that I drive the car.*
conduzca **el carro.**

mandar   *to order, to command*

El sargento *manda* **que todos**   *The sergeant orders everyone to run five miles.*
corran **cinco millas.**

pedir *to request, to ask*
Pedro le *pide* a su padre que lo *escuche*. *Pedro asks his father to listen to him.*

permitir *to permit, to allow*
La maestra *permite* que los estudiantes *sean* originales. *The teacher allows the students to be original.*

preferir *to prefer*
***Prefiero* que mis libros *sean* livianos.** *I prefer my books to be lightweight.*

prohibir *to forbid, to prohibit*
La ley *prohíbe* que la gente *cace* sin licencia. *The law prohibits that people hunt without a license.*

querer *to wish, to want*
Los padres *quieren* que sus hijos *estudien* mucho. *Parents want their children to study a lot.*

rogar *to beg, to request*
Te *ruego* que *vengas*. *I beg you to come.*

sugerir *to suggest*
***Sugieren* que *leamos* la novela.** *They suggest that we read the novel.*

suplicar *to beg, to plead*
Le *suplicamos* que nos *rebaje* el precio. *We begged him/her to lower the price.*

NOTE: 1. In all of the above examples, the verb in the main clause and the verb in the dependent clause have different subjects. If the subjects in both clauses are the same, *que* is omitted and the infinitive is used instead of the subjunctive.

Ellos quieren ir a la playa. *They want to go to the beach.*
Yo prefiero conducir el carro. *I prefer to drive the car.*

2. *Dejar, hacer, mandar, permitir,* and *prohibir* may be followed by either the subjunctive or the infinitive.

Me *manda* que *conteste*.
Me *manda* contestar. } *He orders me to answer.*

***Déjela* que *baile*.**
***Déjela* bailar.** } *Let her dance.*

EJERCICIO A **Esperanzas** Exprese lo que estas personas esperan.

EJEMPLO: el profesor / los alumnos aprender la lección
El profesor **espera** que los alumnos **aprendan** la lección.

1. los padres / los hijos / lograr sus metas

   _____

2. yo / haber / paz en el mundo

   _____

3. el campesino / llover mucho

   _____

4. el comerciante / el cliente / firmar el contrato

   _____

5. los pasajeros / el vuelo / llegar a tiempo

   _____

6. los anfitriones / los invitados / divertirse en la fiesta

   _____

7. el inquilino / los nuevos vecinos / no hacer mucho ruido

   _____

EJERCICIO B   **Así se hace.** La mamá de Raquel tiene su manera de hacer las cosas. Exprese en lo que ella insiste.

EJEMPLO: el niño / lavarse las manos antes de comer
           La mamá **insiste** en que el niño **se lave** las manos antes de comer.

1. el televisor / apagarse a las diez de la noche

   _____

2. toda la familia / comer junta

   _____

3. Raquel / no dejar sus cosas en la sala

   _____

4. todos / ayudar con los quehaceres domésticos

   _____

5. los amigos de Raquel / venir a la casa

   _____

6. los hijos / descansar después de comer

   _____

EJERCICIO C   **Muchas ideas** Cuando Celia y algunas amigas van a ir a España, todo el mundo les ofrece un consejo o una sugerencia. Exprese lo que todo el mundo dice.

EJEMPLO: Armando / aconsejar / ellas / visitar el Museo del Prado
           Armando **aconseja** que ellas **visiten** el Museo del Prado.

1. yo / sugerir / Celia / llamar a mi primo

   _____

2. Nancy / recomendar / ellas / hacer una excursión al Valle de los Caídos

   _____

3. Jorge y yo / aconsejar / ellas / conocer la ciudad de Toledo

   _____

4. el papá de Celia / exigir / Celia / hablarle por teléfono

   _____

5. Elsa / pedir / Celia / comprarle un recuerdo

   _____

6. todos / insistir en / las chicas / enviarles tarjetas postales

   _____

7. Manolo / esperar / ellas / ir a Málaga

   _____

EJERCICIO D   **Una carta**   Antes de salir en el viaje, Celia recibe una carta de un primo que vive en Madrid. Complete la carta con la forma apropiada del verbo indicado.

Querida Celia:

Acabo de enterarme de que tú piensas venir unas amigas a España. ¡Ojalá que _____
1. (ser)
pronto! Quiero que (tú) _____ que estaré a tus órdenes durante tu estancia.
2. (saber)

   Sugiero que Uds. _____ una lista de los lugares que quieren _____ .
   3. (preparar)   4. (conocer)
Nosotros deseamos que Uds. _____ un buen rato aquí. Mis padres han recomendado
5. (pasar)
que yo les _____ de guía y que las _____ a mis lugares favoritos. Pero
6. (servir)   7. (llevar)
prefiero que tú me _____ las cosas que desean _____ . Te pido que tú
8. (decir)   9. (hacer)
me _____ y que me _____ cuáles son los planes que han hecho.
10. (escribir)   11. (contar)
Espero _____ tu respuesta pronto.
12. (recibir)

Hasta pronto.

Vicente

    b. The subjunctive is used after verbs and expressions of feeling or emotion, such as fear, joy, sorrow, regret, or surprise.

      alegrarse (de)   _to be glad_

      Me _alegro_ de que _hayas llegado_ bien.   _I am glad that you arrived well._

temer   *to be afraid, fear*
Tememos** que no haya **boletos.   *We are afraid that there are no tickets.*

tener miedo (de)   *to be afraid, fear*
Tengo miedo de** que el avión **se retrase.   *I'm afraid that the airplane be delayed.*

sentir   *to be sorry, regret*
Ella *siente* que Uds. *tengan* que trabajar tanto.   *She is sorry (regrets) that you have to work so much.*

sorprenderse (de)   *to be surprised*
Te sorprendes** de que ellos te **recuerden.   *You are surprised that they remember you.*

EJERCICIO E   **Reacciones**   Exprese la reacción de la familia de Lidia cuando un grupo de estudiantes de intercambio visitan su casa.

EJEMPLO: el padre / sorprenderse / los jóvenes / hablar español
El padre **se sorprende** de que los jóvenes **hablen** español.

1. Juan / alegrarse / ellos / ser fanáticos del fútbol

_____

2. la mamá / sentir / varios jóvenes / no saber mucho de su cultura

_____

3. la abuela / temer / no haber suficiente comida

_____

4. Lidia y yo / estar contentos / los estudiantes / divertirse

_____

5. tú / tener miedo / ellos aburrirse fácilmente

_____

6. la hermana menor / sentir / el grupo / no poder quedarse más tiempo

_____

EJERCICIO F   **¿Qué sienten?**   Exprese lo que sienten las siguientes personas en varias circunstancias.

EJEMPLO: Jorge va al zoológico. Los animales son feroces.   *(temer)*
Jorge **teme que** los animales **sean** feroces.

1. Alfredo va al parque a jugar al fútbol. Nadie está jugando al fútbol.   *(sorprenderse)*

_____

2. La abuela visita el pueblo en que nació. Todo ha cambiado.   *(lamentar)*

_____

3. Luis y Daniel oyen que el equipo de la escuela ganó el campeonato.   (*alegrarse*)

   _____

4. Laura se enteró de que Migdalia tuvo un accidente automovilístico.   (*sentir*)

   _____

5. La mamá preparó una comida especial. Los hijos siempre llegan tarde.   (*tener miedo*)

   _____

EJERCICIO G   **Noticias locales** Exprese la reacción de varias personas al oír las siguientes noticias.

los pasajeros	alegrarse
todo el mundo	lamentar
los empleados	sentir
los ciudadanos	sorprenderse
el público	temer
los jóvenes	tener miedo de

EJEMPLO: Cierran el aeropuerto a causa del mal tiempo.
       Los pasajeros **temen** que **cierren** el aeropuerto a causa del mal tiempo.

1. Habrá un concierto en el estadio por un artista muy popular.

   _____

2. Muchas compañías despiden a sus trabajadores.

   _____

3. Buscan donativos para mantener los programas para los ancianos.

   _____

4. Cancelan la obra de teatro después de cinco funciones.

   _____

5. Un atleta local recibe una medalla de oro en un campeonato mundial.

   _____

6. La sequía continúa; sólo sol y calor en el pronóstico.

   _____

   c. The subjunctive is used after verbs and expressions of doubt, disbelief, or denial.

   no creer *not to believe*
   No creo que *sea* ella.   *I don't believe it is she.*

   dudar *to doubt*
   Dudamos que *vengan*.   *We doubt that they will come.*

   negar *to deny*
   Niegas que esto *sea* necesario.   *You deny that this is necessary.*

NOTE: 1.   When used interrogatively, *creer* indicates uncertainty and is usually followed by the subjunctive.

   ¿Crees* que ella *haya llamado?   *Do you believe that she called?*

   2.   *Creer, no dudar,* and *no negar* indicate belief or certainty and are usually followed by the indicative.

   ***Creo* (No dudo, No niego) que**   *I believe (don't doubt, don't deny)*
   Miguel la *conoce*.   *that Miguel knows her.*

EJERCICIO H   **Dudas**   Exprese quién duda o no cree lo siguiente.

EJEMPLO: El niño pide pocos juguetes.   *(el padre)*
   El padre **duda que** el niño **pida** pocos juguetes.

1.   El piano es el instrumento musical más antiguo.   *(el músico)*

_____

2.   Los dulces tienen valor nutritivo.   *(los médicos)*

_____

3.   A los niños les gusta acostarse temprano.   *(los padres)*

_____

4.   Todo saldrá bien.   *(el pesimista)*

_____

5.   Los pronosticadores del tiempo siempre tienen razón.   *(el público)*

_____

6.   Los exámenes son justos.   *(el estudiante mal preparado)*

_____

7.   Hay buenas noticias en el periódico de hoy.   *(los lectores)*

_____

EJERCICIO I   **¿Qué crees?**   Exprese lo que Luis duda cuando sus amigos le comentan sobre una fiesta que planean.

EJEMPLO: Ricardo traerá su cámara de video.   **Yo dudo (No creo) que Ricardo la traiga.**

1.   Todo el mundo llegará a la hora indicada.   _____

2.   Las chicas van a preparar los bocadillos.   _____

3.   Javier tocará la guitarra.   _____

4.   La fiesta terminará temprano.   _____

5.   Habrá muchas personas en la fiesta.   _____

6. Nosotros nos divertiremos muchísimo. _____

7. Marisol sacará muchas fotografías. _____

| **EJERCICIO J** | **Negación** Exprese quién niega las siguientes cosas.

EJEMPLO: Hay escasez de legumbres frescos. (los campesinos)
          Los campesinos **niegan** que **haya** escasez de legumbres frescos.

1. La familia Vargas vive aquí. (*el dueño*)
_____

2. Los taxistas están en huelga. (*el jefe del sindicato*)
_____

3. Van a cancelar las clases mañana. (*el director*)
_____

4. Habrá una depresión económica. (*el presidente*)
_____

5. El perro mordió al niño. (*la señora*)
_____

6. El equipo cometió muchos errores. (*el entrenador*)
_____

d. The subjunctive is used after impersonal expressions of possibility, doubt, uncertainty, necessity, emotion, etc. If the impersonal expression indicates certainty, the indicative is used.

es dudoso *it is doubtful*

Es *dudoso* que *haga* frío.   *It is doubtful that it will be cold.*

es importante *it is important*

Es *importante* que Uds. *escuchen*.   *It is important that you listen.*

es (im)posible *it is (im)possible*

Es (im)posible que no haya espacio.   *It's (im)posible that there's no room.*

es una lástima *it is a pity*

Es *una lástima* que ella *esté* ausente.   *It's a pity she is absent.*

es mejor
más vale } *it is better*

(Es mejor / Más vale) que lo hagamos ahora.   *It's better that we do it now.*

> **es menester**
> **es necesario** } *it is necessary*
> **es preciso**
>
> **Es (***menester* / *necesario* / *preciso***)**   *It's necessary that I also go.*
>   **que yo *vaya* también.**
>
> **es probable**   *it is probable*
> **Es *probable* que *llueva*.**   *It's probable that it will rain.*
>
>   NOTE: **Es cierto que hará frío.**   *It's certain that it will be cold.*
>   **Es evidente que ella está ausente.**   *It's evident that she is absent.*
>   **Es verdad que yo soy su tío.**   *It's true that I am his uncle.*

EJERCICIO K   **Consejos**   Exprese que lo que la mamá de Elvira le dice cuando la ayuda a instalarse en la residencia de la universidad.

EJEMPLO: Es importante / mantener todo en orden.
          Es importante que **mantengas** todo en orden.

1. Es preciso / tú / poner el despertador cada noche

   _____

2. Es dudoso / tu compañera de cuarto / ser responsable

   _____

3. Es probable / yo / regresar la semana que viene.

   _____

4. Es importante / tú / dedicarse a los estudios.

   _____

5. Es posible / las otras chicas / querer usar tu teléfono celular

   _____

6. Es menester / tú / llamarme todos los días

   _____

7. Es verdad / tú / ir a aprender a hacer muchas cosas por ti misma

   _____

EJERCICIO L   **Comentarios**   Nick está en la Ciudad de México y toma una excursión turística. Exprese lo que el guía les dice a los miembros del grupo.

EJEMPLO: Es probable / Uds. / necesitar más tiempo en los lugares que visitamos hoy
          Es probable que Uds. **necesiten** más tiempo en los lugares que visitamos hoy.

1. Es importante / nadie / alejarse del grupo

   _____

2. Es probable / haber mucha cola en todos los sitios

_____

3. Es imposible / Uds. / ver todo en esta excursión

_____

4. Será necesario / Uds. / tomar otras excursiones durante su estancia

_____

5. Es dudoso / permitirse el uso de las cámaras en los salones de exhibición

_____

6. Es verdad / venderse tarjetas postales en la tienda del museo

_____

7. Es preciso / Uds. / no dejar cosas de valor en el autobús

_____

8. Es importante / todo el mundo / seguir el horario de la excursión

_____

EJERCICIO M   **Reglas y más reglas**   Hilda y su familia viven en un condominio y asisten a una reunión de la asociación del condominio. Exprese lo que el presidente de la asociación dice.

EJEMPLO: Es preciso / todo el mundo / obedecer los reglamentos de la asociación
Es preciso que todo el mundo **obedezca** los reglamentos de la asociación.

1. Es posible / Uds. / no estar de acuerdo con todos los reglamentos

_____

2. Es imposible / los reglamentos / satisfacer a todo el mundo

_____

3. Es necesario / todos / participar en el programa de reciclaje

_____

4. Es prohibido / cortar las flores

_____

5. Más vale / todo el mundo / saber los reglamentos

_____

6. Es importante / todos / respetarse

_____

7. Es menester / Uds. / informarme de cualquier problema

_____

EJERCICIO N | **Una carta** Selene va a estar en Buenos Aires por una temporada. Complete el mensaje que ella le manda a una amiga que vive allí.

Querida Lupita:

Quiero que tú _____ que yo voy a estar en Buenos Aires al fin del mes. Espero
　　　　　　1. (saber)

_____ un mes allí y deseo que nosotras _____ tiempo juntas. Pienso
2. (pasar)　　　　　　　　　　　　　　　　3. (pasar)

tomar un curso intensivo en el Instituto Interamericano y es posible que yo _____
　　　　　　　　　　　　　　　　　　　　　　　　　　　　　　　　　　　4. (buscar)

alojamiento cerca de donde tú vives. Es menester que yo _____ el curso intensivo
　　　　　　　　　　　　　　　　　　　　　　　5. (terminar)

porque la compañía donde solicito trabajo exige que todos los empleados _____
　　　　　　　　　　　　　　　　　　　　　　　　　　　　　　　　　　6. (ser)

bilingües en inglés y en español. Es probable que yo _____ tu ayuda porque es
　　　　　　　　　　　　　　　　　　　　　　　　7. (pedir)

importante que yo _____ esta meta. Es necesario que yo _____ una
　　　　　　　8. (lograr)　　　　　　　　　　　　　　　　　　9. (tener)

referencia local y pido que tú me _____ en eso. Es una lástima que mi viaje no
　　　　　　　　　　　　　　　10. (ayudar)

_____ a ser de puro placer, pero me alegro de que tú y yo _____ renovar
11. (ir)　　　　　　　　　　　　　　　　　　　　　　　　　　12. (poder)

nuestra amistad.

Hasta pronto.

Selene

EJERCICIO O | **Una invitación** Complete la invitación que Elsa escribe a unos amigos.

Queridos amigos:

Quiero que Uds _____ a una fiesta de sorpresa que tendrá lugar en mi casa este
　　　　　　　1. (venir)

sábado a las ocho. Celebramos el cumpleaños de mi hermana mayor. Es importante que Uds.

no _____ de la fiesta porque queremos que _____ una sorpresa. Es preciso
　2. (hablar)　　　　　　　　　　　　　　　　　　　3. (ser)

que todos los invitados _____ a las ocho en punto porque mi hermana llegará a las
　　　　　　　　　　　　4. (estar)

ocho y media. No es necesario que Uds. le _____ un regalo. Solamente esperamos
　　　　　　　　　　　　　　　　　　　　　5. (dar)

que Uds. _____ la felicidad de la ocasión con nosotros. Es un cumpleaños especial
　　　　　6. (compartir)

pero ella prefiere que nadie _____ su edad. ¡Ojalá que Uds. _____
　　　　　　　　　　　　　　7. (saber)　　　　　　　　　　　　　　8. (poder)

acompañarnos!

　　Ruego que Uds. me _____ por teléfono y _____ su asistencia.
　　　　　　　　　　　　9. (llamar)　　　　　　　　　10. (confirmar)

Elsa

EJERCICIO P   **Actividad oral**   Trabaje con un(-a) compañero(-a), convénzalo(-a) de lo que debe hacer para salir bien en el curso de español. Use el presente o el presente perfecto del subjuntivo donde sea posible.

EJEMPLO: Me sorprendo de que no hayas salido bien en el examen. Es importante que tú recibas buenas notas. Te recomiendo que prepares la tarea con cuidado… etc.

CHAPTER 11

The Imperfect and Pluperfect Subjunctive; Sequence of Tenses; Conditional (If) Sentences

1. The Imperfect and Pluperfect Subjunctive

a. Forms

1. The imperfect subjunctive of all verbs is formed by dropping the *-ron* ending of the third-person plural of the preterit tense and adding either the *-ra* or the *-se* endings.

INFINITIVE	PRETERIT THIRD-PERSON PLURAL	IMPERFECT SUBJUNCTIVE	
		-RA FORM	-SE FORM
jugar *to play*	**jugaron**	jugara jugaras jugara jugáramos jugarais jugaran	jugase jugases jugase jugásemos jugaseis jugasen
vender *to sell*	**vendieron**	vendiera vendieras vendiera vendiéramos vendierais vendieran	vendiese vendieses vendiese vendiésemos vendieseis vendiesen
recibir *to receive*	**recibieron**	recibiera recibieras recibiera recibiéramos recibierais recibieran	recibiese recibieses recibiese recibiésemos recibieseis recibiesen
dormir *to sleep*	**durmieron**	durmiera durmieras durmiera durmiéramos durmierais durmieran	durmiese durmieses durmiese durmiésemos durmieseis durmiesen
pedir *to ask, to request*	**pidieron**	pidiera pidieras pidiera pidiéramos pidierais pidieran	pidiese pidieses pidiese pidiésemos pidieseis pidiesen

INFINITIVE	PRETERIT THIRD-PERSON PLURAL	IMPERFECT SUBJUNCTIVE	
		-RA FORM	-SE FORM
decir to say, to tell	**dijeron**	dijera dijeras dijera dijéramos dijerais dijeran	dijese dijeses dijese dijésemos dijeseis dijesen
ir to go **ser** to be	**fueron**	fuera fueras fuera fuéramos fuerais fueran	fuese fueses fuese fuésemos fueseis fuesen
caer to fall	**cayeron**	cayera cayeras cayera cayéramos cayerais cayeran	cayese cayeses cayese cayésemos cayeseis cayesen

NOTE: The *nosotros*-form of the imperfect subjunctive is the only form that has an accent mark (on the vowel immediately before the ending).

2. The pluperfect subjunctive consists of the imperfect subjunctive of *haber* plus a past participle.

hubiera (hubiese) **hubieras (hubieses)** **hubiera (hubiese)**	leído	**hubiéramos (hubiésemos)** **hubierais (hubieseis)** **hubieran (hubiesen)**	leído

b. Uses

1. Like the present and present-perfect subjunctive, the imperfect and pluperfect subjunctive are usually introduced by the conjunction *que*. The imperfect and pluperfect subjunctive are used if the verb in the main clause is in the imperfect, preterit, conditional, or pluperfect tenses.

Yo *quería* **que ellos** *hablaran (hablasen)*.	*I wanted them to speak.*
Insistió **en que yo** *pagara (pagase)*.	*He insisted that I pay.*
No *permitiría* **que los niños** *salieran (saliesen)*.	*She would not permit that the children go out.*
Yo *dudaba* **que** *hubieran (hubiesen)* **llamado**.	*I doubted that they had called.*

2. The imperfect and pluperfect subjunctive are used after verbs and expressions of advice, command, demand, desire, hope, permission, preference, prohibition, request, or suggestion that are in the imperfect, preterit, conditional, or pluperfect tenses.

Te *aconsejé* **que** *viajaras* **en avión.**	*I advised you to travel by plane.*
Le *dijeron* **que llegara a tiempo.**	*They told him/her to arrive on time.*
La maestra *dejó* **(***permitió***) que los niños** *jugaran* **en el patio.**	*The teacher allowed the children to play in the patio.*
Desearía **(***Querría***) que tú me** *acompañases.*	*I would wish / want you to accompany me.*
Esperaba **que nos** *viéramos* **pronto.**	*I hoped that we would see each other soon.*
La ley *exigía* **que los ciudadanos** *pagasen* **impuestos.**	*The law required that the citizens paid taxes.*
El padre *hizo* **que su hijo** *pidiera* **una disculpa.**	*The father made his son apologize.*
Mis amigos *preferían* **(***insistían en***) que yo** *condujese* **el carro.**	*My friends preferred (insisted) that I drive the car.*
Te *supliqué* **(***rogué***) que vinieras.**	*I begged you to come.*
Sugirieron **que** *leyéramos* **la novela.**	*They suggested that we read the novel.*

EJERCICIO A **Recuerdos familiares** Exprese lo que varios amigos dicen que recuerdan de sus padres.

EJEMPLO: mi papá / exigir / mis hermanos y yo / trabajar

Mi papá **exigió** que mis hermanos y yo **trabajáramos.**

1. mi mamá / aconsejar / yo / ahorrar dinero

_____

2. mis padres / prohibir / mi hermana / volver a casa tarde

_____

3. mis padres / insistir / nosotros / asistir a la universidad

_____

4. mi papá / hacer / mi hermano / aprender otro idioma

_____

5. mis padres / suplicar / mi hermana y yo / ser muy unidos

_____

6. mi mamá / querer / yo / aprovecharse de cualquier oportunidad

_____

7. mis padres / permitir / nosotros / desarrollar nuestros intereses

_____

EJERCICIO B **La obra teatral** Exprese los sentimientos de la directora del departamento de drama de la escuela.

EJEMPLO: esperar / los actores / aprender el guión

Ella **esperaba** que los actores **aprendieran** el guión.

1. pedir / todo el mundo / tomar la obra en serio

_____

2. exigir / el protagonista / llegar a tiempo a los ensayos

_____

3. aconsejar / los actores / ensayar más

_____

4. prohibir / Gerardo / leer el guión

_____

5. suplicar / los ayudantes / terminar el escenario para el estreno

_____

6. esperar / haber mucho público

_____

7. querer / la obra / tener éxito

_____

3. The imperfect and pluperfect subjunctive are used after verbs and expressions of feeling or emotion, such as fear, joy, sorrow, regret, or surprise that are in the imperfect, preterit, conditional, or pluperfect tenses.

Me alegré de que tú *hubieras llegado* **bien.**	*I was glad that you had arrived well.*
Ella *sintió* **que Uds.** *trabajasen* **tanto.**	*She was sorry (regretted) that you work so much.*
Te *sorprendías* **de que ellos te** *recordaran.*	*You were surprised that they remembered you.*
Temíamos **que no** *hubiera* **boletos.**	*We feared there weren't any tickets.*

EJERCICIO C   **Recuerdos de un viaje** Exprese lo que Vicente dijo que fueron los comentarios de su familia durante un viaje a Bogotá.

EJEMPLO: mi papá / sorprenderse / haber tantos edificios modernos
            Mi papá se sorprendió de que **hubiera** tantos edificios modernos.

1. mis hermanas / alegrarse / muchos jóvenes / hablar inglés

_____

2. mi mamá / sorprenderse / las personas / ser muy amigables

_____

3. yo / sentir / nosotros / no poder pasar más tiempo allí

_____

4. nosotros / sorprenderse / haber muchos restaurantes de comida rápida

_____

5. Hilda / temer / a mí / no gustarme la comida tradicional

_____

6. yo / tener miedo / los colombianos / no comprenderme al hablar español

_____

| **EJERCICIO D** | **Sentimientos** Complete las siguientes frases con la forma apropiada del verbo indicado para expresar los sentimientos de las personas que viajan juntos en una excursión. |

EJEMPLO: Javier se alegró de que Sara **hubiera encontrado** su pulsera.
                                              (encontrar)

1. Felipe estaba contento de que nosotros _____ boletos para el concierto.
                                          (conseguir)

2. Jenny se sorprendió de que el guía le _____ flores.
                                        (mandar)

3. Yo sentí que María _____ tantos chismes durante el viaje.
                      (contar)

4. Nosotros temimos que las figuras que mandamos a casa por correo _____ sin
                                                                  (llegar)
   romperse.

5. Alberto lamentó que nadie le _____ cuando salieron del museo.
                               (esperar)

6. El guía se alegró de que todos _____ mucho.
                                 (divertirse)

4. The imperfect and pluperfect subjunctive are used after verbs and expressions of doubt, disbelief, or denial that are in the imperfect, preterit, conditional, or pluperfect tenses.

Dudábamos que *vinieran.*	*We doubted that they would come.*
No creía **que** *fuera* **ella.**	*I didn't believe it was she.*
Negaste **que esto** *fuese* **necesario.**	*You denied that this was necessary.*

NOTE: 1.   When used interrogatively, *creer* indicates uncertainty and is usually followed by the subjunctive.

¿*Creíste* **que ella hubiera** **llamado?**	*Did you believe that she had* *called?*

2. *Creer, no dudar,* and *no negar* indicate belief or certainty and are usually followed by the indicative.

Creía **(No dudaba, No negaba)** **que Miguel la** *conocía.*	*I believed (didn't doubt, didn't* *deny) that Miguel knew her.*

| **EJERCICIO E** | **Dudas** Cuando eran pequeños, Fernando le contaba muchas cosas falsas a su hermano menor. Exprese lo que el hermano le dice, ahora que son mayores. Use *dudar, no creer o negar* en cada frase. |

EJEMPLO: La luna es de queso.   Yo **dudaba que** la luna **fuera** de queso.

1. Los títeres son personas humanas.

   _____

2. Hay carros que vuelan.

   _____

3. El sol sale cuando apagamos la luz.

   _____

4. Un avión puede volar sin piloto.

   _____

5. No necesitaremos un reloj para marcar el tiempo.

   _____

6. Podemos cavar un hoyo para llegar al Oriente.

   _____

7. La nieve produce toda el agua potable.

   _____

5. The imperfect and pluperfect subjunctive are used after impersonal expressions of possibility, doubt, uncertainty, necessity, emotion, etc., that are in the imperfect, preterit, conditional or pluperfect tenses. If the impersonal expression indicates certainty, the indicative is used.

Era _dudoso_ **que** _hiciera_ **frío.**	_It was doubtful that it would be cold._
Era _importante_ **que Uds.** _escucharan._	_It was important that you listen._
Era _imposible_ **que no** _hubiese_ **lugar.**	_It was impossible that there was no room._
Sería _una lástima_ **que ella** _estuviera_ **ausente.**	_It would be a pity that she were absent._
Sería _mejor_ **que lo** _hiciéramos_ **ahora.**	_It would be better for us to do it now._
Fue _necesario_ **que yo** _fuera_ **también.**	_It was necessary for me to go too._
Era _probable_ **que** _lloviera._	_It was probable that it would rain._

But:

Era _seguro_ **que** _hacía_ **frío.**	_It was certain that it was cold._
Era _evidente_ **que ella** _estaba_ **ausente.**	_It was evident that she was absent._
Era _verdad_ **que yo** _era_ **su tío.**	_It was true that I was his uncle._

EJERCICIO F   **Una demora**   Cuando Clarisa iba a volver a los Estados Unidos de Madrid, hubo una demora de ocho horas en el aeropuerto. Complete las oraciones con el tiempo apropiado para expresar lo que un agente de la aerolínea les dijo a los pasajeros.

Era una lástima que nosotros no _____ darles más información hasta ahora. Era
1. (poder)

evidente que _____ un problema serio con el avión. A principios, era dudoso que
2. (haber)

el vuelo _____ hoy y era probable que Uds. _____ que ir a un hotel.
3. (salir)   4. (tener)
Cuando suceden estas cosas, es imposible _____ el resultado de la revisión
5. (pronosticar)
mecánica.

Fue necesario que nosotros _____ otra tripulación y le fue difícil llegar tan
6. (buscar)
pronto al aeropuerto. Sobre todo, era preciso que la aerolínea _____ la seguridad
7. (asegurar)
de cada pasajero. Era indispensable que nosotros _____ todas las precauciones
8. (tomar)
necesarias sin que Uds. _____ demasiadas inconveniencias. Muchas gracias a
9. (sufrir)
todos. Ahora estamos listos para abordar el avión.

EJERCICIO G | **Comentarios** Use la expresión impersonal indicada para expresar lo que Diego les comentó a sus amigos.

Ejemplo: Yo no salí anoche. (*Era mejor…*)
Era mejor que tú **no hubieras salido** anoche.

1. Nuestro equipo no ganó el campeonato. (*Era una lástima*)

_____

2. Alicia escribió ese mensaje. (*Era probable*)

_____

3. Miguel rompió la piñata en la fiesta. (*Era imposible*)

_____

4. El servicio de Internet no funcionaba anoche. (*Era dudoso*)

_____

5. Nosotros no llegamos tarde al partido. (*Más valía*)

_____

6. Ellos no leyeron el aviso que les llegó por correo. (*Era menester*)

_____

2. Sequence of Tenses

The tense of the subjunctive depends on the form of verb in the main clause.

VERB IN MAIN CLAUSE	VERB IN DEPENDENT CLAUSE
Present Indicative Present Perfect Future Command	Present Subjunctive OR Present-Perfect Subjunctive

Él insiste en
He insists

Él insistirá en
He will insist

Él ha insistido en
He has insisted

Insista en
Insist

} **que los niños *naden* en el lago.**
that the children swim in the lake.

No *creo* que los niños *hayan nadado* en el lago.
I don't believe that the children have swum in the lake.

VERB IN MAIN CLAUSE	VERB IN DEPENDENT CLAUSE
Imperfect Preterit Conditional Pluperfect	Imperfect Subjunctive OR Pluperfect Subjunctive

Él insistía en
He insisted (He used to insist)

Él insistió en
He insisted

Él insistiría en
He would insist

Él había insistido en
He had insisted

} **que los niños *nadaran* (*nadasen*) en el lago.**
that the children swim in the lake.

No *creía* que los niños *hubieran* (*hubiesen*) nadado en el lago.
I didn't believe that the children had swum in the lake.

| EJERCICIO H | **Cuentitos** Complete los siguientes párrafos con la forma apropiada de los verbos indicados entre paréntesis.

1. Me alegro de que Uds. _____ a esta reunión porque es importante que los padres

1. (venir)

   _____ las reglas que imponemos durante los quince días que sus hijos pasarán en
   2. (saber)

   el campamento. Es importante que cada explorador _____ todos los artículos
   3. (tener)

   indicados en la lista que ya han recibido. Queremos que _____ una experiencia buena
   4. (ser)

   para ellos y que ellos _____ de la vida de un explorador y que _____
   5. (disfrutar)   6. (aprender)

   mucho. Permitimos que los exploradores _____ su teléfono celular y que lo _____
   7 (traer)   8. (usar)

   solamente por la noche. Es prohibido _____ el teléfono celular durante el día
   9. (usar)

tanto para hacer llamadas como recibirlas. Tampoco se permite que ellos _____ 10. (entretenerse) con los juegos electrónicos portátiles durante el día. Es evidente que esto _____ ser 11. (poder) una distracción peligrosa.

2. Habían pronosticado mal tiempo pero era preciso que nosotros _____ de la casa. 1. (salir) Era dudoso que ninguno de los invitados _____ a tiempo por las malas condi- 2. (llegar) ciones de los caminos. Era abril y todo el mundo quería que _____ buen tiempo. 3. (hacer) Nadie creía esperaba que _____ una nevada durante la noche. Los novios estaban 4. (caer) nerviosos porque pensaban que _____ necesario cancelar todos los arreglos que 5 (ser) habían hecho para su boda. Lamentaban que sus padres les _____ en tener una 6. (convencer) boda grande con muchos invitados. Ellos querían _____ una boda pequeña e 7. (tener) íntima, pero era evidente que sus padres _____ otra decisión. Los novios estaban 8. (tomar) seguros de que el mal tiempo haría que su deseo inicial _____ . Pero los novios 9. (realizarse) se sorprendieron de que todos los invitados _____ llegar a la boda a tiempo. 10. (poder)

3. Cuando José llegó al teatro era difícil _____ a la taquilla por tanta muchedumbre. 1. (acercarse) «¿Por qué le dije a ella que me _____ aquí? _____ más fácil que nosotros 2. (encontrar) 3. (ser) _____ en un café. Pero ella no quería _____ eso. Prefería que yo 4. (reunirse) 5. (hacer) la _____ en la taquilla del teatro. Temo que ella no me _____ y se irá.» se 6. (esperar) 7. (ver) murmuró.

3. Conditional (If) Sentences

a. Conditional sentences are made up of two clauses: a *si*-clause (if-clause) and a main or result-clause. The *si*-clause may precede or follow the main clause. Possible conditions are expressed with the present tense in the *si*-clause and the future tense in the main or result clause.

Si **llueve, no saldremos.** *If it rains, we will not go out.*

b. To express a condition that is contrary to fact in the present time, the imperfect subjunctive is used in the *si*-clause and the conditional in the main or result clause.

Si lloviera (lloviese), **no** *saldríamos (saliéramos).* *If it rained, we would not go out.*

c. To express a condition that is contrary to fact in the past time, the pluperfect subjunctive is used in the *si*-clause and the conditional perfect or the pluperfect subjunctive in the main or result clause.

> **Si *hubiera* (*hubiese*) llovido, no habríamos (hubiéramos) salido.**   *If it had rained, we wouldn't have gone out.*

d. The imperfect and pluperfect subjunctives are used after *como si* (*as if*).

> **Adolfo habla *como si fuera* experto.**   *Adolfo speaks as if he were an expert.*
> **Ella gastó dinero *como si hubiera tenido* millones de dólares.**   *She spent money as if she had had millions of dollars.*

e. Summary

	SI CLAUSE	MAIN OR RESULT CLAUSE
PRESENT TIME	Imperfect Subjunctive (-se or -ra form)	Conditional OR Imperfect Subjunctive (-ra form only)
PAST TIME	Pluperfect Subjunctive (-se or -ra form)	Conditional Perfect OR Pluperfect Subjunctive (-ra form only)

EJERCICIO I   **Condiciones reales**   Complete las frases para expresar lo que las personas harán.

EJEMPLO: Si no **ahorro** dinero, lo **gasto** .
(ahorrar) (gastar)

1. Si tú me _____ (llamar), yo _____ (saber) dónde encontrarte.

2. Si yo _____ (buscar) trabajo, lo _____ (encontrar) .

3. Si ellos _____ (estudiar), _____ (pasar) los exámenes.

4. Si nosotros _____ (terminar) temprano, _____ (poder) ir al cine.

5. Si el maestro _____ (estar) ausente, no _____ (haber) clase.

6. Si los niños _____ (portarse) bien, yo les _____ (comprar) helado.

7. Si yo _____ (dormirse) ahora, no _____ (dormir) en toda la noche.

| EJERCICIO J | **Yo haría…**   Exprese lo que Ud. haría si hiciera en las siguientes circunstancias. |

EJEMPLO: ir al centro comercial / comprar mucha ropa
Si yo **fuera (fuese)** al centro comercial, compraría mucha ropa.

1. pasar un año en México / hablar el español perfectamente

2. tener un loro / enseñarle a hablar

3. participar en un maratón / no ganar el premio

4. conocer a una persona famosa / pedirle su autógrafo

5. entrevistar al presidente / hacerle muchas preguntas

6. pintar bien / tener muchas exposiciones de mis cuadros

7. no poder resolver un problema / buscar la ayuda de alguien

| EJERCICIO K | **Un mundo nuevo**   Exprese lo que las siguientes personas dicen de sus deseos de viajar. |

EJEMPLO: Rafael / ir a México / visitar las pirámides de Tenochtitlán
Si Rafael **fuera** a México, **visitaría** las pirámides de Tenochtitlán.

1. Elena / pasar tiempo en Barcelona / aprender el catalán

2. nosotros / estar en Madrid / ver muchas obras de arte en el Museo del Prado

3. yo / viajar a Costa Rica / pasar mucho tiempo en los parques nacionales

4. tú / hacer un viaje a Guatemala / conocer la cultura precolombina

5. David y Marco / pasar las vacaciones en la República Dominicana / descansar en las playas

6. tú y yo / ir a Chile / poder esquiar en las montañas de los Andes

7. Paula / visitar a Colombia / comprar muchas esmeraldas

_____

EJERCICIO L   **Añoranza (Nostalgia)**   Exprese lo que un grupo de ancianos añoran.

EJEMPLO: aprender a conducir / ser más independiente
Si yo **hubiera aprendido** a conducir, **habría (hubiera)** sido más independiente.

1. quedarme en la escuela / llegar a ser dentista

_____

2. seguir los consejos de mis padres / casarme con otra persona

_____

3. no salir de mi pueblo / no conocer otras culturas

_____

4. tener dinero / establecer mi propia empresa

_____

5. ser menos impaciente / tener más oportunidades

_____

6. tomar la música en serio / ser un músico profesional

_____

7. ser más sabio / no invertir tanto dinero en la Bolsa

_____

EJERCICIO M   **Actividad oral**   Trabaje con un(a) compañero(a) y tomen turnos haciendo preguntas sobre qué haría en diferentes circunstancias. Use las siguientes circunstancias o piense en otras.

perder un anillo de oro
tener mucho dinero
recibir una beca a la universidad
tener un boleto para volar a cualquier ciudad del mundo
ser suspendido en un curso
ser el presidente del país, etc.

EJEMPLO: ¿Qué harías si perdieras un anillo de oro?
Si yo **perdiera** un anillo de oro, lo **buscaría** por todas partes.

CHAPTER 12
The Subjunctive With Conjunctions, Adverbial Clauses, and Adjectival Clauses

1. The Subjunctive With Conjunctions

There are conjunctions in Spanish that require the subjunctive if uncertainty, doubt, anticipation, or indefiniteness is implied. Otherwise, the indicative is used.

aunque *although, even though, even if*

SUBJUNCTIVE	INDICATIVE
Aunque me pida una disculpa, no se la daré. *Although he may ask for an apology, I will not give it to him.*	*Aunque me pidió una disculpa, no se la di.* *Although he asked for an apology, I didn't give it to him.*

cuando *when*

SUBJUNCTIVE	INDICATIVE
Te hablaré *cuando te vea*. *I will speak to you when I see you.*	**Siempre te hablo *cuando te veo*.** *I always speak to you when I see you.*

de manera que
de modo que } *so that*

SUBJUNCTIVE	INDICATIVE
Caminaron despacio, *de manera (de modo) que* ellos *pudieran* sacar fotografías. *They walked slowly, so that they could take pictures.*	**Caminaron despacio, *de manera (de modo) que* ellos pudieron sacar fotografías.** *They walked slowly, so they were able to take pictures.*

después (de) que
luego de que } *after*

SUBJUNCTIVE	INDICATIVE
Nos reuniremos *después de que* yo *regrese* de mi viaje. *We will meet after I return from my trip.*	**Siempre nos reunimos *después de que* yo *regreso* de mi viaje.** *We always meet after I return from my trip.*

en cuanto
tan pronto como } *as soon as*

SUBJUNCTIVE	INDICATIVE
Confirma tu participación *en cuanto que (tan pronto como) recibas* la invitación. *Confirm your participation as soon as you receive the invitation.*	Confirmé mi participación *en cuanto que (tan pronto como) recibí* la invitación. *I confirmed by participation as soon as I received the invitation.*

hasta que *until*

SUBJUNCTIVE	INDICATIVE
Esperen *hasta que ellos lleguen.* *Wait until they come.*	Esperamos *hasta que ellos llegaron.* *We waited until they arrived.*

mientras *while*

SUBJUNCTIVE	INDICATIVE
No aprenderás *mientras* no prestes atención. *You will not learn while you don't pay attention.*	No aprendiste *mientras* no prestaste atención. *You did not learn while you did not pay attention.*

NOTE: If the subjects of the main and dependent clauses are the same, *que* is usually omitted and the infinitive is used.

Entró sin saludar a nadie.	*She entered without greeting anyone.*
Espere hasta llegar a casa.	*Wait until you arrive home.*
Caminaron despacio para sacar fotos.	*They walked slowly in order to take photos.*

EJERCICIO A   ¿Qué hacer? Exprese lo que Marisol cuenta de cómo pasó el día. Use el indicativo o el subjuntivo como sea necesario.

EJEMPLO: Iré al centro con tal que Uds. **vayan** también.
                                        (ir)

1. Llamé a Rosa temprano para que ella —————— mis planes.
                                          (saber)

2. Decidimos encontrarnos en un café del centro aunque —————— por la tarde.
                                                          (llover)

3. En cuanto que yo —————— de la casa, cayó un aguacero.
                        (salir)

4. Me quedé en casa hasta que _____ de llover.
   (dejar)

5. A fin de _____ a tiempo, tomé un taxi.
   (llegar)

6. Rosa me vio tan pronto como yo _____ en el café.
   (entrar)

7. Juan estaba con Rosa y en cuanto que él me _____ , se levantó para saludarme.
   (ver)

8. Tuvimos que prestarle dinero a Juan para que él _____ pagar la cuenta.
   (poder)

9. Aunque _____ tarde, decidimos ir al cine.
   (ser)

10. En cuanto _____ la película, volví a casa.
    (terminar)

EJERCICIO B   **Así son las madres.**   Unas amigas hablan de lo que sus madres les dicen antes de salir con los amigos. Exprese lo que dicen.

EJEMPLO: Llámame aunque tú **vuelvas** a casa temprano.
(volver)

1. ¿Has dejado un número de teléfono en caso de que yo te _____ ?
   (necesitar)

2. Estaré preocupada hasta que tú _____ en casa.
   (estar)

3. Llámame luego que tú _____ a la fiesta.
   (llegar)

4. Vuelve a casa temprano de modo que yo _____ acostarme tranquilamente.
   (poder)

5. No hagas mucho ruido cuando tú _____ en la casa.
   (entrar)

6. Aunque yo _____ durmiendo, despiértame cuando tú _____ .
   (estar)   (llegar)

2.   The Subjunctive in Adverbial Clauses

a. Adverbial clauses function as adverbs by providing information about when, where, how, or why something happens. Such clauses are usually introduced by the following conjunctions:

a fin de que
para que } *in order that, so that*

Compraré la revista *a fin de que* (*para que*) la leas.   *I will buy the magazine so that you read it.*

a condición de que   *on the condition that*

Iremos al cine a condición de que hagas la tarea.   *We will go to the movies on the condition that you do your homework.*

a menos que *unless*

No iré *a menos que* tú *vayas* también.   *I will not go unless you go too.*

a no ser que *lest, unless*

El partido comenzará a las 7:00,   *The game will start at 7:00,*
  ***a no ser que* llueva.**   *unless it rains.*

antes (de) que *before*

Prepararé la cena *antes de que* ellos   *I will prepare dinner before*
  lleguen.   *they arrive.*

con tal de que *provided that*

Me prestó el dinero *con tal de que*   *He lent me the money provided that*
  se lo *devolviera* en quince días.   *I returned it in two weeks.*

en caso de que *in case (that)*

Llamaré *en caso de que haya* un   *I will call in case there is a*
  cambio en tus planes.   *change in your plans.*

sin que *without*

No puedes entrar *sin que* te *vean*.   *You can't enter without being seen.*

b. In Spanish, the subjunctive is used in an adverbial clause if the situation described in the clause is viewed as something hypothetical or anticipated.

Queremos salir *sin que* nos *vean*.   *We want to leave without them seeing us.*

c. The subjunctive is also used after compounds of -*quiera* and similar indefinite expressions.

dondequiera *wherever*

***Dondequiera* que yo *vaya*, llevaré**   *Wherever I go, I will take*
  la cámara.   *the camera.*

Cualquier(a) *whatever*

***Cualquier* hotel que *escoja*, le**   *Whatever hotel he chooses, he*
  parecerá caro.   *will find expensive.*

quienquiera (pl. **quienesquiera**) *whoever*

***Quienquiera* que *conteste*, déjele**   *Whoever answers, leave him a message.*
  un recado.

cuandoquiera *whenever*

***Cuandoquiera tengas* tiempo,**   *Whenever you have time, please*
  llámame, por favor.   *call me.*

por + adv. / adj. + **que** *however, no matter how*

***Por* rápido que *corran* los trenes,**   *No matter how fast the trains run,*
  hay demoras.   *there are delays.*

| EJERCICIO C | **Buenos amigos** Exprese lo que dice Ernesto de Paco y cómo trata a sus amigos usando la expresión adverbial indicada en cada frase. |

EJEMPLO: Paco / no ir / sin que / Enrique / ir también
Paco no va **sin que** Enrique **vaya** también.

1. Paco / no jugar en el partido / a menos que / Enrique / jugar también

2. Paco / dar muchas fiestas / para que / sus amigos / divertirse

3. Paco / hacer todos los preparativos / antes de que / sus amigos / llegar

4. Paco / no ir a ninguna parte / sin que / un amigo / acompañarle

5. Paco / ayudarles a los amigos / con tal que / ellos ayudarle

6. Paco / darme el número de su teléfono celular / en caso de que / yo / tener que hablar con él

| EJERCICIO D | **Una excursión** Vicente y unos amigos van a hacer el alpinismo. Exprese lo que dicen antes del viaje. |

EJEMPLO: Nosotros saldremos temprano / a menos que / quedarnos dormidos
Nosotros saldremos temprano **a menos que nos quedemos** dormidos.

1. Haremos el alpinismo / con tal que / no llover

2. Yo debo comprarme botas nuevas / antes de que / nosotros / hacer la excursión

3. Lucas llevará una brújula / para que / nosotros / no perderse

4. Llevaremos una malla / en caso de que / bajar la temperatura

5. No debemos salir / sin que / las cantimploras / estar llenas de agua

6. Debemos desayunarnos bien / antes de que / nosotros / salir

EJERCICIO E   ¿**Por qué?** Exprese por qué el señor Montoya hizo estas cosas. Complete las frases a continuación.

1. Compró un televisor con pantalla grandísima / para que / su familia / ver bien sus programas favoritos

_____

2. Lo metió en la casa / sin que / sus hijos / verlo

_____

3. Hizo una reservación en un restaurante elegante / a fin de que / su esposa y él / poder celebrar su aniversario

_____

4. Apuntó la cita en su agenda / antes de que / él / olvidarlo

_____

5. Guardó cien dólares en su escritorio / en caso de que / faltarle dinero

_____

6. Les prometió un regalo a los hijos / con tal que / ellos / recibir buenas calificaciones

_____

EJERCICIO F   **Un mensaje electrónico** Complete, con la forma apropiada del verbo indicado, el mensaje electrónico que Miguel le mandó a un amigo de España.

Querido Adrián:

Me alegro de que hayas aceptado mi invitación de pasar las vacaciones con nosotros.

Cuandoquiera que tú _____ , serás bien recibido. Yo sé que nosotros nos llevamos
1. (llegar)

bien y cualesquiera que _____ sus intereses en este viaje, los cumpliremos.
2. (ser)

Quienquiera que te _____ en el viaje será bien recibido también. Dondequiera
3. (acompañar)

que tú _____ , te encontraré. Me doy cuenta de que por económico que te
4. (estar)

_____ el vuelo, el viajar es caro. Haremos lo más posible para que el viaje no
5. (parecer)

te _____ un dineral.
6. (costar)

Hasta pronto,

Miguel

3.   The Subjunctive in Adjectival Clauses

a. An adjectival clause modifies a noun in the same way an adjective modifies a noun. The noun modified by an adjective clause is referred to as the antecedent.

Es un restaurante *caro.*	*It's an expensive restaurant.*
Es un restaurante que *se llama* **«Cielito Lindo».**	*It's a restaurant called Cielito Lindo.*

b. In Spanish, there are two types of antecedents: those that are part of reality—definite or existent—and those that are not part of reality —indefinite or nonexistent. The subjunctive is used with adjectival clauses that modify antecedents that are not part of reality or the speaker's experience (indefinite, nonexistent, or negative antecedents).

Busco un restaurante que *tenga* **mesas al aire libre.**	*I'm looking for a restaurant that has tables outdoors.*
Quiero un restaurante que *tenga* **un menú internacional.**	*I want a restaurant that has an international menu.*
Necesito un restaurante que *quede* **cerca de la casa.**	*I need a restaurant that is close to the house.*
No hay ningún restaurante que *quede* **cerca de la casa.**	*There is no restaurant near to the house.*

> **NOTE:**   If the antecedent is definite and identifiable, the adjectival clause is in the indicative.
>
> | | |
> |---|---|
> | **Busco un restaurante que** *se llama* **«Cielito Lindo».** | *I am looking for a restaurant called Cielito Lindo.* |
> | **Me gustan los restaurantes que sirven platos internacionales.** | *I like restaurants that serve international dishes.* |

c. The sequence of tenses rules also apply in adjectival clauses.

Quiero **un restaurante que** *sirva* **buena comida.**	*I want a restaurant that serves good food.*
Quería **un restaurante que** *sirviera* **buena comida.**	*I wanted a restaurant that served good food.*
No *hay* **película que le** *agrade.*	*There is no film that he likes.*
No *había* **película que le** *agradara.*	*There was no film that he liked.*

d. Other relative words such as *donde* and *quien* can also introduce adjectival clauses.

Busca **un quiosco donde** *vendan* **revistas en español.**	*He's looking for a kiosk where they sell magazines in Spanish.*
Quería **una amiga con quien** *pudiera* **bailar.**	*He wanted a friend with whom he could dance.*

e. In Spanish, a noun may be followed by a relative clause introduced with *que* that has a verb in the indicative or the subjunctive. If the indicative is used in the relative clause, it means that the antecedent has already been identified. If the subjunctive is used in the relative clause, it means that the antecedent has not been identified.

> *Encontré* **el suéter** *que* me *gusta.*   *I found the sweater that I like.*
> *No encontré* **un suéter** *que* me *gustara.*   *I didn't find a sweater that I liked.*

EJERCICIO G   **En la galería de arte** Fernando va a una galería de arte para ver una exposición. También quiere comprar una pintura para su nuevo apartamento. Exprese lo que Fernando le dice al dependiente.

EJEMPLO: illustrar un estilo moderno   Busco un cuadro que **illustre** un estilo moderno.

1. no costar mucho   _____

2. tener pocos colores vibrantes   _____

3. no necesitar un marco elegante   _____

4. expresar el espíritu del pintor   _____

5. representar un tema universal   _____

6. dar un ambiente dramático al cuarto _____

EJERCICIO H   **Un nuevo empleado** Jorge y Felipe son socios de una empresa. Exprese lo que ellos dicen cuando solicitan un nuevo empleado.

EJEMPLO: Nosotros buscamos una persona que **tenga** buena presentación.
_____ (tener)

1. Queremos encontrar un empleado que _____ (saber) inglés y español.

2. Necesitamos una persona que _____ (poder) aprender el negocio rápidamente.

3. Buscamos un empleado que no _____ (pedir) un salario alto.

4. Necesitamos una persona que _____ (practicar) la coordinación de esfuerzo.

5. No queremos ninguna persona que _____ (buscar) un ascenso en seguida.

6. Queremos un empleado que _____ (cumplir) con sus responsabilidades.

EJERCICIO I   **Mis experiencias** Lois acaba de volver de Costa Rica donde vivió con una familia. Exprese lo que ella dice de su experiencia.

EJEMPLO: No había ninguna familia que **pudiera** ser más simpática.
_____ (poder)

1. La señora ofreció preparar cualquier comida que me _____ (gustar) .

2. Dondequiera que yo _____ (ir) , la gente me trató con cortesía.

3. No había nadie en la familia que ―――― inglés.
(hablar)

4. Por más que yo ―――― de expresarme en español, muchas veces no me entendían.
(tratar)

5. Me hacía falta un diccionario que ―――― muchas expresiones comunes sobre la vida diaria.
(presentar)

6. No encontré ninguna librería que ―――― tal diccionario.
(vender)

7. No había experiencia tan difícil que no ―――― algo de beneficio.
(tener)

EJERCICIO J **Actividad oral** En su escuela hay un programa extensivo de actividades extra-curriculares en que los alumnos pueden participar. Trabajando con un compañero, exprese qué clase de actividad le interesa a Ud. Por ejemplo, *Busco una actividad en que ..., Necesito una actividad que ..., Me interesa una actividad que ...,* etc.

PARA EXPRESARSE MEJOR
Actividades extra-curriculares

el ajedrez *chess* 　　**el debate** *debate*
el coro *chorus* 　　**los deportes** *sports*
la danza *dance* 　　**el drama** *drama*

EJERCICIO K **Lectura** Lea la siguiente carta que fue publicada en un periódico local. Luego conteste las preguntas.

PARA EXPRESARSE MEJOR

someterse *to submit* 　　**el cupo** *quota*
retirar *to take back* 　　**recurrir** *to resort, to have recourse*
el atraso *delay, lag* 　　**remitir** *to refer*
la matrícula *enrollment, registration* 　　**subvencionado** *subsidized*
el vacante *vacancy* 　　**marginar** *to marginalize; to exclude*

Cancelación de matrícula a niña por enfermedad

En abril, nuestra hija de 6 años —Isabel— cayó gravemente enferma. A causa de esto, fue preciso que se sometiera a exámenes y tratamientos por lo que dejó de asistir al colegio, lo que informamos oportunamente con certificado médico. Retiramos sus tareas para que el atraso fuera lo menor posible, pero le cancelaron la matrícula por inasistencia y la dejaron sin vacante para el próximo año escolar, ya que a estas alturas los colegios municipalizados ya no cuentan con cupos. Aunque recurrimos a la directora de la escuela, al Departamento Provincial de Educación y a la Corporación de Educación de Las Estrellas, a la cual dicho Departamento Provincial nos remitió, no hemos encontrado solución alguna, y ni siquiera un argumento razonable que explique por qué enfermarse es motivo para que un colegio subvencionado margine a una niña del sistema.

1. ¿Qué le pasó a la niña?

    (a) Fue herida en un accidente automovilístico.

    (b) Padeció de una enfermedad.

    (c) Se mudó a otro pueblo.

    (d) Fue a vivir con otros parientes.

2. ¿Por qué le cancelaron la matrícula?

    (a) Sus padres no pudieron pagar las colegiaturas.

    (b) Se suspendió en todas las materias.

    (c) Fingió estar enferma.

    (d) Faltó a las clases.

3. ¿Qué resultado tuvo esta cancelación?

    (a) No habría lugar para ella en la escuela al año siguiente.

    (b) Tendría que repetir el año.

    (c) Estudiaría con la directora del colegio.

    (d) No recibiría los tratamientos médicos.

4. ¿Qué buscan los padres de la niña?

    (a) Dinero para matricular a la niña en un colegio privado

    (b) Una explicación razonable de esta clase de discriminación

    (c) Cambios en las leyes sobre la educación pública

    (d) La ayuda de varios funcionarios gubernativos

CHAPTER 13
Formal, Informal, and Indirect Commands; Commands With Object Pronouns

1.   Formal Commands

a. Formal commands (*Ud.* and *Uds.*) are always expressed by the present subjunctive.

Hable / Hablen **más fuerte.**	*Speak louder.*
Vuelva / Vuelvan **pronto.**	*Return soon.*
Diga / Digan **la verdad.**	*Tell the truth.*
Vaya / Vayan **a la playa.**	*Go to the beach.*

b. Negative commands are formed by placing *no* before the affirmative command.

No **hable más fuerte.**	*Don't speak louder.*
No **vuelvan pronto.**	*Don't return soon.*
No **diga la verdad.**	*Don't tell the truth.*
No **vayan a la playa.**	*Don't go to the beach.*

c. Reflexive pronouns are attached to the affirmative reflexive command and there is an accent mark on the next-to-last syllable of the verb. In negative commands, the reflexive pronoun precedes the verb.

Lávese / Lávense la cara.	*Wash your face.*
No *se* **lave / laven la cara.**	*Don't wash your face.*
Despídase. / Despídanse.	*Say goodbye.*
No *se* **despida / despidan**	*Don't say goodbye.*

NOTE: Subject pronouns are usually omitted with commands.

EJERCICIO A   **Una nueva cafetera** Rosalía tiene una nueva cafetera y va a usarla por primera vez. Exprese las instrucciones que ella debe seguir.

EJEMPLO: enjuagar la jarra   **Enjuague** la jarra.

1. llenar el depósito con agua fría

   _____

2. usar una taza llena de agua por cada cucharada sopera de café molido

   _____

3. sacar el soporte del filtro

   _____

4. echar el café molido en un filtro desechable dentro del soporte del filtro

   _____

5. colocar de nuevo el soporte del filtro en su posición de bloqueo correcta

    _____

6. poner la jarra sobre la placa de calentamiento

    _____

7. enchufar el cable eléctrico

    _____

8. pulsar el interruptor para poner en funcionamiento la cafetera

    _____

9. no interrumpir el ciclo

    _____

10. servir el café

    _____

| EJERCICIO B | **Estudiantes activos** Durante una orientación para la nueva clase de estudiantes en la secundaria, el director les dice lo que deben hacer para ser estudiantes activos. Exprese lo que les dice el director. |

EJEMPLO: asistir a la escuela todos los días   **Asistan** a la escuela todos los días.

1. no faltar a las clases

    _____

2. comprobar cada ausencia con una nota de los padres

    _____

3. preparar la tarea cada día

    _____

4. llegar temprano

    _____

5. estudiar para los exámenes

    _____

6. no dejar el trabajo hasta el último momento

    _____

7. hacerse socios de algún club o equipo

    _____

8. obedecer el código de conducta

    _____

9. no tirar papeles en el piso

    _____

10. participar activamente en el proceso educativo

_____

EJERCICIO C   **En casa ajena**   Ricardo y Luis van a pasar el fin de semana en casa de unos amigos. Exprese lo que les dice su mamá.

EJEMPLO: portarse bien   **Pórtense** bien.
           no portarse mal   **No se porten** mal.

1. lavarse las manos antes de comer _____

2. cepillarse los dientes _____

3. bañarse rápidamente _____

4. no quedarse en el patio _____

5. no levantarse de la mesa sin pedir permiso _____

6. no dormirse en el sofá _____

7. acostarse temprano _____

8. despertarse sin dificultad _____

9. vestirse rápidamente _____

10. despedirse de los anfitriones _____

2. Informal Commands

a. *Tú* and *VOSOTROS* Commands

1. Regular Verbs

(a) The singular (*tú*) form of the familiar affirmative command is the same as the third-person singular of the present indicative.

INFINITIVE	cantar *to sing*	beber *to drink*	dormir *to sleep*
TÚ COMMAND	canta	bebe	duerme

(b) The plural (*vosotros*) form of the familiar affirmative command is formed by changing the -r ending of the infinitive to -d.

INFINITIVE	cantar *to sing*	beber *to drink*	dormir *to sleep*
VOSOTROS COMMAND	cantad	bebed	dormid

(c) The negative familiar command forms are all expressed by the present subjunctive.

INFINITIVE	cantar *to sing*	beber *to drink*	dormir *to sleep*
NEGATIVE FAMILIAR COMMAND	no *cantes* (tú) no *cantéis* (vosotros)	no *bebas* (tú) no *bebáis* (vosotros)	no *duermas* (tú) no*durmáis* (vosotros)

NOTE: The *vosotros* command is rarely used in Spanish America. Formal plural commands (*Uds.*) are used instead.

EJERCICIO D | **Una amiga nueva** Emma quiere entablar amistad con la hija de sus nuevos vecinos, que tiene la misma edad que ella. Exprese lo que Emma le dice a la muchacha.

EJEMPLO: jugar conmigo / no jugar con las otras niñas
Juega conmigo; **no juegues** con las otras niñas.

1. pasearse conmigo / no pasearse con las otras niñas

_____

2. montar en mi bicicleta / no montar en la bicicleta de ellas

_____

3. leer mis cuentos / no leer los cuentos de ellas

_____

4. buscarme / no buscarlas a ellas

_____

5. reunirse conmigo / no reunirse con ellas

_____

EJERCICIO E | **La maestra española** La nueva maestra es de España. Exprese lo que ella les dice a sus alumnos.

EJEMPLO: Niños, **mirad** el mapa de España; no **miréis** el mapa de Venezuela.
(mirar)   (mirar)

1. Niños, _____ los libros; no _____ las bocas.
(abrir)   (abrir)

2. Niños, _____ las plumas; no _____ los marcadores.
(sacar)   (sacar)

3. Niños, _____ a la pizarra; no _____ a la ventana.
(acercarse)   (acercarse)

4. Niños, _____ la mochila debajo del escritorio; no _____ debajo de la silla.
(poner)   (poner)

5. Niños, _____ una foto; no _____ un álbum de fotos.
(traer)   (traer)

6. Niños, _____ bien; no _____ mal.
(portarse)   (portarse)

| EJERCICIO F | **Una personalidad difícil**   El señor Villareal tiene una personalidad pesada y difícil. Exprese lo que su esposa le sugiere al respecto. |

EJEMPLO: Adán, **quéjate** conmigo; no **te quejes** con tus hermanos.
                (quejarse)   (quejarse)

1. Adán, ——————— conmigo; no ——————— con los vecinos.
              (pelear)   (pelear)

2. Adán, ——————— en voz baja; no ——————— en voz alta.
              (hablar)   (hablar)

3. Adán, ——————— conmigo; no ——————— con otras personas.
              (contar)   (contar)

4. Adán, ——————— lo que yo te digo; no ——————— lo que te dicen las
              (creer)   (creer)
otras personas.

5. Adán, ——————— más abiertamente; no ——————— de vez en cuando.
          (comunicar)   (comunicar)

6. Adán, ——————— antes de hablar.
              (pensar)

2. Irregular Verbs

The following verbs have irregular commands in the affirmative singular (*tú*). All other familiar commands are regular.

INFINITIVE	AFFIRMATIVE COMMAND	NEGATIVE COMMAND
dec**ir**	*di* / decid	no digas / no digáis
hac**er**	*haz* / haced	no hagas / no hagáis
ir	ve / id	no vayas / no vayáis
pon**er**	*pon* / poned	no pongas / no pongáis
sal**ir**	*sal* / salid	no salgas / no salgáis
ser	*sé* / sed	no seas / no seáis
ten**er**	*ten* / tened	no tengas / no tengáis
val**er**	*val* / valed	no valgas / no valgáis
ven**ir**	*ven* / venid	no vengas / no vengáis

EJERCICIO G   **Consejos** Ken siempre se pone muy alborotado cuando va a hacer algo. Exprese los consejos que le da su mamá.

EJEMPLO: Ken, **haz** todo con calma.
                    (hacer)

1. Ken, ——————— paciente.
            (ser)

2. Ken, no ——————— nervioso.
              (ponerse)

3. Ken, no ——————— tanta prisa.
              (tener)

4. Ken, ——————— en seguida.
            (salir)

5. Ken, ——————— la verdad.
            (decir)

6. Ken, ——————— acá.
            (venir)

7. Ken, ——————— mucho cuidado.
            (tener)

8. Ken, no ——————— tan listo.
              (ser)

9. Ken, no ——————— a hacer eso.
              (ir)

10. Ken, ——————— mucha atención a lo que haces.
             (poner)

EJERCICIO H   **¿Qué dirían?** Exprese lo que dirían las siguientes personas en estas circunstancias.

EJEMPLO: YO: Llegamos tarde y ya empezó la película.

            TÚ: **No te pongas furioso.**
                  (no ponerse furioso)

1. LAURA: Esta calle está muy oscura.

    ELISA: ——————————————————————————
                          (no tener miedo)

2. ALICIA: No sé si debo salir con Frank o no.

    VERA: ——————————————————————————
                      (no ser tonta / salir con él)

3. PAUL: ¿Quieres saber mi contraseña?

    JANE: ——————————————————————————
                      (no decírsela a nadie)

4. VICKI: ¿Dónde pongo el regalo?

    ELSA: ——————————————————————————
                      (ponerlo allí con los otros)

5. JACK: No comprendo lo que dice el maestro.

   RUDY: _____
                          (hacer muchas preguntas)

6. MARÍA: ¿A qué hora es la fiesta?

   GUY: _____
                          (venir a las ocho y media)

EJERCICIO I   **Un mensaje**   Exprese lo que Diego le escribe a un amigo que piensa visitarlo.

Querido Enrique:

_____ a mi casa el sábado por la tarde. _____ (tú) todas las diligencias
   1. (venir)   2. (hacer)

por la mañana. No _____ a pie; _____ en bicicleta. _____
              3. (venir)   4. (venir)   5. (salir)

de tu casa a las doce y media y no _____ prisa. _____ cuidado al
                              6. (tener)   7. (tener)

llegar a la Avenida Luces porque hay mucho tránsito. _____ tu traje de baño
                                                  8. (poner)

en la mochila. _____ a tus padres que vamos a nadar en la piscina. No
            9. (decirles)

_____ malo y no _____ a desilusionarme. Es todo por ahora.
10. (ser)   11. (ir)

Cordialmente,

Diego

EJERCICIO J   **No necesitas mapa.**   Exprese las instrucciones que Betty le da a una amiga
para llegar a su gimnasio.

EJEMPLO: tomar la ruta 80   **Toma** la ruta 80.

1. ir hacia el oeste   _____
2. continuar de frente por cinco millas _____
3. salir en tercera salida   _____
4. dar vuelta a la izquierda   _____
5. pasar un centro comercial   _____
6. mantenerse en el carril derecho   _____
7. pararse en el semáforo   _____
8. doblar a la derecha   _____
9. seguir derecho una cuadra   _____
10. buscar estacionamiento en la calle _____

b. *Nosotros* Commands

1. The *nosotros* command is formed with the present-subjunctive form of *nosotros*.

***Comamos* más tarde.**	*Let's eat later.*
No *descansemos* ahora.	*Let's not rest now.*

2. *Vamos a* + infinitive is often used to replace the affirmative *nosotros* command, but the present subjunctive must always be used to form the negative *nosotros* command.

***Veamos* una película.**	
***Vamos* a *ver* una película.**	*Let's see a movie.*
No *veamos* esa película.	*Let's not see that movie.*

   NOTE: *Vamos*, not *vayamos*, is used to express "let's go." *No vayamos* is used to express "let's not go."

***Vamos* al teatro.**	*Let's go to the theater.*
***No vayamos* al museo.**	*Let's not go to the museum.*

3. With reflexive verbs, the final *-s* of the verb ending is dropped when the reflexive pronoun *nos* or the indirect-object pronoun *se* is added to the affirmative *nosotros* form. An accent mark is required over the stressed syllable.

Sentémonos.	*Let's sit down.*
Vámonos.	*Let's go.*
Levantémonos.	*Let's get up.*
Démoselo.	*Let's give it to them.*
Expliquémoselo.	*Let's explain it to her.*

EJERCICIO K   **Vamos a...**   Exprese lo que sugieren dos amigos cuando escuchan lo que otro amigo les dice.

EJEMPLO: Tom tiene muchos discos compactos nuevos. (*pedirlos prestados*)
Vamos a pedírselos prestados.
Sí, **pidámoselos** prestados.

1. Elena no entiende la decisión que el grupo tomó. (*explicarla*)

   _____

   _____

2. Fred no encuentra su raqueta de tenis. (*devolverla*)

   _____

   _____

3. Lynn y Clara buscan entradas para el concierto. (*darlas*)

   _____

   _____

4. Ya me cansé de caminar. (*sentarse*)

_____

_____

5. Tengo ganas de ir a nadar. (*irse*)

_____

_____

6. Antonia nunca tiene paraguas cuando llueve. (*regalarlo*)

_____

_____

7. Nos gusta mucho este lugar. (*quedarse*)

_____

_____

3.   Indirect Commands

Indirect commands are also expressed by the present subjunctive and are usually introduced by *que*.

Que entren **ellos.**	*Let them enter.*
Que diga **ella la verdad.**	*Let her tell the truth.*
Que lo busque **él.**	*Let him look for it.*

EJERCICIO L   **Un esfuerzo cooperativo**   Leslie coordina una fiesta para el fin del año escolar. Exprese lo que ella les dice a sus compañeros.

EJEMPLO: Leslie / ser la coordinadora de la fiesta
Que Leslie **sea** la coordinadora de la fiesta.

1. Nick / colgar los adornos   _____

2. Linda y Don / inflar los globos   _____

3. todo el mundo / preparar un bocadillo   _____

4. Miguel / traer los discos compactos   _____

5. Pablo y Juan / comprar los refrescos   _____

6. Antonio / buscar cosas para una rifa   _____

7. Myrna / organizar las competencias   _____

8. Hilda / enviar invitaciones a los profesores   _____

$\boxed{\textbf{EJERCICIO M}}$ **Que otra persona lo haga.** Jerry es muy perezoso y nunca quiere hacer nada. Exprese quién debe hacer estas cosas.

EJEMPLO: lavar el carro (*mi papá*)   Que mi papá **lo lave.**

1. poner la mesa (*Adela*)

_____

2. regar el jardín (*Faustino*)

_____

3. devolver los libros a la biblioteca (*Nancy*)

_____

4. comprarle un regalo de cumpleaños a Jane (*Suzy y Jack*)

_____

5. pedir el número de teléfono de Rafael (*Arturo*)

_____

6. apagar las luces (*Uds.*)

_____

7. recoger el periódico (*Eddie*)

_____

4.   Command Forms With Object Pronouns

a. Object pronouns (including reflexive pronouns) are attached to the verb in affirmative commands and precede the verb in negative commands. An accent mark is required if the verb's original stress is on the next-to-last syllable.

Háble*me*.	*Talk to me.*
No *me* hable.	*Don't talk to me.*
Póngan*lo* aquí.	*Put it here.*
No *lo* pongan aquí.	*Don't put it here.*
Busquémos*lo*.	*Let's look for it.*
No *lo* busquemos.	*Let's not look for it.*
Siéntate.	*Sit down.*
No te sientes.	*Don't sit down.*
Leedla.	*Read it.*
No la leáis.	*Don't read it.*
Hazlo.	*Do it.*
No lo hagas.	*Don't do it.*

b. With indirect commands, object pronouns always precede the verb.

| Que *lo* busque Lisa. | *Let Lisa look for it.* |
| Que no *lo* busque Lisa. | *Let not Lisa look for it.* |

| Que *se* queden aquí. | *Let them stay here.* |
| Que no *se* queden aquí. | *Let them not stay here.* |

c. Reflexive verbs in the affirmative *vosotros* command drop the final *-d* before adding the reflexive pronoun.

| **Levantaos.** | *Get up.* |
| **Reuníos.** | *Meet.* |

NOTE: *Idos* (Go away) is the only exception.

EJERCICIO N **En el restaurante** El señor Gómez ha invitado a algunos amigos a comer en un restaurante. Exprese las respuestas, en forma de imperativo, que el señor Gómez da a las preguntas que le hace el mesero.

EJEMPLO: ¿Les digo las especialidades del día ahora? (*sí*)   Sí, **díganoslas.**

1. ¿Les traigo los menús? (*sí*) _____

2. ¿Les sirvo la sopa ahora? (*sí*) _____

3. ¿A quiénes les doy más pan? (*a ellos*) _____

4. ¿Les repito las especialidades del día? (*sí*) _____

5. ¿Les quito los platos ahora? (*no*) _____

6. ¿A quién le doy la cuenta? (*a mí*) _____

EJERCICIO O **¿Qué hacer?** Unas amigas van a hacerle una fiesta de despedida a Norma. Exprese lo que dicen mientras preparan la lista de invitados. Use pronombres-objeto en la respuesta.

EJEMPLO: Hace mucho que no recibo carta de Patricia. (*escribirle una carta*)
Escríbesela.

1. ¿Sabrá la noticia de Norma? (*contarle la noticia*)

_____

2. ¿Vendría a la fiesta? (*invitarla*)

_____

3. ¿Tendría dinero para el viaje? (*enviarle el dinero*)

_____

4. ¿Dónde se quedaría? (*ofrecerle la casa*)

_____

5. Tenemos que saber si vendrá.   (*llamarle por teléfono*)

EJERCICIO P   **Amigas**   Exprese lo que Juana le dice a su amiga Alejandra cuando se encuentran en el centro. Use la forma imperativa.

1. Alejandra, —————— lo que sucedió.
(decirme)

2. No —————— tú, todo saldrá bien.
(preocuparse)

3. No —————— , Alejandra, tú no tuviste la culpa.
(enfadarse)

4. Que —————— ellos en la fiesta.
(divertirse)

5. —————— nosotras en este café y —————— un café.
(sentarse) (tomar)

6. No —————— tú a pedir ningún postre.
(ir)

7. Que él —————— una disculpa.
(pedirte)

8. —————— nosotras porque ya es tarde.
(irse)

9. —————— nosotras hablando de eso por teléfono.
(seguir)

10. —————— cuando llegues a casa.
(llamarme)

EJERCICIO Q   **Actividad oral**   Trabajando solo o con un compañero, prepare una explicación y demostración de cómo hacer algo. Por ejemplo: jugar un juego, preparar un plato especial, hacer algo en la computadora, armar algo que ha comprado, etc. Use el imperativo en esta actividad.

EJERCICIO R   **Lectura**   Lea los siguientes anuncios y conteste las preguntas.

Oferta de viajes fuera de temporada desde $999

Ahorre hasta $1100 por persona cuando viaje en tour fuera de temporada.

Seleccione de una variedad de destinaciones populares.

Imagínese, de 8 a 14 días, desde $999, incluyendo tarifas aéreas y hoteles de primera clase.

Conozca ciudades encantadoras e inolvidables.

Visite nuestro sitio en la red:
www.viajes.com o vaya a su agencia de viajes.

1. ¿Por qué ofrecen precios reducidos?

    (a) Es la época en que no hay mucho turismo.

    (b) Viajar en grupo es más económico.

    (c) Visitan lugares poco frecuentados por turistas.

    (d) Hay muchos hoteles encantadores.

> ¿Te gustaría aprender una profesión paso a paso? Aprende corte, confección y alta costura. Ofrecemos cursos prácticos, fáciles de comprender y de rápido aprendizaje. Evaluación de estudios por correspondencia, correo electrónico, fax o teléfono. Consigue un diploma que acreditará tus conocimientos y capacidad. Pídenos información de tu curso preferido. Llama ahora mismo al 52 578 3333.

2. ¿Cuál es la ventaja de estos cursos?

    (a) Dan facilidades de pago.

    (b) Ofrecen empleo a los más capacitados.

    (c) Toman el curso por correspondencia.

    (d) Los cursos duran poco tiempo.

> *Alcance su bienestar y manténgase en forma en el Hotel Emporio.*
>
> Disfrute de su deporte favorito, incluyendo un campo de golf de 36 hoyos, 3 piscinas de agua salada, 3 cabinas de belleza, 4 duchas a presión, baño turco, sauna y un amplio surtido de tratamientos para mantenerse en forma. Disponga de un servicio gratuito a la playa.
>
> *Este verano, cuídese.*
> *Llame al 52 973 4500 para más información.*

3. ¿A qué se dedica este hotel?

    (a) Al descanso completo de sus huéspedes.

    (b) A mejorar el estado físico de los huéspedes.

    (c) Al entrenamiento de los atletas.

    (d) A ofrecer una variedad de clases de meditación.

CHAPTER 14
Constructions With Infinitives

1. Verb + Infinitive

In Spanish, the infinitive of a verb is frequently used to serve as a complement in verb + infinitive constructions. Many conjugated verbs can be followed directly by an infinitive.

Quiero comer **a las dos.**   *I want to eat at two o'clock.*
Debes estudiar **más.**   *You should study more.*

a. Verbs that may be followed directly by an infinitive:

conseguir (e to **i)** *to succeed in, to manage to*
creer *to think, to believe*
deber *should, ought to*
decidir *to decide*
dejar *to let, to allow*
desear *to want, to wish*
esperar *to hope, to expect, to wait*
hacer *to make*
impedir (e to **i)** *to impede, to prevent from*
intentar *to try to*
lograr *to succeed in*
mandar *to order*
merecer *to deserve, to merit*
necesitar *to need, to have to*
oír *to hear*
olvidar *to forget*
parecer *to seem*

pensar (e to **ie)** *to intend*
permitir *to permit*
poder (o to **ue)** *to be able to, can*
preferir (e to **ie; e** to **i)** *to prefer*
procurar *to try to*
prohibir *to prohibit*
prometer *to promise*
querer (e to **ie)** *to want*
recordar (o to **ue)** *to remember*
saber *to know how to*
sentir (e to **ie; e** to **i)** *to regret, to be sorry*
soler (o to **ue)** *to be used to, to be accustomed to*
temer *to be afraid to, to fear*
ver *to see*

EJERCICIO A **Sí o no** Use el verbo entre paréntesis y exprese lo que hizo cada una de las siguientes personas. Conserve el mismo tiempo en la nueva oración.

EJEMPLO: María apuntó la nueva dirección electrónica de su amiga. (*recordar*)
María **recordó apuntar** la nueva dirección electrónica de su amiga.

1. Ellos llegaron al teatro a tiempo. (*procurar*)

   _____

2. Carlos comprende el español pero contesta en inglés. (*soler*)

   _____

3. Lisa no nos acompañó. (*poder*)

   _____

4. Nosotros visitamos la exposición otra vez. (*deber*)

   _____

5. Tú me escribías a menudo. (*querer*)

   _____

6. El señor compró otra marca de carro. (*decidir*)

   _____

7. Yo arreglé la computadora. (*saber*)

   _____

8. Jerry devolvió los libros a la biblioteca. (*prometer*)

   _____

9. Nadya regó las plantas de su vecina. (*olvidar*)

   _____

10. Alex tenía bastante dinero para comprar un anillo de compromiso. (*esperar*)

   _____

| **EJERCICIO B** | **Preguntas generales**   Conteste las preguntas que un(a) amigo(a) nuevo(a) le hace. |

1. ¿Qué sueles hacer durante tu tiempo libre?

   _____

2. ¿Qué piensas hacer después de graduarte de la escuela?

   _____

3. ¿Cuando asistes a actividades culturales, adónde prefieres ir: al cine, al teatro o al museo?

   _____

4. ¿Sabes esquiar?

   _____

5. ¿Qué debes hacer hoy después de las clases?

   _____

6. ¿Necesitas comprar algo en el centro comercial?

   _____

7. ¿Podrás acompañarme al centro comercial esta tarde?

   _____

8. ¿Procuras terminar la tarea temprano por la noche?

   _____

9. ¿Prometes ayudarme a conocer la ciudad?

   _____

10. ¿Dónde piensas pasar el día feriado?

---

2.   Preposition + Infinitive

a. The following prepositions are generally used before an infinitive:

a   *to, at*

Deseamos ir *a* pescar.   *We want to go fishing.*

al + inf.   *upon, on*

Al entrar en la casa, se quitó   *Upon entering the house, he took off*
  el abrigo.   *his coat.*

antes de   *before*

Se despidieron *antes de* salir.   *They said goodbye before leaving.*

con   *with (sometimes to, of, or by)*

No ganas nada *con* huir.   *You don't gain anything by running away.*

de   *of, to*

No tengas miedo *de* decirnos la verdad.   *Don't be afraid of telling us the truth.*

después de   *after*

Después de apagar el televisor, ella se   *After shutting off the TV, she began*
  puso a trabajar.   *to work.*

en   *in, on, of*

Tardé *en* llegar porque hubo un   *I was late coming in because there*
  accidente.   *was an accident.*

en lugar de ⎫
en vez de   ⎬   *instead of*

Lucy estudiará *en lugar de*   *Lucy will study instead of*
  (*en vez de*) salir.   *going out.*

hasta   *until*

La rana tomó agua *hasta* explotar.   *The frog drank water until it exploded.*

para   *in order to, for*

Llegó temprano *para* comprar   *He arrived early in order to buy*
  las entradas.   *the tickets.*

sin   *without*

El niño salió *sin* pedir permiso.   *The child left without asking permission.*

NOTE: The construction verb + preposition + infinitive usually occurs in a two-
         clause sentence. If the subjects in the clauses are different, *que* is required and
         a conjugated form of the verb is used instead of the infinitive. For example:

*Ella se alegra de **asistir** a la fiesta.*	*She is happy to attend the party.*
*Ella se alegra de que yo **asista** a la fiesta.*	*She is happy that I am attending the party.*
*Consiente en **llamarme.***	*He agrees to call me.*
*Consiente en que yo lo **llame.***	*He agrees that I call him.*
***Se vistió** antes de **preparar** el café.*	*He got dressed before preparing the coffee.*
***Se vistió** antes de que su esposa **preparara** el café.*	*He got dressed before his wife prepared the coffee.*

EJERCICIO C | **La entrevista** Complete la siguiente narración añadiendo una preposición, de ser necesario.

Carlos procuró ———— 1. llegar temprano a la entrevista. ———— 2. ir a la oficina de la empresa, él decidió ———— 3. entrar en un café ———— 4. tomar un café. No tardaron ———— 5. servírselo.

———— 6. llevar el café a la calle, se sentó en una mesa y empezó ———— 7. tomarlo. También trataba ———— 8. calmarse los nervios. Comenzó ———— 9. fijarse en las otras personas que estaban en el café.

Esperaba ———— 10. ver una cara conocida ———— 11. poder ———— 12. saludarla. Quería ———— 13. distraerse de la entrevista que le esperaba. Dejó ———— 14. tratar ———— 15. formular las respuestas que daría a las preguntas que le hicieran. ———— 16. pensarlo, tomó el café en dos tragos y salió del café. ———— 17. estar en la calle, se puso ———— 18. caminar rápidamente ———— 19. estar delante del edificio. No deseaba ———— 20. llegar tarde.

EJERCICIO D | **Comentarios al azar** Exprese los comentarios que Anita expresó sobre lo que había visto durante el día. Combine los elementos para formar una sola oración usando la preposición indicada

EJEMPLO: al / recibir los regalos / los novios / dar las gracias
   Al recibir los regalos, los novios dieron las gracias.

1. en vez de / leer el periódico / mi padre / escuchar las noticias en la radio

_____

2. antes de / comer / los niños / lavarse las manos

_____

3. sin / aunque / hacer frío / el joven / salir / ponerse un suéter

_____

4. después de / terminar el programa / ellos / apagar el televisor

_____

5. hasta / estar dentro del edificio / la señora / no cerrar el paraguas

_____

b. The following verbs require a preposition before an infinitive:

1. Verbs that require *a* before an infinitive:

acostumbrarse a *to be accustomed / used to*

No *me acostumbro a* levantarme.   *I don't get used to getting up early.*

animar a *to encourage*

Mis profesores *me animan a* estudiar más.   *My teachers encourage me to study more.*

aprender a *to learn to*

Todos *aprendimos a* jugar al ajedrez.   *We all learned to play chess.*

atreverse a *to dare to*

Manuel no *se atreve a* manejar solo.   *Manuel doesn't dare to drive by himself.*

ayudar a *to help*

Gloria *ayuda a* su abuela los fines de semana.   *Gloria helps her grandmother on weekends.*

comenzar a (e to ie) *to begin to*

Los perritos *comenzaron a* abrir los ojos.   *The puppies started to open their eyes.*

decidirse a *to decide to*

Laura *se decidió a* tomarse unas vacaciones.   *Laura decided to take a vacation.*

dedicarse a *to dedicate oneself to*

Martín *se dedica a* los deportes.   *Martín dedicates himself to sports.*

disponerse a *to get ready to*

Las gemelas *se disponen a* comer.   *The twins are getting ready to eat.*

empezar a (e to ie) *to begin to*

***Empezaremos a* cocinar tan pronto lleguen los invitados.**   *We will start cooking as soon as the guests arrive.*

enseñar a *to show how, to teach to*

Los niños quieren que les *enseñe a* nadar.   *The children want me to teach them to swim.*

invitar a   *to invite to*

Ana, ¿quieres *invitar a* cenar a los García?	*Ana, do you want to invite the Garcia's over for dinner?*

ir a   *to be going to*

Las niñas quieren *ir a* jugar al fútbol.	*The girls want to go to play soccer.*

llegar a   *to get to, to succeed in*

Me gustaría *llegar al* trabajo temprano.	*I would like to go to work early.*

negarse a (e to ie)   *to refuse to*

¿Te *niegas a* hacer tus quehaceres?	*Do you refuse to do your chores?*

ponerse a   *to begin to, to start*

Si nos aburrimos, *nos ponemos a* ver una película.	*If we get bored, we start to watch a movie.*

prepararse a   *to get ready to*

Me *preparaba a* salir cuando sonó el teléfono.	*I was getting ready to leave when the phone rang.*

volver a (o to ue)   *to do* (something) *again*

La familia *volverá a* pasar las vacaciones en la playa.	*The family will spend their vacation at the beach again.*

2. Verbs that require *de* before an infinitive:

acabar de   *to have just*

***Acabo de* oír la noticia.**	*I have just heard the news.*

acordarse de (o to ue)   *to remember to*

***Se acordó de* pagar la cuenta.**	*He remembered to pay the bill.*

alegrarse de   *to be glad*

***Nos alegramos de* aprender español.**	*We are happy to learn Spanish.*

arrepentirse (e to ie)   *to regret*

***Te arrepentiste de* decir eso.**	*You regretted saying that.*

dejar de   *to stop*

Ellos *dejaron de* visitarnos.	*They stopped visiting us.*

encargarse de   *to take charge of*

***Se encarga de* comprar los regalos.**	*She takes charge of buying the gifts.*

olvidarse de   *to forget*

No *se olviden de* estudiar para sus exámenes.	*Don't forget to study for your exams.*

terminar de   *to stop*

**Paco, ¿terminaste de organizar
tu cuarto?**

*Paco, did you finish organizing
your room?*

tratar de   *to try to*

Tratarán de **llamar más tarde.**

They will try to call later.

3. Verbs that require *en* before an infinitive:

consentir en (e to **ie; e** to **i)**   *to consent to, to agree*

¿Consentiría **Ud. *en* pagar más
impuestos?**

Would you agree to pay more taxes?

consistir en   *to consist of*

Consintió en **lavar los platos.**

He agreed to wash the dishes.

convenir en   *to agree to*

Convenimos en **reunirnos a la una.**

We agreed to meet a one o'clock.

empeñarse en   *to be determined to; to insist on*

Me empeño en **ser el anfitrión.**

I insist on being the host.

insistir en   *to insist on*

Linda *insiste en* pagar por la cena.

Linda insists on paying for dinner.

pensar en   *to think about*

Pensamos en **nuestros amigos
todos los días.**

*We think about our friends
every day.*

tardar en   *to delay in, to be long in*

Yo *tardé en* entregar la tarea.

I delayed in submitting the assignment.

4. The following verbs require *con* before an infinitive:

amenazar con   *to threaten to*

**Él *amenaza con* presentar los
documentos.**

*He threatens to present the
documents.*

contar con (o to **ue)**   *to count on, to rely on*

Ella *cuenta con* recibir la beca.

She counts on receiving the scholarship.

soñar con (o to **ue)**   *to dream of*

Sueño con **ser célebre.**

I dream about being famous.

EJERCICIO E   **Una introducción**   Un grupo de turistas se reúne con el guía que va a
acompañarlos durante su estancia en Buenos Aires. Complete los comentarios
del guía con la preposición apropiada, cuando sea necesario.

En mi experiencia de guía, muchas personas quieren ———— conocer lo más que puedan,

<u>1.</u>

mientras otras personas desean ———— dedicarse ———— pasar su tiempo en las tiendas.

2.
3.

Yo creo que debe ———— haber una combinación de las dos actividades. Suelo ————

4.
5.

aconsejarles a las personas que procuren ———— aprovecharse de todas las oportunidades

6.

que hay durante el tiempo corto que van ———— estar en Buenos Aires. Yo siempre trato

7.

———— proveerle muchas oportunidades al grupo. Uds. pueden ———— decirme lo que

8.
9.

más les interesa ———— ver. Necesito ———— poder ———— planear una excursión que

10.
11.
12.

les agrade. Espero que Uds. lleguen ———— apreciar la historia y cultura porteñas. No se

13.

olviden ———— llevar sus cosas personales al bajar del autobús. No se acostumbren

14.

———— volver al autobús tarde. Gracias por su atención.

15.

EJERCICIO F   **Escribir un tema**   Exprese lo que el profesor les dice a los estudiantes antes de que ellos escriban su primera composición en su clase. Añada una proposición si es necesario.

EJEMPLOS: Uds. / deber / prestar mucha atención
Uds. **deben prestar** mucha atención.

Volver (Uds.) / escribirlo en limpio.
Vuelvan a escribirlo en limpio.

1. Uds. / ir / escribir su primera composición en esta clase

2. Uds. / deber / leer el tema

3. Empezar (Uds.) / pensar en el tema

4. Uds. / poder / consultar sus apuntes de clase y otros libros

5. Contar (Uds.) / utilizar libros de referencia

6. Aprender (Uds.) / usar el diccionario.

7. No tardar (Uds.) / comenzar / escribir.

8. Tratar (Uds.) / organizar bien las ideas

9. No ir (Uds.) / distraerse

_____

10. Ponerse (Uds.) / escribir un borrador primero

_____

11. Volver (Uds.) / leer lo que han escrito.

_____

12. Pensar (Uds.) / producir un trabajo excelente

_____

13. Uds. / deber / entregar el trabajo al terminar la clase

_____

EJERCICIO G | **Comparaciones**   Exprese las diferencias que Ricardo dice que existen entre él y sus amigos. Use una preposición si es necesario.

EJEMPLO: la hermana de Jimmy / ayudarle / aprender / bailar
La hermana de Jimmy lo **ayuda a** aprender a bailar.

1. el padre de Antonio / enseñarle / conducir

_____

2. los abuelos de Pedro / decidirse / comprarle una moto

_____

3. Los padres de Víctor / dejarlo / tomar clases de equitación

_____

4. la mamá de Felipe / insistir / darle su propio teléfono celular

_____

5. el papá de Luis / acabar / aumentarle su dinero semanal

_____

6. el tío de Tomás / consentir / regalarle un viaje a Puerto Rico

_____

7. los padres de Jorge / soler / llevarlo al teatro con frecuencia

_____

EJERCICIO H | **El poeta**   Ud. asiste a una declamación de poesía en una librería cerca de su casa. Exprese lo que el poeta le dice al público. Añada una preposición si es necesario.

EJEMPLO: yo / acabar / publicar dos libros de mis poesías
Yo **acabo de** publicar dos libros de mis poesías.

1. yo / alegrarse / estar aquí

_____

2. yo / empezar / disfrutar de la poesía a una temprana edad

_____

3. mi madre / empeñarse / recitarme versos cada noche

_____

4. yo / aprender / escribir versos en la escuela primaria

_____

5. la casa editorial / insistir / arreglar eventos como éste

_____

6. yo / consentir / asistir a este evento

_____

7. yo / tratar / expresar mis sentimientos en mis poesías

_____

8. yo / dedicarse / presentar mis experiencias por la poesía

_____

9. los poetas / soler / pasar largas horas solos

_____

10. yo / disponerse / publicar otra edición de poesías pronto

_____

EJERCICIO I   **Actividad oral**   Trabajando con un compañero, prepare un cuento de diez frases en que emplee el uso del verbo + infinitivo, el verbo + preposición + infinitivo o preposición + infinitivo. Puede hablar de la rutina diaria, un evento inesperado, un sueño, etc.

EJERCICIO J   **Lectura**   Lea el siguiente párrafo y conteste las preguntas.

Acaba de lanzarse una página que va a proveer información de índole turística para viajeros de los cinco continentes. Al abrir esta página de la red, el usuario encontrará información concentrada sobre más de doscientos países, más de dos mil regiones, cinco mil lugares naturales y más de cuarenta mil ciudades. Los que han diseñado la página quieren acercar el mundo y la han diseñado no sólo para la gente que quiera visitar otros lugares, sino para cualquier persona que quiera obtener información sobre algún tema. Tanto un viajero como un cocinero o un meteorológico puede aprovecharse de información sobre lugares turísticos, recetas culinarias o el clima, por ejemplo. Además, la gente indígena de los centros turísticos va a poder anexar información que considere importante y hasta crear un álbum de fotos personales o un recetario.

1. ¿Qué se anuncia en este párrafo?

    (a) Un nuevo sistema para hacer reservaciones

    (b) Otro recurso para los diseñadores de páginas en la red

    (c) Una nueva enciclopedia de turismo

    (d) Un fondo de información al alcance de todos

2. El propósito de los diseñadores fue

    (a) atraer a más viajeros a su agencia de viajes.

    (b) ofrecer información a todo el mundo a bajo costo.

    (c) vender excursiones a diferentes partes del mundo.

    (d) facilitar la adquisición de información sin salir de casa.

CHAPTER 15
Nouns and Articles

1. Nouns

a. Gender of Nouns

All nouns in Spanish are either masculine or feminine.

1. The following nouns are masculine:

(a) Nouns that refer to male beings and most nouns that end in *-o*.

el hombre *man*	**el libro** *book*	**el zapato** *shoe*
el príncipe *prince*	**el periódico** *newspaper*	**el padre** *father*
el conde *count*	**el hermano** *brother*	**el señor** *man*
el tío *uncle*	**el dinero** *money*	**el doctor** *doctor*

NOTE: Some exceptions are:

la foto (short for **la fotografía**) *photograph*

la mano *hand*

la moto (short for **la motocicleta**) *motorcycle*

(b) Numbers, days of the week, months of the year, and names of rivers and oceans.

el diez de mayo *May 10*

el viernes *Friday*

el (Río) Amazonas *the Amazon (river)*

el veintitrés de enero *January 23*

noviembre *November*

el (Océano) Atlántico *the Atlantic (Ocean)*

(c) Compound nouns that consist of a verb and a noun.

el abrelatas *can opener*	**el parabrisas** *windshield*
el lavaplatos *dishwasher*	**el paracaídas** *parachute*
el paraguas *umbrella*	**el sacapuntas** *pencil sharpener*
el tocadiscos *record player*	**el salvavidas** *lifeguard, life preserver*

(d) Nouns ending in *-or, -és,* or *-n* that refer to people.

el doctor *doctor*	**el inglés** *Englishman*
el profesor *teacher*	**el alemán** *German man*

NOTE: 1. These nouns have a feminine form, which is formed by adding *-a*. If a masculine noun has an accent mark on the last syllable, the accent is dropped in the equivalent feminine form.

la doctora *doctor*	**la inglesa** *Englishwoman*
la profesora *teacher*	**la alemana** *German woman*

2. Exceptions are: **el actor** (actor) / **la actriz** (actress) and **el emperador** (emperor) / **la emperatriz** (empress).

2. The following nouns are feminine:

   (a) Nouns referring to female beings and most nouns ending in *-a.*

la mujer *woman*	**la ventana** *window*	**la bota** *boot*
la enfermera *nurse*	**la puerta** *door*	**la mesa** *table*
la condesa *countess*	**la lluvia** *rain*	**la fiesta** *party*
la tía *aunt*	**la hermana** *sister*	**la doctora** *doctor*

   NOTE: Some exceptions are:

el día *day*	**el problema** *problem*
el idioma *language*	**el telegrama** *telegram*
el mediodía *noon*	**el sistema** *system*
el programa *program*	**el planeta** *planet*
el mapa *map*	

   (b) Nouns ending in *-dad, -tad, -tud, -umbre, -ie,* or *-ión.*

la ciudad *city*	**la serie** *series*
la seguridad *safety*	**la especie** *species, kind*
la juventud *youth*	**la unión** *union*
la incertidumbre *uncertainty*	**la condición** *condition*
la libertad *liberty*	**la lección** *lesson*

   NOTE: Some exceptions are:

el avión *airplane*	**el camión** *truck*

3. The following nouns are either masculine or feminine depending on their meaning.

MASCULINE	FEMININE
el capital *capital (money)*	**la capital** *(government)*
el cura *priest*	**la cura** *cure*
el orden *order (tidiness)*	**la orden** *order (command)*
el guía *guide (male)*	**la guía** *guidebook, guide (female)*
el policía *policeman*	**la policía** *police force, policewoman*
el radio *the radio (appliance)*	**la radio** *radio (broadcasting system)*

4. Some nouns present special cases:

   (a) The following nouns referring to people distinguish their gender by the article.

el / la **artista**   *artist*   el / la **joven**   *youth*

el / la **dentista**   *dentist*   el / la **testigo**   *witness*

el / la **modelo**   *model*   el / la **mártir**   *martyr*

b. Number of Nouns

1. Nouns ending in a vowel form the plural by adding -s.

   el **vecino** / los **vecinos**   *neighbor / neighbors*

   la **recompensa** / las **recompensas**   *reward / rewards*

   el **paquete** / los **paquetes**   *package / packages*

2. Nouns ending in a consonant (including -y) form the plural by adding -es.

   el **lugar** / los **lugares**   *place / places*

   la **ley** / las **leyes**   *law / laws*

   NOTE: 1. Nouns ending in -z change -z to -c before adding -es.

   el **lápiz** / los **lápices**   *pencil / pencils*

   la **voz** / las **voces**   *voice / voices*

   2. An accent mark is added or dropped to keep the original stress:

   el **joven** / los **jóvenes**   *young man / young men*

   el **inglés** / los **ingleses**   *English man / English men*

   el **examen** / los **exámenes**   *exam / exams*

   la **lección** / las **lecciones**   *lesson / lessons*

   3. Nouns ending in -s, except for those ending in -és, do not change in the plural:

   la / las **dosis**   *dosage / dosages*

   el / los **martes**   *Tuesday / Tuesdays*

   el / los **paréntesis**   *parenthesis / parentheses*

   la / las **síntesis**   *synthesis / syntheses*

   4. In a mixed plural (masculine and feminine), the masculine plural form of the noun is used:

   los **niños** = el **niño** y la **niña** OR los **niños** y las **niñas**

   los **tíos** = el **tío** y la **tía** OR los **tíos** y las **tías**

   los **padres** = el **padre** y la **madre** OR los **padres** y las **madres**

   los **señores** Vargas = el **señor** y la **señora** Vargas

EJERCICIO A   ¿Qué es? Silva trabaja en una guardería de niños. Trata de entretener a un grupo de niños y hace que ellos identifiquen lo que ven en unos dibujos. Exprese lo que dicen los niños.

EJEMPLO: el gato

1. El señor

2. la pelota

3. el avion

4. el libro

5. el telephono

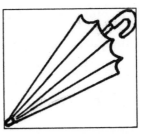

6. la computadora

7. la sombrilla

8. el pero

9. ___El arbol___

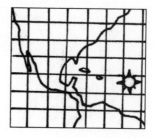

11. ___el mapa___

10. ___la coca___

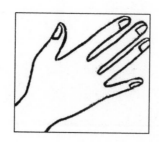

12. ___la mano___

EJERCICIO B **El vocabulario** Esteban estudia para un examen en la clase de español. Tiene que acertar la palabra del significado que le da un amigo. Exprese lo que Esteban dice.

EJEMPLO: cada año tiene doce ___el mes___

1. lo que muestra la extensión de un país ___el mapa___
2. la persona que gobierna una nación democrática ___el presidente___
3. el medio de transporte que corre en una vía ___el tren___
4. el símbolo celestial de la noche ___la luna___
5. el hombre que escribe versos ___el poeta___
6. donde viven los prisioneros ___la carcel___
7. la persona que cuida a los nadadores ___el salvavidas___
8. lo que ilumina la oscuridad ___la lampara___
9. la persona que arregla los dientes ___el dendista___
10. todo el dinero que una persona tiene ___el banco___
11. la parte temprana de la vida ___la adolecensia___
12. lo que practica una cultura _____
13. el transporte más rápido de viajar ___el avion___

14. la celebración _____

15. lo que habla una persona _____

16. el esposo de la reina _____

17. la esposa de mi hijo _____

18. donde se practica la justicia _____

19. lo que se usa para abrir una lata _____

20. veinticuatro horas _____

EJERCICIO C   **El verano**   Complete el párrafo que Larry escribió sobre su estación preferida. Use la forma plural de los sustantivos dados entre paréntesis.

Durante los _____ 1. (mes) de julio y agosto, a los _____ 2. (joven) les gusta pasar

todos los _____ 3. (día) en la playa porque les gustan los _____ 4. (deporte) acuáticos.

Allí los _____ 5. (amigo) se reúnen y pasan las _____ 6. (hora) nadando, buceando o

solamente tomando el sol. Muchas _____ 7. (vez) varios grupos organizan _____ 8. (partido)

de voleibol en la arena. En otras _____ 9. (ocasión) ellos participan en _____ 10. (excursión)

de acampar y hacen esto en las _____ 11. (montaña) o en la playa. En muchas _____ 12. (playa)

hay _____ 13. (concurso). Las _____ 14. (persona) forman _____ 15. (equipo) para construir

_____ 16. (castillo) o _____ 17. (figura) de arena. Siempre hay muchas _____ 18. (actividad)

para disfrutar del buen clima del verano. Casi todo el mundo está de acuerdo de que el verano

es la mejor de las cuatro _____ 19. (estación) porque no necesitan usar _____ 20. (abrigo)

pesados cuando están al aire libre.

2. Definite Articles

a. Forms of the Definite Article

1. There are four definite articles in Spanish corresponding to English *the:*

	SINGULAR	PLURAL
MASCULINE	el	los
FEMININE	la	las

NOTE: 1. Feminine nouns that begin with the stressed *a*-sound (*a* or *ha*) take the article *el* in the singular and *las* in the plural.

el **agua**	*water*	*las* **aguas**	*waters*
el **alma**	*soul*	*las* **almas**	*souls*
el **ave**	*bird*	*las* **aves**	*birds*
el **hacha**	*hatchet*	*las* **hachas**	*hatchets*

2. *El* combines with *a* and *de* to form the contractions *al* and *del*, respectively.

3. The neuter article *lo*, used with adjectives, does not vary in form.

Lo importante es aprender. *That which is important is learning.*

b. Uses of the Definite Article

1. The definite article is used:

(a) before the names of languages, except after *hablar, en,* or *de.*

El español es una lengua útil. *Spanish is a useful language.*
But:
Ella habla español e inglés. *She speaks Spanish and English.*
El cuento está escrito en francés. *The story is written in French.*
La clase de japonés es divertida. *The Japanese class is fun.*

NOTE: 1. If an adverb occurs between *hablar* and a name of a language, the article may be used with the language.

Habla bien *el griego.* *He speaks Greek well.*

2. Current everyday usage tends to omit the definite article after the verbs *aprender, enseñar, escribir, estudiar, leer,* and *saber.*

Yo sé leer chino. *I know how to read Chinese.*
¿Enseña Ud. alemán? *Do you teach German?*

(b) before titles, except when directly addressing the person.

La señorita Rojas está presente hoy. *Miss Rojas is present today.*
¿Cuándo llegó Ud., Señorita Rojas? *When did you arrive, Miss Rojas?*

NOTE: The article is omitted before *don, doña, San, Santo,* and *Santa.*

(c) instead of the possessive adjective with parts of the body or clothing, when the possessor is clear.

Marta se lava *las* **manos.** *Marta washes her hands.*
Se puso *el* **traje de baño.** *He put on his bathing suit.*

(d) to express the time of day and the seasons.

Es *la* **una.** *It's one o'clock.*
Me despierto a *las* **cinco.** *I wake up at five o'clock.*

(e)   with the names of seasons. It can be omitted after *en* when it is suggested that the event referred to occurs in that season each year.

Me encanta *la* **primavera (***el* **verano, el otoño,** *el* **invierno).**	*I love spring (summer, autumn, winter.)*
Voy al Caribe en invierno.	*I go to the Caribbean in winter.*

(f)   when expressing dates with the days of the week, except after *hoy + ser*, *mañana + ser, ayer + ser,* etc.

Vamos a la playa *el* **sábado.**	*We are going to the beach (on) Saturday.*
Los **martes hay tamales.**	*(On) Tuesdays there are tamales.*
La boda fue *el* **domingo pasado.**	*The wedding was last Sunday.*
Hoy es lunes.	*Today is Monday.*
Mañana es viernes y hay examen.	*Tomorrow is Friday and there is an examination.*

(g)   before names of rivers, oceans, and mountains.

los **Pirineos**	*the Pyrenees*	*el* **Amazonas**	*the Amazon* (river)
los **Andes**	*the Andes*	*el* **Tajo**	*the Tagus* (river)
el **Atlántico**	*the Atlantic*	*el* **Caribe**	*the Caribbean* (sea)

(h)   before certain names of countries, states, and cities.

el **Brasil**	*Brazil*	*la* **Argentina**	*Argentina*
los **Estados Unidos**	*the United States*	*el* **Perú**	*Peru*
la **Florida**	*Florida*	*el* **Uruguay**	*Uruguay*
el **Paraguay**	*Paraguay*	*el* **Canadá**	*Canada*
el **Ecuador**	*Ecuador*	*el* **Cairo**	*Cairo*

> **NOTE:** 1.   Current everyday usage tends to omit the definite article before the names of countries.
>
> | | |
> |---|---|
> | **Vivo en Estados Unidos.** | *I live in the United States.* |
> | **Ellos viajan por Argentina.** | *They travel through Argentina.* |
>
> 2.   The definite article is used with geographical **names that are** modified.
>
> | | |
> |---|---|
> | *la* **España** *contemporánea* | *contemporary Spain* |
> | *el* **México** *precolombino* | *pre-Colombian Mexico* |
> | *la* **América** *del Sur* | *South America* |

(i)   before nouns or adjectives that are used in a general or abstract way.

La **libertad es preciosa.**	*Liberty is precious.*
La **nutrición es importante.**	*Nutrition is important.*
El **rojo es un color vibrante.**	*Red is a vibrant color.*
Me gusta *la* **falda larga pero** *la* **corta me queda mejor.**	*I like the long skirt but the short one fits me better.*

(j) before infinitives that function as nouns. The article is often omitted when the infinitive is the subject in a sentence.

(El) reír es bueno. *Laughing is good.*

(El) mentir es un vicio. *Lying is a vice.*

NOTE: Infinitive nouns are always masculine.

(k) before nouns of weight or measure. (The indefinite article is used in English.)

un dólar *la* libra *a dollar a pound*

veinte centavos *la* docena *twenty cents a dozen*

2. The definite article is omitted:

(a) before nouns in apposition.

Buenos Aires, capital de la Argentina, es una ciudad cosmopolita. *Buenos Aires, the capital of Argentina, is a cosmopolitan city.*

Pablo Picasso, pintor español, pintó muchos cuadros. *Pablo Picasso, a Spanish painter, painted many paintings.*

(b) before ordinal numbers expressing the numerical order of rulers.

Felipe Segundo *Phillip the Second*

Carlos Quinto *Charles the Fifth*

(c) before the second noun, when two nouns are joined by *de* to form a compound noun.

el dolor de muelas *toothache*

la carne de cerdo *pork*

libros de arte *art books*

EJERCICIO D **Preguntas** Conteste las preguntas que le hace una compañera de clase.

1. ¿En qué estación naciste? (*primavera*)

_____

2. ¿En qué mes fue? (*mayo*)

_____

3. ¿Sabes en qué día fue? (*lunes*)

_____

4. ¿De qué color tienes los ojos? (*azul*)

_____

5. ¿Cuándo pasas tiempo con los amigos? (*fin de semana*)

_____

6. ¿Cuándo sales a comer con tu familia? (*viernes*)

_____

7. ¿Dónde naciste? (*Estados Unidos*)

_____

8. ¿En qué estado? (*Florida*)

_____

9. ¿Qué idioma estudias? (*francés*)

_____

10. ¿Cómo se llama tu profesor de francés? (*señor Dupont*)

_____

11. ¿Cuál es tu materia favorita? (*biología*)

_____

12. ¿Y tu menos favorita? (*inglés*)

_____

13. ¿A qué hora es tu última clase? (*1:30*)

_____

14. ¿Qué te gustaría llegar a ser? (*contador*)

_____

EJERCICIO E   **Una carta**   Complete la carta que Lisa le escribió a una amiga. Llene los espacios en blanco con la forma apropiada del artículo definido, de ser necesario.

Querida Nora:

Por fin estamos en Madrid, ___1.___ de España. Tenemos mucho interés en visitar ___2.___ sitios de gran interés como ___3.___ Palacio Real, ___4.___ sección antigua de la ciudad y ___5.___ restaurantes típicos. Aunque no puedo hablar bien ___6.___ español, trataré hacerlo lo mejor posible. Llegamos ___7.___ martes a eso de ___8.___ seis de la mañana. Dicen que escogimos ___9.___ mejor estación para estar aquí porque se puede hacer mucho en ___10.___ primavera en Madrid. Y mayo es ___11.___ mes más agradable del año.

___12.___ señorita Burgos sigue acompañándonos y como ella es de Perú, ella comprende todo. ¿Te acuerdas de ella? Es ___13.___ tía de Sofía y es ___14.___ profesora de español. Mañana vamos a ___15.___ Escorial que fue construido por Felipe ___16.___ Segundo. Según ___17.___ guías, ___18.___

día comenzará muy temprano. Hoy por ――― noche vamos a ――― teatro. Pudimos conseguir
$\quad\quad\quad\quad\quad\quad\quad\quad\quad\quad\quad$ 19. $\quad\quad\quad\quad\quad\quad\quad\quad$ 20.

――― entradas para ――― función de ――― noche. Ya he comprado ――― recuerdos en todos
21. $\quad\quad\quad\quad\quad\quad$ 22. $\quad\quad\quad\quad$ 23. $\quad\quad\quad\quad\quad\quad\quad\quad\quad\quad$ 24.

――― lugares que hemos visitado. Me duelen ――― manos de tanto sacar ――― dinero
25. $\quad\quad\quad\quad\quad\quad\quad\quad\quad\quad\quad\quad\quad\quad$ 26. $\quad\quad\quad\quad\quad\quad\quad\quad\quad\quad$ 27.

de ――― cartera. ¡ ――― viajar es muy divertido!
$\quad$ 28. $\quad\quad\quad$ 29.

Saludos de tu amiga,

Lisa

c. The Neuter Article *LO*

1. *Lo* precedes an adjective used as a noun to express a quality or an abstract idea. *Lo* does not change and is used with masculine and feminine adjectives, singular or plural.

Lo caro no es siempre mejor que *lo* barato.	*That which is expensive is not always better than the cheap (what is cheap).*
Ud. piensa *lo* mismo que yo.	*You think the same as I.*

2. *Lo* + adjective or adverb + *que* expresses *how* + adjective or adverb.

Yo sé *lo* difícil que es.	*I know how difficult it is.*
Vemos *lo* bien que se portan.	*We see how well they behave.*

EJERCICIO F | **Impresiones** Ud. acaba de ver una película con unos amigos. Exprese sus impresiones sobre la película usando *lo* y las sugerencias.

EJEMPLO: bonito **Lo bonito** de la película fue el vestuario.

1. emocionante _____

2. cómico _____

3. menos creíble _____

4. curioso _____

5. divertido _____

6. impresionante _____

7. aburrido _____

3. Indefinite Articles

a. Forms of the Indefinite Article

1. In Spanish there are four indefinite articles corresponding to English *a (an)*, *some, several*, and *a few*.

	SINGULAR	PLURAL
MASCULINE	un	unos
FEMININE	una	unas

b. Uses of the Indefinite Article

1. The indefinite article is used to express the English words *a* (*an*) and *some*.

Un reloj de oro es *un* **regalo elegante.**	*A gold watch is an elegant gift.*
Necesito *unas* **vacaciones.**	*I need a vacation.*
Unos **profesores se reunieron ayer.**	*Some teachers had a meeting yesterday.*

   NOTE: Feminine nouns that begin with the stressed *a*-sound (*a* or *ha*) take the article *un* in the singular and *unas* in the plural.

un **agua** *water*	*unas* **aguas** *waters*
un **águila** *eagle*	*unas* **águilas** *eagles*
un **alma** *soul*	*unas* **almas** *souls*
un **área** *area*	*unas* **áreas** *areas*
un **arpa** *harp*	*unas* **arpas** *harps*
un **haba** *(fava) bean*	*unas* **habas** *(fava) beans*
un **hambre** *hunger*	*unas* **hambres** *hungers*

2. The indefinite article is omitted:

   (a) when a noun expressing nationality, profession, or occupation follows a form of *ser, hacerse, convertirse,* and similar verbs.

Es carnicero.	*He is a butcher.*
Somos cubanos.	*We are Cuban.*
Quiero hacerme abogado.	*I want to become a lawyer.*

   NOTE: The indefinite article is used if the noun is modified.

Es *un* **periodista** *listo.*	*He's a clever journalist.*
Quiero hacerme *un* **abogado** *famoso.*	*I want to become a famous lawyer.*

   (b) before or after certain words that ordinarily have the article in English: *cierto* (a certain), *ciento* (a hundred), *mil* (a thousand), *tal ...* (such a ...), *¡qué ...!* (what a ...!).

cierto libro	*a certain book*
cien dólares	*one (a) hundred dollars*
mil personas	*one (a) thousand people*
tal pregunta	*such a question*
¡Qué carro!	*What a car!*

| EJERCICIO G | **Explicación** Exprese la explicación que Alfredo da de las siguientes cosas.

EJEMPLO: novela / obra escrita   **Una** novela es *una* obra escrita.

1. soneto / clase de poesía   _____

2. autobús / medio de transporte   _____

3. haba / legumbre   _____

4. albaricoque / fruta   _____

5. octubre / mes   _____

6. el trigo / grano   _____

7. natación / deporte   _____

8. griego / lengua   _____

9. enciclopedia / recurso de investigación   _____

10. Paraguay / nación   _____

| EJERCICIO H | **Profesiones** Usando las descripciones que dan, exprese lo que estos jóvenes piensan hacerse.

PARA EXPRESARSE MEJOR

el analfabetismo *illiteracy*   **el psicológo** *psychologist*
el astronauta *astronaut*   **el juez** *judge*
el intérprete *interpreter*

EJEMPLO: Me interesa por qué las personas hacen ciertas cosas.
           Pienso hacerme psicólogo.

1. Quiero eliminar el analfabetismo.

   _____

2. Deseo explorar el espacio.

   _____

3. Me gusta la ropa elegante y sé dibujar bien.

   _____

4. Me fascina pasar horas en la cocina creando platos sabrosos.

   _____

5. Me gustaría construir edificios y puentes.

   _____

6. Paso muchas horas en la computadora y creo programas útiles.

_____

7. Yo hablo varios idiomas y me gusta hablar con personas de otras naciones.

_____

8. La ley me interesa mucho y suelo tomar buenas decisiones.

_____

EJERCICIO I   **Un cuento de éxito**   Durante un viaje a México, Neil conoció a los abuelos de su amigo Nick. Complete el cuento que Neil escribió sobre los abuelos con el artículo apropiado (definido o indefinido), una contracción o con *otro, cien, mil* o *¡qué...!*

__Los__(1.) abuelos de Nick son __los__(2.) señores muy simpáticos. Su abuelo era __un__(3.) hombre de negocios exitoso. __la__(4.) abuela de Nick era de __una__(5.) familia humilde y trabajadora. Su abuelo tenía __un__(6.) sueño de ser __el__(7.) dueño de su propio negocio.

__Al__(8.) casarse, abrieron __una__(9.) tienda de __la__(10.) ropa femenina en __el__(11.) sector nuevo de __la__(12.) ciudad. Abrían __la__(13.) tienda a __las__(14.) cinco y media de la mañana y no la cerraban hasta __las__(15.) diez de __la__(16.) noche, __los__(17.) siete días a __la__(18.) semana. Era __un__(19.) horario largo y pesado. Trataban bien a __los__(20.) clientes y se jactaban de venderles sólo __los__(21.) productos de __la__(22.) primera calidad. Muchos clientes iban a __la__(23.) tienda dos o tres veces __por__(24.) día para conseguir __las__(25.) verduras más frescas. __los__(26.) clientes iban solamente cuando necesitaban __los__(27.) ingrediente especial para __una__(28.) nueva receta que elaboraban. Tenían __un__(29.) surtido extensivo de __unas__(30.) especias y más de __mil__(31.) ingredientes para satisfacer __la__(32.) curiosidad y __la__(33.) necesidad de __el__(34.) cocinero profesional. __lo__(35.) curioso es que ninguno de los abuelos sabe cocinar. ¡Pero __el__(36.) buen sentido de __los__(37.) negocios tenían! En __el__(38.) año llegaron a abrir __la__(39.) tiendas en __el__(40.) barrios cercanos. __Al__(41.) jubilarse había más de __cien__(42.) empleados en su negocio.

EJERCICIO J   **Actividad oral**   Ud. y un amigo están organizando una celebración en la escuela. Trabajando con un(a) compañero(a), prepare una lista de diez cosas que van a necesitar y justifique la necesidad de cada cosa. Use los artículos definidos o indefinidos, contracciones o palabras como: *otro, cien, mil* o *qué.*

EJERCICIO K   **Lectura**   Lea el artículo a continuación y conteste las preguntas.

Un invento que puede causar problemas

Quizá no hay un invento que haya sido recibido con tanto afán y popularidad, tanto por los jóvenes como por los mayores, como el teléfono celular. Rara es la vez que no se vea a una persona sola hablando en voz alta mientras camina por la calle, haciendo las compras en una tienda o supermercado, esperando el despegue de un avión o conduciendo un carro en el próximo carril de la carretera. Por medio de esta tecnología hemos llegado a tener más comunicación con los amigos, los familiares y los colegas, pero, ¿a qué precio? Es un invento que puede causar problemas peligrosos, especialmente cuando la persona usa el celular mientras maneja un vehículo.

Se ha llevado a cabo un estudio sobre los efectos del uso del celular mientras se maneja. Las pruebas que hicieron comprobaron que mientras habla por teléfono, el conductor: deja de ponerle atención a la carretera y a los carros que lo rodean; no puede mantener una velocidad constante y —en algunos casos— tampoco una dirección fija; y sus reacciones son 50% más lentas de lo normal.

Se les ha pedido a las autoridades que se prohiba contestar una llamada mientras se maneja, sin importar si el teléfono es de manos libres o no, porque tienen el mismo efecto. Es notable que en más de 30 países, sea ilegal usar el celular mientras se maneja.

1. La popularidad de este invento se nota por

   (a) su uso extensivo por personas de cualquier edad.

   (b) la facilidad con que se encuentra en las tiendas.

   (c) la atención que ha atraído del público.

   (d) su contribución a la sociedad moderna.

2. ¿Qué ha aumentado este invento?

   (a) Las enfermedades auditivas

   (b) La comunicación entre las personas

   (c) El buen uso del tiempo libre

   (d) Los problemas entre los amigos

3. A pesar de su popularidad, se cree que el uso del celular

   (a) puede ser nocivo.

   (b) perjudica la salud.

   (c) daña el medioambiente.

   (d) facilita el crimen.

4. ¿Qué es un síntoma malo de este invento?

    (a) Causa un 50% de los accidentes automovilísticos.

    (b) No se puede controlar su uso.

    (c) Disminuye un 50% las reacciones del conductor.

    (d) Los gobiernos no reconocen sus peligros.

CHAPTER 16
Adjectives and Adverbs; Comparisons; the Superlative

1. Adjectives

a. Gender of Adjectives

1. Adjectives ending in *-o* form the feminine by changing *-o* to *-a*. Most adjectives ending in a consonant form the feminine by adding *-a*.

bonit*o*, bonit*a* *pretty*	**inglés, inglesa** *English*
alt*o*, alt*a* *tall*	**hablador, habladora** *talkative*
limpi*o*, limpi*a* *clean*	**trabajador, trabajadora** *hard-working*
españ*ol*, español*a* *Spanish*	

2. Many adjectives have the same form for both the masculine and the feminine.

difícil *difficult*	**amable** *kind*
popular *popular*	**agrícola** *agricultural*
grande *large*	

b. Plural of Adjectives

The plural of adjectives is formed by:

1. adding *-s* when the singular form ends in a vowel.

   alto / alto*s*   **italiana / italiana*s***   **amable / amable*s***

2. adding *-es* when the singular form ends in a consonant.

   español / español*es*   **popular / popular*es***   **difícil / difícil*es***

   NOTE: 1. Adjectives with singular forms ending in -z change -z to -c in the plural.

   feliz / felices *happy*

   2. Some adjectives add or drop an accent mark in order to keep the original stress.

   joven / jóvenes *young*

   inglés / inglesa / ingleses / inglesas *English*

   alemán / alemana / alemanes / alemanas *German*

   japonés / japonesa / japoneses / japonesas *Japanese*

   cortés / corteses *courteous, polite*

c. Agreement of Adjectives

1. Adjectives agree in gender and number with the nouns they modify.

   Beth es alta.   *Beth is tall.*

Los *niños* son *traviesos*.   *The children are mischievous.*

2. An adjective modifying two or more nouns of different gender is masculine plural.

La *casa* y el *garaje* son *blancos*.   *The house and the garage are white.*

EJERCICIO A   **Mis amigos**   Exprese lo que Diego dice de sus amigos.

EJEMPLO: Alexandra / perezoso   Alexandra es **perezosa.**

1. Estela / generoso   _____

2. Victoria y Alfredo / amable   _____

3. Efraín / inteligente   _____

4. Nora / trabajador   _____

5. María e Inés / cortés   _____

6. Lázaro / diligente   _____

7. Luisa y Luz / encantador   _____

8. Lili / francés   _____

9. Víctor / fuerte   _____

10. Janet y Michelle / bonito   _____

EJERCICIO B   **El mal tiempo**   Un grupo de amigos ha planeado una excursión a la playa pero han tenido que cancelarla a causa de una tormenta. Exprese cómo se sienten los amigos.

EJEMPLO: Héctor / triste   Héctor está **triste.**

1. Virginia / desilusionado   _____

2. Matt y Nick / furioso   _____

3. Ramón / aburrido   _____

4. Hugh y Vicki / deprimido   _____

5. Sarita / nervioso   _____

6. Jane y Ana / preocupado   _____

7. Pablo y Ralph / descontento   _____

EJERCICIO C   **Opiniones**   Después de un debate acalorado en la clase de historia, los compañeros de clase hacen comentarios sobre los que participaron en el debate. Exprese lo que los compañeros dicen.

EJEMPLO: Carlos / arrogante   Carlos fue **arrogante.**

1. Xavier y Sonia / engañoso   _____

2. Esteban / organizado   _____

3. Emma / responsable   _____

4. Lina y Myra / sincero   _____

5. Pedro / insoportable   _____

6. Clara / justo   _____

7. Andy y Jean / listo   _____

d. Position of Adjectives

1. Descriptive adjectives normally follow the nouns they modify.

   el artículo *interesante*   *the interesting article*
   una casa *blanca*   *a white house*

2. Descriptive adjectives may stand before the noun to emphasize the quality of the adjective or its inherent characteristic.

   Vi los rosales con sus *olorosas* **flores.**   *I saw the rose bushes with their fragrant flowers.*
   Las fiestas me traen **bonitos recuerdos.**   *The holidays bring me beautiful memories.*

NOTE: 1. Some adjectives have different meanings, depending on their position.

   Bolívar fue un *gran* **hombre.**   *Bolívar was a great man.*

   But:

   Mi abuelo es un hombre *grande.*   *My grandfather is a big man.*

2. Common adjectives that change their meaning with a change in position are:

	AFTER THE NOUN	BEFORE THE NOUN
antiguo, -a	old (ancient)	old (former) old-time
cierto, -a	sure; true	a certain
grande	large, big	great
mismo, -a	him (her, it)-self	same
nuevo, -a	new	another, different
pobre	poor	unfortunate
simple	silly, simpleminded	simple, mere

3. Limiting adjectives (numbers, possessive and demonstrative adjectives, adjectives of quantity) usually precede the noun.

tres libros	*three books*	*ese* muchacho	*that boy*
algún mes	*some month*	*tal* cosa	*such a thing*
nuestros padres	*our parents*	*más* pan	*more bread*

COMMON LIMITING ADJECTIVES

algunos, (-as) *some*		**poco, (-a, -os, -as)** *little, few*	
cada *each, every*		**tanto, (-a, -os, -as)** *so much, so many*	
cuanto, (-a, -os, -as) *as much*		**todo, (-a, -os, -as)** *all, every*	
más *more*		**unos, (-as)** *some*	
menos *less*		**unos, (-as) cuantos, (-as)** *a few*	
ningunos, (-as) *no, not any*		**varios, (-as)** *several*	
numerosos, (-as) *numerous*			

EJERCICIO D | **Mi quinceañero** Conteste las preguntas que una compañera de clase le hizo a Patricia sobre su quinceañero. Use los adjetivos entre paréntesis.

EJEMPLO: ¿Qué clase de fiesta tuviste? (*uno, grande, bonito*)
Tuve **una** fiesta **grande** y **bonita.**

1. ¿A qué primos invitaste? (*todo, mi*)

   _____

2. ¿En qué salón tuvo lugar la fiesta? (*uno, cómodo, amplio*)

   _____

3. ¿Cuántas personas había en la fiesta? (*tanto*)

   _____

4. ¿Cuántas personas no aceptaron tu invitación? (*varios*)

   _____

5. ¿De qué parte vinieron los invitados? (*diferente*)

   _____

6. ¿Había un radiolocutor en la fiesta? (*dos, animado*)

   _____

7. ¿Qué clase de comida sirvieron? (*uno, mexicano, sabroso*)

   _____

8. ¿Invitaste a tus amigos? (*varios, simpático*)

   _____

9. ¿Cómo eran los regalos que recibiste? (*bonito, caro, numeroso*)

   _____

10. ¿Con cuántos jóvenes bailaste? (*mucho, amable*)

_____

| EJERCICIO E | **Noticias** Complete con la forma apropiada del adjetivo indicado el mensaje que Paul le escribió a un amigo mientras viajaba en España.

Querido Fernando:

Ayer visitamos la parte _____ de Madrid. Todavía hay _____
          1. (antiguo)   2. (mucho)

edificios _____ que datan a siglos _____ . Lo _____ es
          3. (impresionante)   4. (pasado)   5. (interesante)

que los edificios están bien _____ y _____ . También he observado
                            6. (conservado)   7. (mantenido)

_____ construcciones _____ . Fuimos a _____ museos
8. (mucho)   9. (nuevo)   10. (varios)

donde exhiben la herencia y la contribución _____ al mundo de las _____
                                            11. (español)   12. (bello)

artes. Mi hermana es muy _____ a la música y anoche fuimos a un tablao
                        13. (aficionado)

_____ . La experiencia fue muy _____ . Ésta es la _____
14. (flamenco)   15. (divertido)   16. (primero)

vez que visito esta ciudad y es notable ver la mezcla de las tradiciones _____ con
                                                                        17. (antiguo)

costumbres _____ . Creo que ya hemos visitado casi _____ los lugares
          18. (moderno)   19. (todo)

de interés _____ y _____ .
          20. (histórico)   21. (turístico)

    También _____ chica del grupo me ha atraído la atención. Es _____ ,
            22. (cierto)   23. (bonito)

de ascendencia _____ . Hemos pasado juntos _____ ratos muy
              24. (italiano)   25. (uno)

_____ . En _____ ocasión te contaré más de este _____
26. (agradable)   27. (otro)   28. (fabuloso)

viaje. Hasta pronto.

    Tu _____ amigo,
      29. (fiel)

Paul

    e. Shortened Forms of Adjectives

        1. The following adjectives drop the final *-o* when used before a masculine singular noun.

uno *one, a, an*	**primero** *first*
un **plato** *one (a) plate*	**el *primer* mes** *the first month*
bueno *good*	**tercero** *third*
un buen **año** *a good year*	**el *tercer* piso** *the third floor*
malo *bad*	**alguno** *some*
un mal **día** *a bad day*	***algún* día** *some day*

ninguno *no, not any*

ningún dinero *no money*

> **NOTE:** 1. *Alguno* and *ninguno* require an accent mark when the -o is dropped: *algún, ningún.*
>
> 2. If a preposition comes between the adjective and the noun, the full form of the adjective is used.
>
>   **uno** de los niños   *one of the boys*
>
>   **el** *tercero* **del grupo**   *the third (one) of the group*

2. *Santo* becomes *San* before the masculine name of a saint, except with names beginning with *To-* or *Do-*.

   San José *Saint Joseph*   **San** Francisco *Saint Francis*

   But:

   Santo Tomás *Saint Thomas*   **Santo Domingo** *Saint Dominick*

3. *Grande* becomes *gran* when used before a singular noun of either gender.

   un *gran* **actor** *a great actor*   **una** *gran* **señora** *a great lady*

   But:

   un museo grande *a large museum*   **una iglesia grande** *a large church*

4. *Ciento* becomes *cien* before a noun of either gender and before the numbers *mil* and *millones*. This short form is not used with multiples of *ciento* (*doscientos, trescientos*, etc.) or in combination with any other number, for example, *ciento quince* (115).

   cien lápices / *cien* plumas *one hundred pencils / one hundred pens*

   cien mil personas *one hundred thousand people*

   cien millones de dólares *one hundred million dollars*

   But:

   seiscientos carros *six hundred cars*

   seiscientas millas *six hundred miles*

   ciento veinticuatro dólares *one hundred twenty-four dollars*

EJERCICIO F **Comentarios** Complete los comentarios que hacen distintas personas con la forma apropiada del adjetivo entre paréntesis.

1. Yo nací el día de —————— Fermín; mi hermana nació el día de —————— Teresa.
   (santo)   (santo)

2. —————— día yo pienso recorrer todos los —————— museos de Europa.
   (alguno)   (grande)

3. Es la —————— vez que tú haces esa promesa.
   (tercero)

4. Mi padre me dijo que de _____ modo me dejaría conducir su carro nuevo.
   (ninguno)

5. Jorge sirvió de _____ ejemplo para los otros muchachos.
   (malo)

6. ¡Imagínate, Elena gastó más de _____ dólares en el salón de belleza!
   (ciento)

7. Les dije a mis padres que me quedaría contento con _____ modelo de carro.
   (cualquiera)

8. _____ paraguas te servirá en esta tormenta.
   (ninguno)

9. Es una novela muy larga; tiene más de _____ ochenta páginas.
   (ciento)

10. Hoy estamos al día _____ . Odio el _____ día del mes porque hay
    (primero)   (primero)
    que pagar todas las cuentas.

11. Ésa me parece una _____ idea.
    (bueno)

12. Ya hace una semana que lo busco, pero no lo encuentro en _____ tienda.
    (ninguno)

13. Aunque no tengo ganas de hacerlo, debo reunirme con _____ primas esta noche.
    (alguno)

14. Cada semana anuncian una _____ barata en ese almacén.
    (grande)

15. ¡Qué bonitas son las playas de _____ Tomás!
    (santo)

2.   Adverbs and Adverbial Phrases

Adverbs describe the action expressed by a verb and also modify adjectives and other adverbs. Their form does not change according to gender or number. An adverbial phrase is a group of words that together function as an adverb.

a. Adverbs and Adverbial Phrases of Mode (those answering the question *how?* or *in what way?*)

1. Most adverbs of mode are formed by adding *-mente* to the feminine singular form of an adjective. Adjectives that do not have a distinct feminine form add *-mente* to the singular to form the adverb.

ADJECTIVE	ADVERB
rápido *rapid*	**rápidamente** *rapidly*
intenso *intense*	**intensamente** *intensely*
general *general*	**generalmente** *generally*
feliz *happy*	**felizmente** *happily*
triste *sad*	**tristemente** *sadly*

El tren pasó *rápidamente*.	*The train passed rapidly.*
Lo estudié *intensamente*.	*I studied it intensely.*
***Generalmente* llegan a tiempo.**	*They generally arrive on time.*

NOTE: In a series of two or more adverbs, the ending *-mente* is added only to the last one.

Teresa habló *clara y lentamente*.   *Teresa spoke clearly and slowly.*

2. The following adverbs are not formed with *mente: más, menos, poco, mucho, mejor, peor,* and *demasiado.* These adverbs can also function as adjectives; as such, they vary in gender and number.

ADJECTIVE	ADVERB
Ellos tienen *más* dinero que yo. *They have more money than I.*	**Ellos son *más* ricos.** *They are richer.*
Mi vista es *peor* que la tuya. *My sight is worse than yours.*	**Tú ves *mejor* que yo.** *You see better than I.*
Nancy compra *demasiados* zapatos. *Nancy buys too many shoes.*	**Nancy es *demasiado* rica.** *Nancy is too rich.*

NOTE: *Peor* and *mejor* never vary.

3. The following adverbs have forms different from the adjective form:

ADJECTIVE	ADVERB
bueno *good* **malo** *bad*	**bien** *well* **mal** *badly*

Es un buen **concierto; la orquesta toca *bien*.**   *It's a good concert; the orchestra plays well.*

Es una película *mala*; los actores actúan *mal*.   *It's a bad film; the actors act poorly.*

4. Adverbial phrases may be formed by using *con* + noun.

Prepararon la comida *con cuidado*.   *They prepared the meal with care.*

Se saludaron *con cortesía* (cortésmente).   *They greeted each other with courtesy (courteously).*

5. Adverbial phrases of mode are usually formed as follows:

de manera + adjective
Yo hablo *de manera* clara.   *I speak in a clear way.*

de modo + adjective
Yo hablo *de modo* claro.   *I speak in a clear way.*

EJERCICIO G   **Una crítica**   Conteste las preguntas que una amiga le hizo a Tere al volver de un día de compras en el centro comercial. Use el adjetivo entre paréntesis para formular un adverbio.

EJEMPLO: ¿Cómo te fue en el centro comercial? *(magnífico)*   Me fue **magníficamente.**

1. ¿Cómo te saludaron los dependientes? (*cortés*)

   _____

2. ¿Cómo te atendieron? (*amable / rápido*)

   _____

3. ¿Cómo hablaste con los dependientes? (*franco*)

   _____

4. ¿Cómo envolvieron el regalo? (*cuidadoso*)

   _____

5. ¿Cómo se hizo la venta? (*serio / eficaz*)

   _____

6. ¿Cómo se despidieron de ti los dependientes? (*cordial*)

   _____

EJERCICIO H   **El entrenador** Complete lo que dijo el entrenador después de que su equipo perdió un partido. Forme los adverbios con los adjetivos entre paréntesis.

Hoy el equipo jugó _____ . Muchos de los jugadores jugaron _____
                      1. (malo)   2. (distraído)

y fallaron _____ varias jugadas simples. _____ , yo traté de sustituir
            3. (inexplicable)   4. (inmediato)

a otros jugadores pero _____ eso no resultó tampoco.
                        5. (desgraciado)

   Hace poco tiempo que no juegan _____ y van a tener que practicar más
                                    6. (bueno)

_____ y _____ . _____ la derrota de hoy los hará jugar
  7. (serio)   8. (enérgico)   9. (afortunado)

más _____ en el futuro.
     10. (efectivo)

EJERCICIO I   **En otras palabras** Exprese lo que Ruth dice del discurso de un político usando la construcción *con* + sustantivo.

EJEMPLO: El político presentó sus ideas claramente.
           El político presentó sus ideas **con claridad.**

1. Él habló lentamente.   _____

2. Contestó las preguntas cortésmente.   _____

3. Defendió sus argumentos enérgicamente.   _____

4. Explicó las investigaciones hábilmente. _____

5. Repitió su opinión diligentemente.   _____

6. Pidió apasionadamente nuestro apoyo.   _____

7. Ramiro lo prometió sinceramente.   _____

b. Adverbs and Adverbial Phrases of Time or Frequency

1. Adverbs of time or frequency answer the question *when?*

ahora *now*	**hoy** *today*	**siempre** *always*
anoche *last night*	**luego** *then*	**tarde** *late*
ayer *yesterday*	**nunca** *never*	**temprano** *early*
entonces *then*	**pronto** *soon*	**todavía** *still, yet*

2. Adverbial phrases of time or frequency

algún día *some day*	**muchas veces** *often*
a veces *sometimes*	**pocas veces** *seldom*
esta noche *tonight*	**primero** *first*
este fin de semana *this weekend*	**todos los días** *every day*
más tarde *later*	

EJERCICIO J **¿Cuándo o con qué frecuencia?** Exprese cuándo o con qué frecuencia Ud. hace o ha hecho las siguientes acciones. Use el tiempo del verbo apropiado y el adverbio o la expresión adverbial indicado.

EJEMPLO: volver a leer un libro / poco / vez Yo **he vuelto** a leer un libro **pocas veces.**

1. llegar tarde a una cita / siempre

   _____

2. viajar en avión / mucho / vez

   _____

3. perder las llaves / ayer

   _____

4. ponerse a dieta / el año pasado

   _____

5. salir suspendido en una clase / nunca

   _____

6. dormir una siesta / mañana

   _____

7. cantar delante de un público / una vez

   _____

8. pedirle dinero prestado a un amigo / a veces

   _____

9. marcar un número de teléfono equivocado / la semana pasada

   _____

10. encontrar dinero en la calle / algún día

   _____

EJERCICIO K   Frecuencia   Exprese con qué frecuencia las personas hacen varias cosas. Use las expresiones sugeridas.

ahora	nunca	siempre	temprano
cada semana	pocas veces	tarde	todos los días

EJEMPLO: Lidia ha visto todas las películas que estrenan en el cine. Ella va al cine **cada semana.**

1. Luis es un niño mal educado. Él _____ pide permiso ni expresa su agradecimiento.

2. A Victoria le gusta ver la televisión después de terminar la tarea. Por eso ella se acuesta

   _____ .

3. Nelson prefiere el tiempo caluroso, por eso él va a esquiar _____ .

4. Aunque a Sara no le gustan los postres _____ va a pedir un helado.

5. Cuando hay una barata en el almacén, la señora Sosa _____ llega

   _____ para encontrar el mejor surtido.

6. Para estar en forma, muchas personas suelen caminar una milla _____ .

c. Adverbs and Adverbial Phrases of Place

   1. Common adverbs of place that answer the question *where?*

abajo *below, downstairs*	**dentro** *inside*
¿adónde? *(to) where?*	**derecho** *straight ahead*
allí *there*	**detrás** *behind*
aquí *here*	**¿dónde?** *where?*
arriba *above, upstairs*	**enfrente** *in front of, opposite*

   2. Common adverbial phrases of place

a la derecha *to the right*	**delante de** *in front of, ahead of*
a la izquierda *to the left*	**detrás de** *behind*
al lado de *next to, alongside*	**encima de** *on top of*
debajo de *beneath*	**frente a** *facing, in front of*

EJERCICIO L   ¿Dónde?   Exprese dónde ocurren estas acciones. Complete las siguientes oraciones con un adverbio o expresión adverbial, según el caso.

abajo	arriba	dentro de	encima de
al lado	debajo de	delante de	frente a

EJEMPLO: Se guardan los productos lácteos **dentro del** refrigerador para que no se echen a perder.

1. Antes de que hubiera bancos, mucha gente guardaba el dinero en casa _____ colchón.

2. En una casa, el sótano está _____ y el desván está _____ .

3. En el salón de clase, el profesor suele estar _____ la clase.

4. Al poner la mesa, ponen los platos _____ la mesa.

5. Roberto tiene buenas costumbres y siempre cuelga su ropa _____ el guardarropa.

6. Al formar una cola, una persona se pone _____ la otra.

7. La casa de mi vecino está _____ la mía.

8. Para verse en un espejo, hay que ponerse _____ un espejo.

    d. Other Adverbial Phrases

       1. Some adverbial expressions are formed by combining prepositions with other words.

         (a) PREPOSITION (+ ARTICLE) + NOUN

a la vez *at the same time*	**de veras** *really, truly*
al fin *finally*	**en seguida** *immediately, at once*
de día *by day*	**por desgracia** *unfortunately*
de memoria *by heart*	**sin duda** *undoubtedly*
de noche *by night*	**sin embargo** *nevertheless*
de repente *suddenly*	

         (b) PREPOSITION + ADJECTIVE

a menudo *often*	**en general, por lo general** *generally*
de nuevo *again*	**por consiguiente** *consequently*
de pronto *suddenly*	**por supuesto** *of course*

         (c) PREPOSITION + ADVERB

al (a lo) menos *at least*
en cuanto *as soon as*

         (d) PREPOSITION + VERB FORM

al amanecer *at daybreak*	**por escrito** *in writing*
al anochecer *at nightfall*	**por lo visto** *apparently, evidently*

         (e) PREPOSITION + ADJECTIVE + NOUN

de buena (mala) gana *(un)willingly*	**en otra parte** *elsewhere*
en ninguna parte *not anywhere, nowhere*	**en todas partes** *everywhere*

2. Common adverbial expressions formed with other words.

ahora mismo *right now*	**hoy mismo** *this very day*
a pesar de *in spite of*	**junto a** *beside*
cada vez más *more and more*	**mientras tanto** *meanwhile*
cuanto antes *as soon as possible*	**rara vez** *seldom*
de cuando en cuando *from time to time*	**tal vez** *perhaps*
dentro de *poco shortly*	**tan pronto como** *as soon as*
hoy (en) día *nowadays*	**ya no** *no longer*

EJERCICIO M | **Comentarios** A Alberto le gusta comentar sobre muchas cosas. Complete sus comentarios con las expresiones adverbiales sugeridas.

al amanecer	de mala gana	hoy mismo
al anochecer	de memoria	en todas partes
a la vez	de noche	por escrito
a pesar de	de nuevo	rara vez
de cuando en cuando	de repente	sin duda
de día	en ninguna parte	ya no

1. El niño escuchó el cuento tantas veces que lo sabe ＿＿＿＿＿＿＿ .

2. Debemos comprar las entradas para el concierto ＿＿＿＿＿＿＿ , si no, se acaban.

3. Se ven los mejores colores del cielo ＿＿＿＿＿＿＿ .

4. Si vas a prestarle dinero a Juan, pídele un contrato ＿＿＿＿＿＿＿ .

5. Elena volvió a la universidad; ＿＿＿＿＿＿＿ trabaja en el salón de belleza.

6. ¿Los señores Vidal? ＿＿＿＿＿＿＿ los veo en la calle.

7. No soy muy deportista pero ＿＿＿＿＿＿＿ juego al voleibol en la playa.

8. El horario de Pedro ha cambiado porque consiguió un trabajo ＿＿＿＿＿＿＿ y ahora descansa ＿＿＿＿＿＿＿ .

9. Clara pasó la tarde en el museo ＿＿＿＿＿＿＿ que cancelaron la exposición.

10. Luke es perezoso y siempre hace las tareas ＿＿＿＿＿＿＿ .

11. Los pájaros empiezan a cantar ＿＿＿＿＿＿＿ .

12. Busqué esa revista ＿＿＿＿＿＿＿ pero no la encontré ＿＿＿＿＿＿＿ .

13. Hablaba con mi hermano por teléfono pero —————————— se cortó la comunicación.

    Tuve que marcar el número —————————— .

14. Lizette tiene la mala costumbre de escuchar dos conversaciones —————————— .

15. Todo el mundo lleva abrigo, bufanda, gorra y guantes. —————————— hace un

    frío tremendo.

3.   Comparisons of Equality and Inequality

a. Comparisons of Equality

1. The formula *tan* + adjective or adverb + *como* (as . . . as) is used when comparing adjectives.

   Ella *es tan alta como* **él.**   *She's as tall as he.*

   José corre *tan rápidamente como* **Luis.**   *José runs as rapidly as Luis.*

2. The formula tanto (*-a, -os, -as*) + noun + *como* (as much / as many . . . as) is used when comparing nouns.

   Tengo *tantos amigos como* **ella.**   *I have as many friends as she.*

   Necesito *tanto dinero como* **Ud.**   *I need as much money as you.*

3. *Tanto como* is used when comparing verbs.

   Trabajamos *tanto como* **ellos.**   *We work as much as they.*

   Leen *tanto como* **yo.**   *They read as much as I.*

EJERCICIO N   **Todo es igual.**   Según la señora Calderón, todo es igual. Exprese lo que ella dice.

EJEMPLO: el pan / sabroso / el pastel   El pan **es tan sabroso como** el pastel.

1. los dramas / divertidos / las comedias

   _____

2. la plata / valiosa / el oro

   _____

3. los adolescentes / traviesos / los niños

   _____

4. el azúcar / dulce / la miel

   _____

5. la primavera / agradable / el otoño

   _____

6. una película / entretenida / una obra de teatro

_____

7. las amigas / importantes / los parientes

_____

EJERCICIO O   **Más igualdad**   Javier y Rudy son muy parecidos. Compare cómo hacen las siguientes cosas.

Ejemplo: correr rápidamente   Javier **corre tan rápidamente como** Rudy.

1. nadar bien   _____

2. bailar hábilmente   _____

3. expresarse claramente _____

4. hablar francamente   _____

5. vestirse mal   _____

6. reírse alegremente   _____

7. trabajar cuidadosamente _____

EJERCICIO P   **El imitador**   La mamá de Nick cree que él imita mucho a sus amigos. Exprese lo que ella dice.

Ejemplo: jugar / Jaime   Nick **juega tanto como** Jaime.

1. leer / Carlos   _____

2. dormir / Felipe   _____

3. trabajar / Víctor _____

4. divertirse / Tony _____

5. comer / Alfredo   _____

6. estudiar / Miguel _____

7. gastar / Beto   _____

EJERCICIO Q   **La competencia**   Antonio compite mucho con sus amigos. Exprese lo que Antonio hizo.

Ejemplo: participar en concursos
           Antonio **participó en tantos concursos como** sus amigos.

1. ganar trofeos _____

2. ver películas _____

3. comprar ropa   _____

4. gastar dinero   _____

5. tener suscripciones   _____

6. decir mentiras   _____

7. beber refrescos   _____

EJERCICIO R   **Perspectivas**   Alejandra y Nadya pasan mucho tiempo juntas, pero nunca están de acuerdo. Exprese lo que Nadya responde a los comentarios de su amiga.

EJEMPLO: ALEJANDRA: Compramos muchas revistas.   (*regalos*)

          NADYA: Compramos **tantas revistas como regalos.**

ALEJANDRA: Había muchos niños en las tiendas.   (*adultos*)

NADYA: _____

ALEJANDRA: Tomamos muchos autobuses.   (*trenes*)

NADYA: _____

ALEJANDRA: Comimos muchas empanadas.   (*papas fritas*)

NADYA: _____

ALEJANDRA: Nos probamos muchas faldas.   (*suéteres*)

NADYA: _____

ALEJANDRA: Entramos en muchos almacenes.   (*cafés*)

NADYA: _____

b. Comparisons of Inequality

    1. When using comparisons of inequality, adjectives are compared as follows:

ADJECTIVE	rico (-a, -os, -as)	*rich*
COMPARATIVES	más rico menos rico	*richer* *less rich*

Esta familia es rica.   *This family is rich.*

Esta familia es *más* (*menos*) rica que ésa.   *This family is richer (less rich) than that one.*

    2. The comparative forms of *bueno, malo, grande,* and *pequeño* are irregular.

POSITIVE	COMPARATIVE
bueno (-a, -os, -as) *good* **malo (-a, -os, -as)** *bad*	**mejor (-es)** *better* **peor (-es)** *worse*
grande (-s) *great, big*	**mayor (-es)** *greater; older* **más grande (-s)** *larger* **menos grande (-s)** *less large*
pequeño (-a, -os, -as) *small*	**menor (-es)** *minor, lesser; younger* **más pequeño (-a, -os, -as)** *smaller* **menos pequeño (-a, -os, -as)** *less small*

NOTE: 1. *Mejor* and *peor* generally precede the noun. *Mayor* and *menor* generally follow the noun.

mi *mejor* **profesor**	*my best teacher*
mi hermano *menor*	*my younger brother*

      2. The regular and irregular comparative forms of *grande* and *pequeño* have different meanings. *Más grande* and *más pequeño* compare differences in size or height (physical meaning); *mayor* and *menor* compare differences in age or status (figurative meaning).

mi amigo *más pequeño*	*my smaller friend*
mi hermana *mayor*	*my older sister*
de *menor* **importancia**	*of lesser importance*

      3. *Que* (than) is used after a comparative.

Es más inteligente *que* **yo.**	*He is more intelligent than I.*
Tengo más discos *que* **tú.**	*I have more records than you.*

      4. *De* (than) replaces *que* before a number if the sentence is affirmative. If the sentence is negative, *que* is used.

Gastó más (menos) *de* **cinco dólares.**	*She spent more (less) than five dollars.*
But:	
No gastó más *que* **cinco dólares.**	*She didn't spend more than five dollars.*

      5. If the second part of the comparison is a clause with a different verb, *de* is used together with a form of *el (la, los, las) que*.

Gastó más dinero *del* **que ganó
  su esposo.**
	*She spent more money than her
	  husband earned.*

Compró más zapatos *de los* **que
  necesitó.**
	*She bought more shoes than
	  she needed.*

NOTE: In each of these sentences, the nouns *dinero* and *zapatos* are the objects of both verbs: *gastó dinero, ganó dinero; compró zapatos, necesitó zapatos.*

If the noun is not the object of both verbs, or if an adjective or adverb is being compared, *de lo que* is used.

Gasta más dinero *de lo que* te imaginas.	*She spends more money than you imagine.*
Habla más lentamente *de lo que* escribe.	*She speaks more slowly than she writes.*

EJERCICIO S   **Observaciones**   Durante una visita a un pequeño pueblo universitario, Diego hace varias observaciones sobre lo que ve. Exprese sus observaciones usando más y menos por turnos en las oraciones.

EJEMPLO: hay / cafés / restaurantes

        Hay **más** (**menos**) cafés **que** restaurantes en el pueblo.

1. hay / edificios altos / edificios bajos   _____

2. hay / flores / árboles   _____

3. hay / tiendas pequeñas / centros comerciales   _____

4. hay / parques / bosques   _____

5. hay / fuentes / estatuas   _____

6. hay / iglesias / cortes   _____

7. hay / bicicletas / carros   _____

EJERCICIO T   **Los nietos**   La señora Dávila tiene diez nietos y le gusta hacer comparaciones entre ellos. Exprese lo que ella dice alternando *más* o *menos* en cada oración.

EJEMPLO: Nina es estudiosa.   (*Luz*)   Nina **es más** (**menos**) **estudiosa que** Luz.

1. Joaquín es travieso.   (*Linda*)   _____

2. Alfredo es responsable.   (*Susana*)   _____

3. Linda es habladora.   (*Ricardo*)   _____

4. Susana es inteligente.   (*Juana*)   _____

5. Ricardo es serio.   (*Luz*)   _____

6. Norma es cariñosa.   (*José*)   _____

7. José es bondadoso.   (*Alfredo*)   _____

EJERCICIO U   **¿Quién lo hace mejor (peor)?**   Exprese quién hace estas cosas mejor o peor que la persona indicada.

EJEMPLO: Inés / montar a caballo / Emma

Inés monta a caballo **mejor (peor) que** Emma.

1. Fred / dibujar / Luis   _____

2. Anita / bailar / Vicente   _____

3. Celia y Cristina / jugar al fútbol / yo   _____

4. Estela / diseñar joyería / Nora   _____

5. Lázaro / declamar poesía / nosotros   _____

4.   The Superlative

a. The superlative (the most / least . . .) is formed as follows: *el* (*la, los, las*) + noun + *más* (*menos*) + adjective + *de*. The noun stands between the article and the adjective. After the superlative, *de* means *in*.

la pintura más (menos) cara   *the most (least) expensive painting*

Este niño es *el más (menos) travieso*   *This boy is the most (least) mischievous*
de la clase.   *in the class.*

Es *la mejor (peor) película del* **año.**   *It's the best (worst) film of the year.*

b. To express an absolute superlative (when no comparison is involved), *-ísimo* (*-a, -os, -as*) is often added to the adjective. The meaning is the same as *muy* + adjective.

muy bello ⎫
bellísimo ⎬   *very pretty*

NOTE: 1.   *Muchísimo* is equivalent to *very much*.

2.   Adjectives ending in a vowel drop that vowel before adding *-ísimo*.

3.   Adjectives ending in *-co*, *-go*, or *-z* change *c* to *qu*, *g* to *gu*, and *z* to *c*, respectively, before adding *-ísimo*.

fresco   **fres*qu*ísimo**
largo   **lar*gu*ísimo**
feliz   **feli*c*ísimo**

4.   To form adjectives from adverbs in *-ísimo*, add *-mente* to the feminine form of the adjective: *riquísimamente, lentísimamente*.

EJERCICIO V   **Opiniones**   Exprese su opinión sobre cuál es el (la) mejor (peor) de las cosas indicadas. Justifique su respuesta.

EJEMPLO: deporte

El fútbol es el mejor deporte porque los jugadores deben ser habilísimos.

1. programa de televisión   _____

2. comida   _____

3. refresco   _____

4. grupo musical   _____

5. cantante popular   _____

6. político   _____

7. disco compacto   _____

8. equipo de fútbol americano   _____

EJERCICIO W   **Fotografías**   Elvira muestra las fotos que sacó en un viaje a Puerto Rico. Exprese lo que ella dice con superlativos.

EJEMPLO: éste es / hotel / grande / ciudad   Éste es **el hotel más grande de la** ciudad.

1. éstas son / calles / estrechas / zona colonial

_____

2. éste es / árbol / antiguo / jardín botánico

_____

3. ésta es / iglesia / famosa / isla

_____

4. ésta es / playa / bonita / Caribe

_____

5. éste es / monumento / conocido / Viejo San Juan

_____

6. éstas son / flores / fragantes / jardines

_____

EJERCICIO X   **Exageraciones**   A muchas personas les fascina exagerar mucho cuando hablan de su familia. Exprese lo que dicen usando un superlativo con *-ísimo.*

EJEMPLO: mi padre / ser / médico / famoso   Mi padre es un médico **famosísimo.**

1. mis padres / hacer viajes / largos   _____

2. mi tío / ser / rico   _____

3. mis padres / darme / carro / caro   _____

4. yo / recibir / notas / altas   _____

5. mi novia / ser / guapa _____

6. mi madre / comprar / flores / frescas _____

7. yo / vivir / casa / grande _____

EJERCICIO Y **Actividad oral** Trabajando con un compañero de clase, describa a un amigo o a un miembro de su familia. La descripción debe incluir características físicas y de la personalidad. Luego compare a esta persona con otros amigos o parientes.

CHAPTER 17
Demonstrative Adjectives and Pronouns; Possession

1. Demonstrative Adjectives

a. Demonstrative adjectives precede the nouns they modify and agree with them in gender and number.

este **hombre**	*this man*
esas **mujeres**	*those women*

b. There are three demonstrative adjectives in Spanish.

MASCULINE	FEMININE	MEANING
este estos	esta estas	this these
ese esos	esa esas	that those
aquel aquellos	aquella aquellas	that those

Este (*-a, -os, -as*) refers to what is near or directly concerns the speaker. *Ese* (*-a, -os, -as*) refers to what is not so near or directly concerns the person addressed. *Aquel* (*-lla, -llos, -llas*) refers to what is remote from both the speaker and the person addressed, or does not directly concern either.

Esta revista tiene muchas fotos.	*This magazine has many photos.*
Jorge, dame *esa* revista que tienes en la mano.	*Jorge, give me that magazine that you have in your hand.*
Jorge, prefiero *aquella* revista.	*Jorge, I prefer that magazine over there.*

NOTE: The adverbs *aquí* (here), *ahí* (there), and *allí* (over there) correspond to *este*, *ese*, and *aquel*, respectively.

Prefiero	*esta* **lámpara** *aquí.* *esa* **lámpara** *ahí.* *aquella* **lámpara** *allí.*	*I prefer*	*this lamp here.* *that lamp there.* *that lamp over there.*

EJERCICIO A ¿Cuánto vale? Julia está en una joyería y quiere saber el precio de todo lo que ve en los mostradores. Exprese lo que ella le pregunta al dependiente.

EJEMPLO: broche ¿Cuánto vale **este** broche?

1. aretes _____

2. pulsera _____

3. cadenas de oro _____

4. prendedor _____

5. collar de plata _____

6. anillo de rubíes _____

7. llavero de plata _____

8. hebilla _____

EJERCICIO B   **Me parece...**   Vicky y un amigo pasan la tarde caminando en un pueblo pequeño. Exprese lo que dicen de las cosas que ven. Use la forma apropiada de *ese*.

EJEMPLO: café / bueno   **Ese** café **me parece bueno.**

1. galería de arte / interesante _____

2. tienda / elegante _____

3. faroles / antiguos _____

4. parque / grandísimo _____

5. estatuas / históricas _____

6. centro comercial / pequeño _____

7. restaurante / caro _____

8. calles / angostas _____

EJERCICIO C   **Vistas del barco**   Rocío y unas amigas están en un barco y miran a su alrededor. Complete sus comentarios al ver cosas desde el barco. Use la forma apropiada de *aquel*.

EJEMPLO: Miren **aquel** pico cubierto de nieve.

1. Miren _____ rascacielos altos.

2. Fíjense en _____ torre curiosa.

3. Miren _____ lancha deportiva.

4. Miren _____ vapores grandes.

5. Fíjense en _____ nubes oscuras.

6. Miren _____ palmeras elegantes.

7. Miren _____ barcos de vela.

8. Fíjense en —————— faro encantador.

En una casa de antigüedades Los señores Palomares visitan una casa de antigüedades. Exprese lo que dicen mientras ven todas las cosas que hay. Use el adjetivo demostrativo apropiado.

PARA EXPRESARSE MEJOR

el azucarero	*sugar bowl*	**el espejo**	*mirror*
el bronce	*bronze*	**llamativo**	*gaudy*
el candelero	*candlestick*	**el marco**	*frame*
el encaje	*lace*	**la porcelana**	*porcelain*

EJEMPLO: gustarme / pintura / allí   Me gusta **aquella** pintura.

1. azucarero / ser / hermoso / ahí ————————————————————

2. candeleros / ser / elegantes / aquí ————————————————

3. muñeca / estar / en buenas condiciones / ahí ————————————

4. marcos / ser / interesantes / allí ————————————————————

5. espejo / ser / muy llamativo / aquí ————————————————————

6. gustarme / fotografías / allí ————————————————————————

7. armario / ser / de madera fina / allí ————————————————

8. cortinas de encaje / ser / antiguas / ahí ————————————————

9. estatua de bronce / ser / pesada / aquí ————————————————

10. gustarme / figuras de porcelana / allí ————————————————

Preguntas Mientras Felipe camina por el centro con el alumno de intercambio que va a pasar una temporada con su familia, el alumno le hace muchas preguntas. Conteste sus preguntas usando el adjetivo demostrativo apropiado.

EJEMPLO: ¿Venden ropa fina en la tienda de ahí?   Sí, venden ropa fina en **esa** tienda.

1. ¿Se consiguen revistas en español en la librería de allí?

——

2. ¿Podría cambiar mi dinero por dólares en el banco de aquí?

——

3. ¿Hay muchas computadoras en la biblioteca de ahí?

——

4. ¿Hay un buen surtido de tenis en la zapatería de allí?

   _____

5. ¿Se alquilan videos en la tienda de aquí?

   _____

6. ¿Se compra champú en el supermercado de aquí?

   _____

7. ¿Se venden juguetes caros en la juguetería de ahí?

   _____

8. ¿Sirven buen café en el café de ahí?

   _____

9. ¿Hay una piscina en el gimnasio de allí?

   _____

10. ¿Se permiten bicicletas en el parque de aquí?

   _____

2. Demonstrative Pronouns

a. In Spanish, demonstrative pronouns have the same forms as demonstrative adjectives but, as pronouns, they are not followed by a noun. Also, demonstrative pronouns have a neuter form, in addition to the masculine and feminine ones.

MASCULINE	FEMININE	NEUTER	MEANING
éste éstos	ésta éstas	esto	this (one) these
ése ésos	ésa ésas	eso	that (one) those
aquél aquéllos	aquélla aquéllas	aquello	that (one) those

NOTE: 1. Demonstrative pronouns require an accent on their stressed syllable, to differentiate them from the demonstrative adjectives.

2. Neuter pronouns have no accent mark, since there are no corresponding neuter adjectives.

b. Demonstrative pronouns agree in gender and number with the nouns they replace.

este libro y *aquél*　　　*this book and that* (one)

estas camisas y *ésas*　　*these shirts and those* (ones)

c. The neuter forms *esto, eso,* and *aquello* refer to general statements, ideas, or an object of undetermined gender. These forms do not vary in gender and number.

Hay una cola larga, y *eso* no les gusta a los aficionados.	*There's a long line, and the fans don't like that.*

The question *¿Qué es esto (eso, aquello)?* uses the neuter form because the gender of the noun is unknown. After the noun has been mentioned, the form of the demonstrative adjective or pronoun must correspond to the noun.

¿Qué es *eso*? — Es una cadena.	*What is that?—It's a chain.*
¿Es larga *esa* cadena? — Sí.	*Is that chain long?—Yes.*

d. The pronoun *éste (ésta, éstos, éstas)* also means the *latter* (the latest, the most recently mentioned); *aquél (aquélla, aquéllos, aquéllas)* also means the *former* (the most remotely mentioned).

María y Carmen son amigas: *ésta* es alta, *aquélla* es baja.	*María and Carmen are friends: the former is short, the latter is tall.*

NOTE: In English, we usually say "the former and the latter." In Spanish, the order is reversed: *ésta* (the latter) comes first.

e. The definite article (*el, la, los, las*) followed by *de* (that of, the one of) or *que* (the one that) functions like a demonstrative pronoun.

el (la) de **Pepe**	*that of (the one of) Pepe; Pepe's*
los (las) de **Pepe**	*those of (the ones of) Pepe; Pepe's*
el (la) que **llegó primero**	*the one that arrived first*
los (las) que **llegaron primero**	*the ones that arrived first*
El padre de Pepe es más rico que *el de* José.	*Pepe's father is richer than José's.*
La corbata de Ricardo es distinta de *la de* Luis; es muy parecida *a la que* lleva Tony.	*Ricardo's tie is different from Luis'; it's very similar to the one Tony is wearing.*

EJERCICIO F **De compras** Elsa y Marta han pasado mucho tiempo en la tienda. Antes de llegar a la caja de la tienda, Marta revisa lo que ha puesto en el carrito. Exprese lo que ella dice, usando el pronombre demostrativo apropiado.

EJEMPLO: Voy a comprar este suéter porque **ése** de ahí no me queda bien.

1. Estos zapatos son bonitos pero prefiero —————— de allí.

2. No me gusta mucho ese collar; —————— de aquí es más bonito.

3. Estas camisetas son más prácticas que —————— de ahí.

4. Aquellos lentes de sol son más grandes que —————— de aquí.

5. Esta bufanda es más elegante que —————— de allí.

6. Esos guantes son de buena calidad pero me gustan más —————— de allí.

7. Aquel cinturón es más útil que —————— de aquí.

8. A ver qué tarjeta de crédito aceptan, —————— de aquí o —————— de ahí.

EJERCICIO G   **Los preparativos**   Gina y Tomás hacen las compras en el supermercado para una fiesta. No tienen mucho dinero y quieren comprar todo lo que necesitan. Exprese lo que dicen, usando el pronombre demostrativo apropiado.

EJEMPLO: Estos globos son mejores que **aquéllos** de allí.

1. Esos refrescos son ricos pero —————— de aquí están en oferta.

2. Aquel paquete de dulces es grande pero —————— de ahí contiene más dulces.

3. Este queso es bueno pero —————— de allí es más económico.

4. Estas galletas son más baratas que —————— de allí.

5. Aquel pastel es pequeño; —————— de aquí es más grande.

6. Me gusta este jamón pero —————— de ahí cuesta menos.

7. Estos dos aguacates cuestan más que —————— grande de allí.

EJERCICIO H   **Un niño preguntón**   El hermano de Tony siempre hace muchas preguntas. Complete las preguntas que hace con el pronombre demostrativo apropiado según la sugerencia.

EJEMPLO: ¿Qué significa **esto**? (*aquí*)

1. ¿Oíste —————— ? (*ahí*)

2. ¿Tú crees —————— ? (*aquí*)

3. ¿Recuerdas —————— ? (*allí*)

4. ¿Quiénes dijeron —————— ? (*aquí*)

5. ¿De quién es —————— ? (*allí*)

6. ¿Quién te contó —————— ? (*ahí*)

7. ¿Cuándo descubriste —————— ? (*aquí*)

8. ¿Cómo supiste —————— ? (*allí*)

9. ¿Por qué dices —————— ? (*ahí*)

10. ¿Dónde pusieron —————— ? (*allí*)

EJERCICIO I   **Comparaciones**   Virginia siempre hace comentarios sobre todo lo que oye. Exprese lo que ella dice, usando la forma apropiada de *éste* y *aquél*.

EJEMPLO: Jack es el hermano mayor de Silvia.   Sí, **ésta** es menor que **aquél**.

1. Los amigos de Celia son más corteses que las amigas de Pablo.

   _____

2. Un crucero es más agradable que una excursión en autobús.

   _____

3. Los actores jóvenes son menos hábiles que los actores mayores.

   _____

4. Una fiesta en casa es más económica que una fiesta en un restaurante.

   _____

5. Un grabado fino puede valer tanto como una pintura buena.

   _____

6. Las comedias son tan populares como los dramas.

   _____

> **EJERCICIO J**   **Un mensaje electrónico**   Complete el mensaje que Teresa les mandó a sus suegros con el pronombre demostrativo, usando la forma apropiada del artículo (*el, la, los, las*).

Queridos suegros:

Hoy tuve un día más activo que _____ de mi vecina porque ella me pidió varios
                                    1.

favores. El jardinero vino temprano para cortar el césped y _____ de mi vecina
                                                                    2.

también. Luego llegó el plomero y salí de la casa con mis llaves pero olvidé _____
                                                                                3.

de ella. Por la tarde tuve que recoger a mis hijos en la escuela, y a _____ de mi
                                                                          4.

vecina también. Después llevé a mi hija a la clase de baile mientras _____ de ella
                                                                         5.

asistió a una fiesta. Al entregar el correo, el cartero dejó mis cartas en la puerta

con _____ de otros vecinos y tuve que remediar eso. David no pudo comunicarse
        6.

con Uds. durante el día porque yo me llevé mi teléfono celular y _____ de él tam-
                                                                      7.

bién. Ahora espero pasar una noche tan tranquila como _____ de Uds.
                                                            8.

Saludos a todos,

Teresa

3.   Possession

    a. Possession is generally expressed in Spanish by *de* + possessor.

la cámara *de Lucy*   *Lucy's camera*
los nietos *de los señores Arenas*   *the Arenas' grandchildren*
los libros *del profesor*   *the teacher's books*
el carro *de mi padre*   *my father's car*

NOTE: When *de* is followed by *el*, the contraction *del* is formed.

b. When followed by a form of *ser*, *¿De quién(-es)...?* is equivalent to the English interrogative *whose . . .?*

¿De *quién* **es la muñeca?**	*Whose doll is it?*
¿De *quién* **son los libros?**	*Whose books are they?*
¿De *quiénes* **es la tienda?**	*Whose store is it?*
¿De *quiénes* **son las reglas?**	*Whose rules are they?*

c. The possessive relative *cuyo* (*-a, -os, -as*) is equivalent to the English relative *whose*. *Cuyo* agrees in number and gender with the person or thing possessed and not with the possessor. (See Chapter 19, page 243).

El señor *cuya* **cartera encontré acaba de llamar.**	*The man whose wallet I found has just called.*

EJERCICIO K	*¿De quién es?* Antes de despedirse de los abuelos, la abuela quiere saber de quién son las cosas que ella encontró en la sala. Exprese lo que ella pregunta y lo que responden los nietos.

EJEMPLO: oso de peluche / el bebé   **¿De quién es** el oso de peluche? **Es del** bebé.

1. bolsa / mi mamá _____

2. anteojos / Marco _____

3. juego electrónico / Javier _____

4. gorras / los gemelos _____

5. guantes / Frida _____

6. muñecas / Amanda _____

7. cámara de video / mi papá _____

d. Possessive Adjectives

SHORT FORM	LONG FORM	MEANINGS
mi, mis	mío, -a, -os, as	*my*
tu, tus	tuyo, -a, -os, -as	*your* (familiar singular)
su, sus	suyo, -a, -os, -as	*your, his, her, its, their*
nuestro, -a	nuestro, -a	*our*
vuestro, -a	vuestro, -a	*your* (familiar plural)

1. The short forms of possessive adjectives precede the noun. They agree in gender and number with the person or thing possessed, not with the possessor.

mi **dinero**	*my money*	*tus* **clases**	*your classes*
su **fiesta**	*his (your, her, its, their) party*	*nuestros* **boletos**	*out tickets*
nuestra **bicicleta**	*our bicycle*		

2. The long forms of possessive adjectives follow the noun and agree in number and gender with the person or thing possessed, not with the possessor.

una corbata *mía*	*a tie of mine*
un primo *suyo*	*a cousin of hers*
un amigo *mío*	*a friend of mine*
unos papeles *nuestros*	*some papers of ours*

    NOTE: To avoid ambiguity, *su (sus)* and *suyo (suya, suyos, suyas)* may be replaced by the article + *de Ud. (Uds.)*, *de él (ella)*, or *de ellos (ellas)*.

Pensaba en *su* **hermano.**	*I was thinking about his (her, your, their) brother.*
Pensaba en *el hermano de ella.*	*I was thinking about her brother.*

3. The definite article is used instead of the possessive adjective with parts of the body or clothing, when the possessor is clear.

Hugo levantó *la* **mano.**	*Hugo raised his hand.*
Ella se puso *el* **suéter.**	*She put on her sweater.*
Él cerró *el* **paraguas.**	*He closed his umbrella.*

    But:

María se puso *mi* **anillo.**	*María put on my ring.*

EJERCICIO L   **Cosas antiguas**   Los señores Rivas se van a mudar e invitan a sus hijos a reclamar las cosas de su niñez. Conteste las preguntas de los hijos, según el ejemplo.

EJEMPLO: ¿Eran mis patines?   Sí, eran **tus** patines.

1. ¿Era la muñeca de Sarita?   _____

2. ¿Eran los carteles de Rogelio?   _____

3. ¿Eran estos juegos de mesa de Beto?   _____

4. ¿Era mi mochila?   _____

5. ¿Eran tus palos de golf, papá?   _____

6. ¿Era el juego de té de Lidia?   _____

7. ¿Eran nuestras tarjetas de béisbol?   _____

EJERCICIO M   **Después de un buen día**   Al salir de la playa, Laura se encarga de identificar de quién son las cosas. Exprese a quién pertenecen las cosas, usando las palabras entre paréntesis y un adjetivo posesivo.

EJEMPLO: Esta pelota será de María, ¿verdad?   (*no, Beth*)
          No es la pelota **suya.** Será **la de** Beth.

1. Estas toallas serán de Eduardo y Miguel, ¿verdad?   (*no, Felipe y Víctor*)

   _____

2. Esta loción de broncear será mía, ¿verdad?   (*sí*)

   _____

3. Esta canasta será de Eva, ¿verdad?   (*no, Ana*)

   _____

4. Estos salvavidas serán de Jorge y Brian, ¿verdad?   (*no, Jenny y Pedro*)

   _____

5. Estos anteojos de sol serán de Clara, ¿verdad?   (*no, Frida*)

   _____

6. Estos sombreros serán de Tina y yo, ¿verdad?   (*no, Pepe*)

   _____

7. Estas revistas serán de June, ¿verdad?   (*sí, ella*)

   _____

EJERCICIO N   **¡Ay, qué niños!**   Rebeca es voluntaria en una guardería de niños. Complete los comentarios que ella hace sobre sus experiencias allí, usando el artículo definido apropiado.

1. Inés brincó y se lastimó _____ tobillo.

2. Ricky se puso _____ chaqueta de Mario.

3. Vicky lloró mucho porque perdió _____ pañuelo.

4. Rafael y Antonio nunca quieren cepillarse _____ dientes.

5. Brian siempre se quita _____ zapatos y _____ calcetines.

6. A Felipe le dolió _____ estómago después de comer muchos dulces.

7. Fred levantó _____ puños para pelear con Jack.

     e. Possessive Pronouns

el mío, la mía, los míos, las mías	*mine*
el tuyo, la tuya, los tuyos, las tuyas	*yours* (familiar singular)
el suyo, la suya, los suyos, las suyas	*yours, his, hers, its, theirs*

el nuestro, la nuestra, los nuestros, las nuestras   *ours*

el vuestro, la vuestra, los vuestros, las vuestras   *yours* (familiar plural)

1. Possessive pronouns consist of the definite article + the long form of the possessive adjective.

2. The possessive pronoun agrees in number and gender with the noun it replaces, not with the possessor.

Mi hijo es más aplicado que *el* **(hijo)** *suyo.*   *My son is more studious than yours.*

Esta sugerencia y *las* **(sugerencias)** *suyas* **son valiosas.**   *This suggestion and his are valuable.*

NOTE: 1. The specific meaning of *el suyo* (*la suya, los suyos, las suyas*) may be made clear by replacing the possessive with the expression *de Ud.* (*Uds.*), *de él* (*ella*), or *de ellos* (*ellas*) after the article.

mi hijo y *el de Ud.*   *my son and yours*

tus sugerencias y *las de ella*   *my suggestions and hers*

2. After forms of *ser*, the article preceding the possessive pronoun is usually omitted.

Esta cartera es mía.   *This wallet is mine.*

Aquellos patines son suyos.   *Those skates are hers.*

EJERCICIO O   **Comparaciones**   A Norma le gusta comparar las cosas que tiene con las de sus amigas. Exprese lo que ella dice usando los pronombres posesivos apropiados.

EJEMPLO: Mi pelo es más largo que el pelo de Luisa.
El mío es más largo que **el suyo (el de ella)**.

1. Mis aretes son más finos que los aretes de Brenda.

   _____

2. Mis botas son más cómodas que tus botas.

   _____

3. Nuestro carro es más lujoso que los carros de Uds.

   _____

4. Mi abrigo es más elegante que el abrigo de Celia.

   _____

5. Mis amigas son más simpáticas que las amigas de Margarita.

   _____

6. Mi familia es más unida que tu familia.

   _____

7. Mis ideas son más creativas que las ideas de Silvia y Julia.

_____

EJERCICIO P **¿Dónde está?** Exprese dónde están las cosas que busca tu mamá. Use las palabras entre paréntesis.

EJEMPLO: ¿Dónde están mis llaves?   (_en tu bolsa_)
            Las tuyas están en **tu bolsa.**

1. ¿Dónde están los guantes de tu papá?   (_en el cajón_)

_____

2. ¿Dónde está tu paraguas?   (_cerca de la puerta_)

_____

3. ¿Dónde está mi pluma?   (_en el escritorio_)

_____

4. ¿Dónde están las píldoras de tu abuela?   (_en el baño_)

_____

5. ¿Dónde están los abrigos de Uds.?   (_en el armario_)

_____

6. ¿Dónde está mi calculadora?   (_en la mesa_)

_____

7. ¿Dónde está tu reloj de oro?   (_en la cómoda_)

_____

EJERCICIO Q **Mal preparado** Cuando Jorge va al parque a jugar con sus amigos nunca lleva su propio equipo y debe tomar prestado el equipo de sus amigos. Exprese lo que él dice cuando quiere jugar.

EJEMPLO: ¿Un guante de béisbol? Antonio puede prestarte **el suyo.**

1. ¿Una pelota de voleibol? Yo te presto _____ .

2. ¿Una raqueta de tenis? Jimmy va a prestarte _____ .

3. ¿Una pelota de fútbol? No usamos la de Luis ahora. Allí está _____ .

4. ¿Un monopatín? No estamos usando _____ ahora.

5. ¿Patines? Tú usas el mismo número que Juan. Puedes usar _____ .

6. ¿Un cronómetro? Yo tengo uno pero _____ no funciona bien. Puedes usar

_____ si quieres.

EJERCICIO R   **Actividad oral**   Ud. estudia en la universidad durante el verano y comparte un dormitorio en la residencia con otro estudiante. Para que no haya ningún problema al terminar el programa, Uds. hacen un inventario de lo que hay en el cuarto. Trabajando con un compañero, háganse preguntas para saber a quiénes pertenecen las cosas que hay en el cuarto. Use tantos demostrativos y posesivos como puedan. Por ejemplo: *¿De quién es este televisor?—Este televisor es mío.*

EJERCICIO S   **Lectura**   Lea el siguiente comentario sobre las mujeres actuales y luego conteste las preguntas.

PARA EXPRESARSE MEJOR

el azucarero	*sugar bowl*	**el espejo**	*mirror*
desempeñar	*to act, perform*	**el hogar**	*home*
la empresa	*enterprise: company*	**la jornada**	*day's work*
la exigencia	*demand*	**lograr**	*to achieve, attain*
la factibilidad	*feasibility*	**la red**	*network*
factible	*feasible*	**el respaldo**	*backing, support*

Hoy día las mujeres representan un gran porcentaje de la fuerza laboral y la mayoría de ellas desempeñan simultáneamente los papeles de trabajadora, madre y ama de casa. La factibilidad de cumplir bien con esas responsabilidades y exigencias de siempre ofrece un buen tema para los debates y las entrevistas.

Hay personas que opinan que no es posible hacer bien ambas cosas a la vez porque siempre existirá tensión entre oficina y hogar, y la mujer tendrá que privilegiar ésta o aquélla. Sin embargo, cada día más y más mujeres demuestran que sí es posible manejar esta tensión más o menos sanamente. Esto dependerá de muchos factores como su horario laboral, el respaldo de la empresa, las redes sociales que establezca y la participación del marido u otros familiares. Aunque no existe un modelo ideal de madre trabajadora, éste debe ser una elección libre de parte de la mujer. Lo importante es que el modelo suyo sea factible para ella, para su familia y para su empresa. Para lograr esto, es muy importante que el tradicional contrato de trabajo de jornada completa deje espacio a otros modelos laborales, como las medias jornadas, y aprovechar la tecnología que permite cumplir con las responsabilidades laborales sin estar presente en la empresa. Lo más seguro es que el eterno dilema de ser madre y profesional a la vez nunca desaparecerá, pero cada día habrá más opciones para esta mujer y la sociedad reconocerá y apreciará más el papel valioso que las mujeres desempeñan tanto en las empresas y las profesiones como en el hogar.

1. ¿Qué sabemos de las mujeres hoy día?

   (a) La mayoría prefiere quedarse en casa con sus hijos.

   (b) Su presencia en la fuerza laboral ha aumentado mucho.

   (c) Se quejan de los papeles distintos que tienen que hacer.

   (d) Hay poco respeto para la mujer que trata de hacer dos papeles.

2. Muchos críticos creen que

   (a) las mujeres deben dedicarse a una sola cosa.

   (b) las mujeres deben tener metas alcanzables.

   (c) es imposible hacer bien dos cosas a la vez.

   (d) es fácil disminuir la tensión entre casa y oficina.

3. Según el autor, las mujeres que quieren tener profesión y familia deben

   (a) ser más agresivas en tomar las decisiones.

   (b) crear libremente un horario personal para sí mismas.

   (c) decidir cuál de éstas tiene mayor importancia.

   (d) organizar un sindicato para lograr sus metas.

CHAPTER 18
Personal Pronouns

1.   Subject Pronouns

SINGULAR	PLURAL
yo *I* **tú** *you* (informal) **usted (Ud.)** *you* (formal) **él** *he* **ella** *she*	**nosotros, -as** *we* **vosotros, -as** *you* (informal) **ustedes (Uds.)** *you* (formal) **ellos** *they* (masculine) **ellas** *they* (feminine)

In Spanish, subject pronouns are not used as often as in English. Since the verb ending indicates the subject, subject pronouns are used for clarity, emphasis, and politeness.

Ella **trabajaba mientras yo leía.**	*She worked while I read.*
No se lo diga *Ud.; yo* **se lo diré.**	*Don't tell it to him; I will tell it to him.*
Pasen y siéntense *Uds.* **, por favor.**	*Please come in and be seated.*

NOTE: 1. The *vosotros* form (informal plural) is used in Spain but rarely in Spanish America, where the *ustedes* form is preferred.

2. The English pronoun *it* is not expressed as a subject in Spanish.

¿De quién es? — Es de ella.	*Whose is it? It's hers.*
¿Dónde está? — Está en la mesa.	*Where is it? It's on the table.*

EJERCICIO A   **Las profesiones**   La señora Galdós quiere saber las profesiones de los amigos de Héctor. Use el pronombre apropiado en las respuestas.

EJEMPLO: Rafaela / profesor   **Ella** es profesora.

1. Miguel e Inés / dentista   _____

2. Roberto y tú / abogado   _____

3. Luisa y Marta / futbolista   _____

4. Jenny / contador   _____

5. Beatriz y Sara / médico   _____

6. Pablo / enfermero   _____

7. Alejandra / arquitecto   _____

8. Esteban y Pedro / ingeniero   _____

EJERCICIO B   **Preguntas**   Conteste las preguntas que Enrique le hace a un amigo. Use las sugerencias dadas y el pronombre apropiado.

EJEMPLO: ¿Cuándo viene a visitarte tu prima?   (*este verano*)
              Ella viene a visitarme este verano.

1. ¿Tienes el nuevo videojuego?   (*sí*)

   _____

2. ¿Me lo prestarías?   (*sí*)

   _____

3. ¿Tienen Uds. el mismo juego que tiene Larry?   (*sí*)

   _____

4. ¿Adónde vas esta noche?   (*un concierto*)

   _____

5. ¿Irán Linda y Felipe también?   (*sí*)

   _____

6. ¿A qué hora van Uds. a reunirse?   (*7:00*)

   _____

7. ¿Cómo son los miembros del grupo musical?   (*talentosos*)

   _____

8. ¿Podrás acompañarme al centro comercial mañana?   (*sí*)

   _____

9. ¿Podremos ir temprano?   (*sí*)

   _____

10. ¿Tendrás el carro de tu mamá?   (*sí*)

   _____

2.   Object Pronouns

a. Direct-Object Pronouns

1. Direct-object pronouns replace direct-object nouns. The direct-object pronouns in Spanish are:

SINGULAR	PLURAL
me *me*	**nos** *us*
te *you* (familiar)	**os** *you* (familiar)
lo *you, him, it* (masculine)	**los** *you, them* (masculine)
la *you* (feminine), *her, it* (feminine)	**las** *you, them* (feminine)

NOTE: 1.   *Lo, la, los,* and *las* refer to both people and things.

2.   *Lo, la, los,* and *las* are also the direct-object pronouns for *Ud.* and *Uds.* They mean *you* as well as *him, her, it,* and *them.*

3.   In Spain, *le* is often used in place of *lo* when referring to people. *Lo* is preferred in Spanish America.

2. In Spanish, direct-object pronouns precede the conjugated verb. In compound tenses, direct-object pronouns are placed before the auxiliary verb *haber.*

Lola *me* acompaña.	*Lola accompanies me.*
Ellos *nos* ven.	*They see us.*
Hace una hora que *lo* busco.	*I have been looking for it for an hour.*
Lola *me* ha acompañado siempre.	*Lola has always accompanied me.*

3. When a direct-object pronoun is used in a verb + infinitive construction, it may either precede the conjugated verb or be attached to the infinitive.

_La_ quiero ver.
Quiero ver_la_.   } *I want to see it.*

4. In the progressive tenses, *estar* + gerund (or present participle), a direct-object pronoun may be placed either before the conjugated form of *estar* or attached to the gerund. When the pronoun is attached to the gerund, an accent mark is added to the stressed vowel to retain the original stress.

_La_ estoy comprando.
Estoy comprándo_la_.   } *I am buying it.*

5. The direct-object pronoun is attached to the affirmative command forms. An accent mark is added to the stressed vowel of the command form, except in the case of one-syllable commands. In the case of a negative command, the direct-object pronoun precedes the verb.

Cómpre_la_.	*Buy it.*
Pon_lo_ aquí.	*Put it here.*
But:	
No *la* compre.	*Don't buy it.*
No *lo* pongas aquí.	*Don't put it here.*

6. If a direct-object noun (person or thing) precedes the verb, the direct-object pronoun must be used.

Visito a mis abuelos a menudo.
But:
A mis abuelos *los* visito a menudo.   } *I visit my grandparents often.*

Yo tengo el dinero.
But:
El dinero *lo* tengo yo.   } *I have the money*

EJERCICIO C   **Una ensalada de frutas**   Ruth está ayudando a su mamá a preparar una ensalada de frutas. Conteste las preguntas que la madre le hace a Ruth.

EJEMPLO: ¿Lavaste la pera?   (*sí*)   Sí, **la** lavé.

1. ¿Lavaste las uvas?   (*sí*)   _____

2. ¿Encontraste la sandía?   (*no*)   _____

3. ¿Compraste los plátanos?   (*sí*)   _____

4. ¿Escogiste las manzanas?   (*no*)   _____

5. ¿Cortaste el melón?   (*sí*)   _____

6. ¿Preparaste el melocotón?   (*no*)   _____

7. ¿Buscaste las fresas?   (*sí*)   _____

8. ¿Conseguiste un mango?   (*sí*)   _____

EJERCICIO D   **La fiesta**   Una amiga ayuda a Sarita a hacer los preparativos para una fiesta. Conteste las preguntas que la amiga le hace a Sarita.

EJEMPLO: ¿Compraste los adornos?

   No, no **los** compré. Voy a comprar**los** (**Los** voy a comprar) mañana.

1. ¿Preparaste la lista de invitados?

   _____

2. ¿Mandaste las invitaciones?

   _____

3. ¿Escogiste los discos compactos?

   _____

4. ¿Compraste los refrescos?

   _____

5. ¿Pediste el pastel de cumpleaños?

   _____

6. ¿Conseguiste los platos desechables?

   _____

7. ¿Planeaste el menú?

   _____

8. ¿Organizaste las actividades?

   _____

9. ¿Envolviste el regalo?

   _____

EJERCICIO E | **Una madre nerviosa** La señora Aragón siempre está muy nerviosa cuando sale y deja a los niños al cargo de una vecina. Exprese lo que la vecina le dice cuando la señora Aragón llama para saber cómo va todo.

EJEMPLO: ¿Comió Luis el almuerzo?   No **lo** comió pero está comiéndo**lo** ahora.

1. ¿Terminó Elsa la tarea?
   _____

2. ¿Miraron los gemelos los dibujos animados en la televisión?
   _____

3. ¿Pidieron los niños helado?
   _____

4. ¿Tomó Luis las vitaminas?
   _____

5. ¿Guardaron los niños los juguetes?
   _____

6. ¿Llamó Elsa a su amiga?
   _____

7. ¿Aprendió Andy el poema de memoria?
   _____

EJERCICIO F | **Indecisos** Los señores Tamayo acaban de comprar una casa y son muy indecisos al dar órdenes a los albañiles que están arreglando la casa. Exprese los mandatos afirmativos y negativos que dan los señores Tamayo.

PARA EXPRESARSE MEJOR
el empapelado *wallpaper*   **podar** *to prune*

EJEMPLO: pintar / Uds. / el cuarto   ¡Pínten**lo**! ¡No **lo** pinten Uds.!

1. sacar / Ud. / los arbustos
   _____

2. instalar / Uds. / el sistema de intercomunicación
   _____

3. podar / Ud. / ese árbol
   _____

4. poner / Ud. / el banco en el patio
   _____

5. cortar / Uds. / todas las flores

_____

6. quitar / Uds. / el empapelado

_____

7. colgar / Ud. / la lámpara

_____

| EJERCICIO G | **Todo hecho.**   Exprese lo que Amelia le dice a su mamá cuando le pregunta si ha hecho ciertas cosas. |

EJEMPLO: ¿Has puesto la mesa?   **Sí, la he puesto.**

1. ¿Han colgado los abrigos tus hermanos?

_____

2. ¿Has arreglado las flores en la mesa?

_____

3. ¿Han quitado Uds. sus cosas de la sala?

_____

4. ¿Ha traído Ricky el postre?

_____

5. ¿Has pasado la aspiradora?

_____

6. ¿Han probado Uds. los bonbones?

_____

b. Indirect-Object Pronouns

1. Indirect objects generally refer to people. The indirect-object pronouns in Spanish are:

SINGULAR	PLURAL
me (to) me	**nos** (to) us
te (to) you (familiar)	**os** (to) you (familiar)
le (to) you (to) him, (to) her	**les** (to) you, (to) them

2. Indirect-object pronouns are joined to the verb by the preposition _a_, which is often expressed for clarity or emphasis.

No le dije nada _a_ **ella.**   _I didn't tell her anything._
No te dije nada _a_ **ti.**   _I didn't tell you anything._

3. Indirect-object pronouns follow the same rules of position as direct-object pronouns.

| No *les* escribí. | I didn't write to them. |

Les **voy a escribir.**
Voy a escribir*les.* } I am going to write to them.

Les **estoy escribiendo.**
Estoy escribiéndo*les.* } I am writing to them

No *les* he escrito.	I haven't written to them.
Escríba*les.*	Write to them.
No *les* escriba.	Don't write to them.

4. To clarify or emphasize indirect-object pronouns, a phrase consisting of *a* + noun or the corresponding stressed pronoun is added to the sentence.

¿Qué le regalaste *a María*?	What did you give María as a gift?
¿Qué le regalaste *a ella*?	What did you give her as a gift?
A mí **me regalaste un disco.**	You gave me a record as a gift.

5. Before an indirect-object pronoun, English *to, for,* and *from* are not expressed in Spanish.

Nos dio el libro.	He gave the book to us.
Nos compró un regalo.	He bought a gift for us.
Nos cobró el dinero.	He collected the money from us.

EJERCICIO H   **Regalos** Adriana habla de los regalos que sus padres dieron durante las fiestas de Navidad. Exprese lo que ella dice.

EJEMPLO: a Nina / regalar aretes de oro   Ellos **le regalaron** aretes de oro.

1. a mis tíos / comprar boletos para el teatro

_____

2. a Tomás / dar un videojuego

_____

3. a mí y a mis hermanos / regalar discos compactos

_____

4. a mis abuelos / mandar un álbum para fotos

_____

5. a la vecina / llevar una planta exótica

_____

6. a ti / dar una bufanda de seda

_____

7. a mí / comprar una suscripción de revista

_____

| **EJERCICIO I** | **La cadena de un chisme** Unos amigos quieren saber cómo todo el mundo se enteró de un chisme falso. Exprese lo que dicen los amigos. |

EJEMPLO: a nosotros / Jaime / contar el chisme   A nosotros Jaime **nos contó** el chisme.

1. a Verónica / nosotros / decir el chisme

   _____

2. a Pablo y a Elena / Verónica / contar el chisme

   _____

3. a ti / Pablo / decir el chisme

   _____

4. a Norma / tú / contar el chisme

   _____

5. a Justino / Norma / decir el chisme

   _____

6. a mí / Justino / contar el chisme

   _____

7. a Jaime / yo / decir el chisme

   _____

| **EJERCICIO J** | **¡Qué niños más malcriados!** Después de una reunión familiar la señora Olivares está muy apenada porque todos los niños se portaron mal en la fiesta. Exprese lo que los niños deben hacer, según ella. |

EJEMPLO: Jorge / mandar flores a los abuelos
          Jorge debe mandar**les** flores. OR Jorge **les** debe mandar flores.

1. Rafael y Marta / enviar una explicación a la tía Anita

   _____

2. Susana / escribir una carta a su primo

   _____

3. tú / hablar por teléfono a los tíos

   _____

4. Carlos / ofrecer una explicación a mí

   _____

5. yo / dar un regaño a mis hijos

   _____

6. Antonio / confesar el por qué de sus acciones a ti

   _____

7. nuestros hijos / pedir una disculpa a nosotros

_____

EJERCICIO K | **Reglas de cortesía** La tía Imelda es experta en las reglas de etiqueta. Exprese lo que ella aconseja hacer en varias circunstancias.

EJEMPLO: Un amigo me da un regalo.
            Déle la gracias.
            _____
            (_dar las gracias al amigo_)

1. ¿Qué debo decir cuando hablo con un amigo enfermo?

_____
            (_decir al amigo que Ud. espera que se mejore pronto_)

2. Yo quiero salir con mis amigos por la noche.

_____
            (_pedir permiso a sus padres_)

3. Hay dos asientos desocupados en el cine pero tenemos que pasar por delante de unas personas para llegar a los asientos.

_____
            (_decir «con permiso» a las personas_)

4. Una amiga mía sufre de alergias y estornuda mucho.

_____
            (_decir «salud» a la amiga_)

5. Un peatón va a atravesar la calle y no ve que viene un carro a toda velocidad.

_____
            (_gritar «cuidado» al peatón_)

6. Me gusta pedirle muchos favores a mis amigos.

_____
            (_decir «por favor» a sus amigos_)

EJERCICIO L | **Advertencias** Termine lo que dice un amigo en estas circunstancias. Use un pronombre indirecto en su respuesta.

EJEMPLO: Yo soy mejor amigo que Alex.
            Pídeme ayuda; no **le** pidas ayuda a Alex.
            (_pedir ayuda a mí / no pedir ayuda a Alex_)

1. Tú acabas de oír un gran secreto.

_____
            (_no contar el secreto a nadie_)

2. Vicente no aprecia los regalos.

_____
            (_no regalar nada a él_)

3. Mis primos no comprenden inglés.

_____
            (_no hablar a ellos en inglés; hablar a ellos en español_)

4. El teléfono está sonando y estoy ocupado.

_____

(contestar el teléfono por mí)

5. Tú vas a ver a Dalia antes que yo.

_____

(dar estas fotos a ella)

6. ¿Quieres mi comentario sobre la carta que escribes?

_____

(mostrar la carta a mí; no esconder la carta a mí)

6. *Gustar* is used with indirect objects or indirect-object pronouns.

   (a) *Gustar* (to please) expresses English *to like.*

Me gustó la película.	*I liked the film.*
Le gustaron los regalos.	*She liked the gifts.*
Nos gustaría hacer otro viaje.	*We would like to make another trip.*

   Gustar is preceded by an indirect-object pronoun. Note that *gustar* agrees with the subject, which generally follows it.

Te gusta *esta canción.*	*You like this song.*
Te gustan *estas canciones.*	*You like these songs.*
Les gustó *el dibujo.*	*They liked the drawing.*
Les gustaron *los dibujos.*	*They liked the drawings.*
Nos gusta *correr.*	*We like to run.*

   NOTE: If the thing liked is not a noun but an "action" (expressed by a verb or clause), *gustar* is used in the third-person singular.

Nos gusta correr y nadar.	*We like to run and swim.*
Me gustaría que llegaras a tiempo.	*I would like you to arrive on time.*

   (b) The following verbs function like *gustar:*

   agradar   *to be pleasing*
   Le agradaron las flores.   *She was pleased with the flowers.*

   bastar   *to be enough, to suffice*
   Me bastan diez dólares.   *Ten dollars are enough for me.*

   convenir   *to suit someone, to be good for someone*
   Te convendrá llevar un paraguas.   *It will be good for you to take an umbrella.*

   doler   *to be painful*
   ¿Te duele la cabeza?   *Does your head ache?*

   encantar   *to love*
   Nos encantan las fiestas.   *We love parties.*

faltar   *to be lacking, to need*
Me faltan **tres dólares.**   *I need three dollars.*

hacer falta   *to need*
Me hace falta **otra pluma.**   *I need another pen.*

importar   *to care about something, to mind*
Les importa **mucho su opinión.**   *They care a lot about his opinion.*

interesar   *to be interested in something*
Nos interesa **mucho el arte**   *We are very interested in*
   moderna.   *modern art.*

parecer   *to seem*
Me parece **que estás triste hoy.**   *It seems to me that you are sad today.*

quedar   *to remain (to someone), to have left*
¿Cuánto dinero *nos queda*?   *How much money do we have left?*

sobrar   *to be left over, to have too much*
Le sobró **mucha comida.**   *She had a lot of food left over.*

tocar   *to be someone's turn*
A ti *te toca* **llamar.**   *It's your turn to call.*

EJERCICIO M   **Gustos** Exprese lo que las siguientes personas dicen de sus gustos y los gustos de otros.

EJEMPLO: a Tina / no gustar / el tiempo frío   A Tina **no le gusta** el tiempo frío.

1. a mí / gustar / pasar mucho tiempo con los amigos

   _____

2. a Uds. / no gustar / gastar mucho dinero

   _____

3. a ti / fascinar / los postres muy dulces

   _____

4. a Rosa / encantar / tomar el sol y nadar

   _____

5. a nosotros / gustar / las obras dramáticas

   _____

6. a ellas / no gustar / el arte moderna

   _____

7. a ti y a mí / no gustar / las flores exóticas

   _____

8. a nadie / gustar / oír las malas noticias

_____

9. a los alumnos / no gustar / los exámenes

_____

10. a Cynthia / fascinar / la ropa fina y cara

_____

EJERCICIO N | **Preguntas** Un grupo de amigos está en una excursión. Conteste las preguntas que se hacen usando las sugerencias entre paréntesis.

EJEMPLO: ¿Qué les agradan más a Uds., las tiendas o los museos?
            Nos agradan más las tiendas.
            (*a nosotros / agradar/ las tiendas*)

1. ¿Cuántas fotos te quedan en la cámara?

_____
                        (*a mí / quedar / uno*)

2. ¿Por qué no ha bajado Luz del autobús en ningún sitio?

_____
                    (*a ella / no interesar / nada*)

3. Franco no se ve bien. ¿Qué tendrá él?

_____
                    (*a él / doler la cabeza*)

4. ¿Qué les pareció el tráfico en la carretera a Uds.?

_____
                (*a nosotros / parecer / muy congestionado*)

5. ¿Les convendrá a Uds. descansar un poco en un café?

_____
                    (*a nosotros / convenir / sí*)

6. ¿Hay bastante tiempo para hacer eso?

_____
                (*sí / a nosotros / sobrar / tiempo*)

7. ¿Quién va a pagar la cuenta?

_____
                    (*a ti / tocar / esta vez*)

8. ¿Podré pedir un postre también?

_____
                (*sí / a mí / no importar lo que pides*)

9. ¿Tendrás que sacar dinero de una caja automática bancaria?

_____
                (*no / a mí / quedar veinte dólares*)

10. ¿Por qué está cojeando Enrique?

_____
                    (*a él / doler / una pierna*)

c. Double-Object Pronouns

1. When a verb has two object pronouns, the indirect-object pronoun (usually a person) precedes the direct-object pronoun (usually a thing).

Rosa *me lo* dijo.	*Rosa told it to me.*
Rosa *te lo* dijo.	*Rosa told it to you.*
Rosa *se lo* dijo.	*Rosa told it to you (him, her, them).*
Rosa *nos lo* dijo.	*Rosa told it to us.*

2. When the third person indirect-object pronoun (*le* or *les*) precedes a third person direct-object pronoun (*lo, la, los, las*), the indirect-object pronoun changes to *se*. The various meaning of *se* may be clarified by adding *a Ud., (Uds.), a él (ellos), a ella (ellas)*.

   Rosa se lo dijo [a ella (a ellas)].

3. Double-object pronouns cannot be separated from each other. The position of double-object pronouns follows the same rules as single-object pronouns. When double-object pronouns are added to an infinitive, gerund (present participle), or affirmative command, an accent mark is always added, even to infinitives and command forms of one syllable.

Deseo decír*telo*.	*I want to tell it to you.*
Pón*telo*.	*Put it on.*
No *se lo* dije.	*I didn't tell it to them.*
Se lo **voy a decir.** / **Voy a decír*selo*.**	*I am going to tell it to them.*
Se lo **estoy diciendo** / **Estoy diciéndo*selo*.**	*I am telling it to them.*
No *se lo* he dicho	*I haven't told it to them.*
Dí*gaselo*.	*Tell it to them.*
No *se lo* diga.	*Don't tell it to them.*

EJERCICIO O | **Fin de vacaciones** La familia Burgos alquiló una casa en la playa donde pasaron las vacaciones. Ahora se preparan a dejar la casa. Exprese lo que deben hacer antes de irse, sustituyendo pronombres en las oraciones.

EJEMPLO: devolver estos platos a los vecinos
Debemos devolvér*selos*.
OR
Se los **debemos devolver.**

1. escribir una carta de gracias a los dueños

2. comprar unos vasos nuevos a los dueños

_____

3. devolver el ventilador a la vecina

_____

4. dar nuestra dirección al agente

_____

5. decir adiós a los nuevos amigos

_____

6. entregar la llave al dueño

_____

7. pedir la devolución del depósito al agente

_____

EJERCICIO P   **Una niña consentida**   La familia de Alicia la consiente mucho y para evitar líos y gritos le da todo lo que pida. Exprese lo que Alicia les dice cuando quiere algo y lo que su familia le responde.

EJEMPLO: Sergio / prestarme / tu monopatín
Sergio, **préstamelo.**
Sí, Alicia, **te lo presto.**

1. Mamá / comprarme / esa muñeca

_____

_____

2. Abuela / ponerme / tu pulsera de oro

_____

_____

3. Papá / regalarme / una bicicleta nueva

_____

_____

4. Diego / servirme / más refresco

_____

_____

5. Tía / prestarme / tu estuche de maquillaje

_____

_____

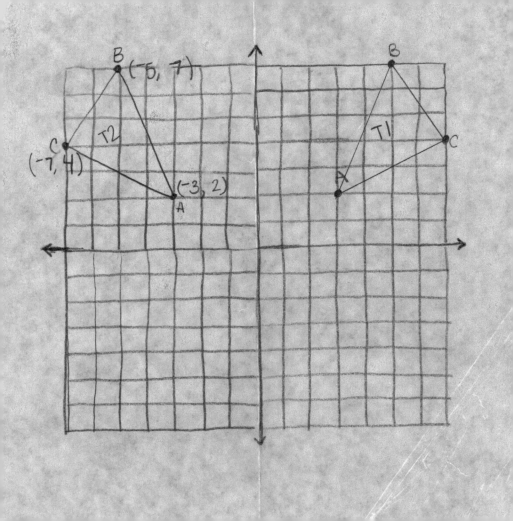

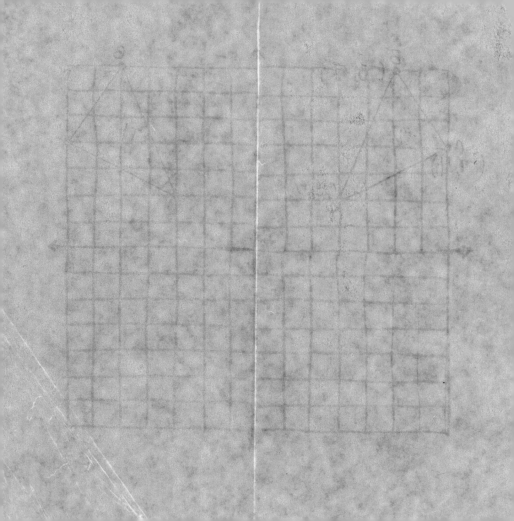

6. Mamá / darme / dulces de chocolate

_____

_____

7. Abuela / contarme / un cuento chistoso

_____

_____

EJERCICIO Q   **Confusión**   Siempre hay mucha confusión en casa de los Cordero porque se cambian de opinión de un momento a otro. Exprese lo que dicen.

EJEMPLO: servirme la sopa
¡Sírve*mela*!   ¡No *me la* sirvas!

1. dar el periódico a tu papá

_____

2. buscarme el teléfono celular

_____

3. traernos las pantuflas

_____

4. prestar la calculadora a tu hermana

_____

5. pedir un favor a tus amigos

_____

6. comprarnos un televisor de pantalla grandísima

_____

7. devolver los discos compactos a tus amigos

_____

3.   Prepositional Pronouns

SINGULAR	PLURAL
mí *me* **ti** *you* (familiar) **él** *him, it* **ella** *her, it* **sí** *yourself, himself, herself, itself*	**nosotros, -as** *us* **vosotros, -as** *you* (familiar) **ellos** *them* (masculine) **ellas** *them* (feminine) **sí** *yourself, themselves*

a. Prepositional pronouns are identical with the subject pronouns, except for *mí*, *ti*, and *sí*. *Mí* and *sí* have a written accent but *ti* does not.

Esto no *es para ti; es para mí.*	*This isn't for you; it's for me.*
El reloj es *de ella.*	*The watch is hers.*

b. The pronouns *mí*, *ti*, and *sí* combine with the preposition *con* (*with*) to form *conmigo* (*with me*), *contigo* (*with you* [familiar]), and *consigo* (*with you* [yourself], *with him*[self], *with her*[self], *with them*[selves]). The forms *conmigo*, *contigo*, and *consigo* do not change in gender and number.

Vamos *contigo.*	*We are going with you.*
No andes *conmigo.*	*Don't walk with me.*
Ella debe estar enojada *consigo.*	*She should be angry with herself.*

c. Common Prepositions

a	*to, at*	**durante**	*during*
acerca de	*about*	**en**	*in, on*
además de	*besides*	**encima de**	*above, on top of*
alrededor de	*around*	**enfrente de**	*in front of, opposite*
ante	*before, in the presence of*	**entre**	*between, among*
antes de	*before*	**frente a**	*in front of*
cerca de	*near*	**fuera de**	*outside of; aside from*
con	*with*	**hacia**	*toward*
contra	*against*	**hasta**	*until*
de	*of, from*	**lejos de**	*far from*
debajo de	*beneath, under*	**para**	*for, in order to*
delante de	*in front of*	**por**	*for, by, through*
dentro de	*within, inside*	**según**	*according to*
desde	*from, since*	**sin**	*without*
después de	*after*	**sobre**	*over, above*
detrás de	*behind*	**tras**	*after*

EJERCICIO R	**¡No quiero!** Ricardo está de mal humor y no quiere hacer lo que su mamá le sugiere. Exprese lo que Ricardo dice al oír sus sugerencias.

EJEMPLO: Cristina y sus amigas van a la piscina.   No quiero ir **con ellas.**

1. Yo voy al centro comercial.

_____

2. Tu papá va al lavacoches.

_____

3. Héctor piensa ir al cine.

_____

4. Después tu papá y yo tenemos que ir a casa de tu tío.

_____

5. Tomás y Nick van al parque.

_____

6. Los papás de José llamaron y van al parque de atracciones.

_____

EJERCICIO S   **Preguntas**   Al volver de un crucero, un amigo le hace preguntas sobre el viaje. Conteste sus preguntas usando el pronombre apropiado.

1. ¿Fuiste en el crucero con tu familia?
   Si, fui al crucero con mi familia

2. ¿Tuviste que pasar todo el tiempo con tus hermanos?
   Si, tuve que pasar todo el tiempo con mi hermano

3. ¿Participaste en las actividades que ofrecían?
   Si participe en las actividades que ofrecían

4. ¿Me vas a contar algo del crucero?
   No, no te voy a contar

5. ¿Estaba tu cabina cerca del comedor?
   No mi cabina no estaba serca del comedor

6. ¿Saliste alguna vez sin tus hermanos?
   Si, sali a la alberca sola

7. ¿Entablaste amistad con otros jóvenes?
   no porque soy muy timida

8. ¿Piensas reunirte con tus compañeros de viaje?

   _____

9. ¿Puedo ir contigo?

   _____

10. ¿Es el capitán quien está detrás de ti en la foto que me enseñó tu hermana?

    _____

11. ¡Tú no sacaste ninguna foto! ¿Siempre viajas sin la cámara?

    _____

12. ¿Compraste regalos para tus amigos?

    _____

EJERCICIO T   **Actividad oral**   Trabajando con un compañero, hablen de una fiesta a la cual Ud. haya asistido. Discutan el propósito de la fiesta, los invitados, las actividades, la comida, etcétera. Usen cuántos pronombres de complemento directo e indirecto que puedan.

EJERCICIO U   **Lectura**   Lea las cartas de unos lectores que aparecieron en una revista y conteste las preguntas.

El buzón de los lectores

> Es la primera vez que les escribo y quiero felicitarlos por su revista. Soy una fiel lectora y me gusta mucho leer todos los artículos interesantes y completos que publican. Por medio de ellos me entero de muchísimas cosas y he aprendido mucho. Les deseo más éxitos de los que ya tienen.

1. Según esta persona, la revista que publican

   (a) presenta temas que le interesan mucho.

   (b) carece de artículos educativos para ella.

   (c) le ofrece poco surtido al lector.

   (d) debe ser más accesible a los lectores.

> Desde hace mucho tiempo estoy suscrita a su revista y me encantan los reportajes que hacen, especialmente sobre las películas. Sin embargo, me gustaría pedirles un favor. Cuando ponen los nombres de las películas, me gustaría que los pusieran en español. Les recuerdo que en algunos casos cuando los traducen o los presentan en inglés, les dan otro nombre. Esto nos puede confundir a nosotros los lectores.

2. ¿Cuál es el propósito de esta carta?

   (a) Aplaudir el buen trabajo que hace la revista

   (b) Quejarse de las demoras en recibir la revista por correo

(c) Ofrecerles una sugerencia para mejorar la calidad de la revista

(d) Pedir más artículos sobre distintos temas

> *Su revista me acompaña desde hace muchos años. Les doy las gracias por hacernos sentir parte de ella. Es una publicación maravillosa y mis amigas y yo siempre la compartimos entre nosotras. Nos fascinan los reportajes, las novelas, las recetas de cocina y más que nada, las entrevistas exclusivas que les hacen a las personas célebres. Pero sí nos hace falta una cosa . . . nos encantaría tener una dirección electrónica o página de Internet donde pudiéramos informarnos de todo lo relacionado con los temas de los artículos o donde encontráramos una galería de fotos de las personas entrevistadas por Uds. Tanto mis amigas como yo les aseguramos que seguiremos comprando su revista y que la continuaremos leyendo en el futuro. Les repito las gracias y las felicitaciones.*

3. ¿Qué busca esta lectora?

   (a) Amigas con quienes puede compartir la revista

   (b) Una manera de comunicarse con las personas famosas

   (c) Una amplificación de la información que provee la revista

   (d) Información sobre la tecnología electrónica

CHAPTER 19
Relative Pronouns

Relative pronouns are used to join two sentences into a single one. The clause introduced by the relative pronoun is the relative clause.

1. QUE

a. *Que* is the most frequently used relative pronoun. *Que* refers to both persons and things. After a preposition, however, *que* refers only to things; *quien(-es)* refers to persons.

	NO PREPOSITION	PREPOSITION
PERSONS	el señor *que* cantó *the man who sang*	el amigo *con quien* estudié *the friend with whom I studied*
THINGS	la revista *que* leo *the magazine that I read*	la pluma *con que* escribo *the pen with which I write*

El señor *que* cantó es mi tío.	*The man who sang is my uncle.*
Este señor, *que* canta bien, es mi tío.	*This man who sings well, is my uncle.*
Las flores *que* acaban de entregar son para ti.	*The flowers that they just delivered, are for you.*
El libro *que* compré es caro.	*The book that I bought is expensive.*
La pluma *con que* escribo no es mía.	*The pen with which I am writing, isn't mine.*

NOTE: 1. The relative pronoun is never omitted in Spanish, as it may be in English.

Los videojuegos *que* buscaba llegarán mañana.	*The video games (that) I was looking for will arrive tomorrow.*

2. In Spanish, a comma is used to set off nonrestrictive relative clauses.

Este restaurante, *que sirve buena comida*, no abre hasta las ocho.	*This restaurant, which serves good food, doesn't open until eight o'clock.*

But:

El restaurante que escogieron está cerrado hoy.	*The restaurant that they chose is closed today.*

3. In Spanish, the preposition always precedes the relative pronoun.

La escuela *a que* asisto tiene una buena reputación.	*The school which I attend has a good reputation.*

EJERCICIO A | **El desfile de modas** Lidia y una amiga asisten a un desfile de modas. Exprese lo que dice Lidia al ver los nuevos diseños.

EJEMPLO: la tela / usar / los diseñadores   Fíjate en la tela **que** usan los diseñadores.

1. los colores / incluir / este diseñador   _____

2. los adornos / poner / la modista   _____

3. el sombrero / llevar / esa modelo   _____

4. los precios / cobrar / los diseñadores   _____

5. los zapatos / usar / aquella modelo   _____

6. el diseño / crear / ese diseñador   _____

7. el vestido largo / llevar / esta modelo   _____

EJERCICIO B | **Claridad** Enrique trabaja de dependiente en un almacén y se molesta cuando los clientes no se expresan con claridad. Exprese lo que los clientes le responden cuando les pide más información.

EJEMPLO: ¿Qué corbata quiere? (*La corbata está encima del mostrador.*)
Quiero la corbata **que** está encima del mostrador.

1. ¿Qué guantes busca Ud.? (*Los guantes son parecidos a éstos.*)

_____

2. ¿Qué bata quiere Ud.? (*El maniquí lleva la bata.*)

_____

3. ¿Qué abrigos busca Ud.? (*Los abrigos fueron anunciados en el periódico.*)

_____

4. ¿Qué camisas quiere Ud.? (*Las camisas están rebajadas de precio.*)

_____

5. ¿Qué botas busca Ud.? (*Las botas son especiales para el alpinismo.*)

_____

EJERCICIO C | **La orquesta escolar** Jeremy muestra una fotografía de la orquesta escolar en que toca y explica quiénes son los otros músicos. Exprese lo que Jeremy dice.

EJEMPLO: los jóvenes / tocar en la orquesta conmigo
Éstos son los jóvenes **que** tocan en la orquesta conmigo.

1. la chica / acompañarme a un baile

_____

2. los chicos / ir a un campamento de música

_____

3. el joven / querer ser conductor de una orquesta

_____

4. la joven / llegar tarde al concierto el año pasado

_____

5. los jóvenes / pensar formar su propio grupo músico

_____

6. la chica / no practicar ni asistir a los ensayos

_____

7. mi amigo / recibir una beca

_____

8. el joven / saber tocar todos los instrumentos

_____

| EJERCICIO D | **Recuerdos del pasado**   José Luis acompaña a su papá en una visita a su pueblo natal. Exprese lo que el padre dice mientras dan un paseo por el pueblo.

EJEMPLO: la escuela primaria / en / aprender a leer
Ésta es la escuela primaria **en que** aprendí a leer.

1. la farmacia / en / trabajar _____

2. el parque / en / jugar al fútbol _____

3. el restaurante / a / ir con tus abuelos _____

4. la escuela / en / estudiar el inglés _____

5. el café / en / reunir con los amigos _____

6. la biblioteca / en / pasar muchas horas _____

7. el cine / a / ir con los amigos _____

2.   QUIEN(-ES)

a. *Quien* and *quienes* can serve as the subject of a relative clause, if that clause is a nonrestrictive clause (set off by commas).

Anoche hablé con el dueño, *quien* me había ofrecido un trabajo.   *Last night I spoke to the owner, who had offered me a job.*

b. *El (la, los, las) que* can be substituted for *quien* or *quienes* when it is used as a subject to express *he (she, those, the one, the ones)* who.

> *Quien* busca, siempre halla. — *He (She) who seeks always finds.*
> *Los que* buscan, siempre hallan. — *Those who seek always find.*

c. When *que* is the direct object of the verb in a relative clause and has an antecedent that is a person, it can be replaced by *a quien;* or *a quienes*, if the antecedent is plural.

> **La mesera (*que*) *a quien* conozco acaba de salir.** — *The waitress whom I know has just left.*
> **Busco a los meseros (*que*) *a quienes* saludé en la puerta.** — *I'm looking for the waiters whom I greeted at the door.*

EJERCICIO E   **Una ceremonia**   Jorge trata de convencer a su abuelo a asistir a una ceremonia de la escuela. Combine las dos frases para expresar lo que Jorge dice.

EJEMPLO: El señor Olmeda es el director de la escuela. Presentará los premios.
El señor Olmeda, **quien** es director de la escuela, presentará los premios.

1. Miguel Andorra ganó muchos premios. Hablará por todos los estudiantes.

   _____

2. Celia Esteves toca bien el piano. Va a acompañar al cantante en el piano.

   _____

3. Aquellos alumnos participan en muchos concursos. Recibirán un aplauso.

   _____

4. Los hermanos Silva saben mucho de computadoras. Explicarán su nuevo programa.

   _____

5. Los padres apoyan mucho a los hijos. Serán reconocidos.

   _____

6. Mi amigo Alberto es el presidente de la clase. Presentará un regalo a la escuela.

   _____

7. Tu nieto es muy listo. Recibirá un premio también.

   _____

EJERCICIO F   **Así es.**   Unos amigos hablan de varias cosas. Combine las dos frases usando *a quien* o *a quienes* para expresar lo que dijeron.

EJEMPLO: El joven me llamó anoche. / Lo conocí en la fiesta de Elena.
El joven, **a quien** conocí en la fiesta de Elena, me llamó anoche.

1. Le presté mi raqueta de tenis a Andrés la semana pasada. / Me la devolvió ayer.

   _____

2. Invité a Luz al baile. / Ella negó la invitación.

   _____

3. Los hermanos Pacheco van mucho al gimnasio. / Tú los viste en la clase de yoga.

_____

4. La amiga de Sonia no me ha dado las gracias. / Yo le compré un refresco.

_____

5. Federico y Adán son los hermanos de Jaime. / Los encontraste en la calle ayer.

_____

6. Mis tíos están en un crucero. / Querías hacerles una pregunta.

_____

7. El señor Aponte cerró su tienda. / Mis padres lo buscaban.

_____

| EJERCICIO G | **Consejos** Exprese lo que el consejero en el campamento les dijo a los muchachos de su grupo. Usen _quien, quienes, el que, la que, los que_ o _las que_. |

EJEMPLO: **Los que** cooperan, tendrán éxito.

1. _____ prestan atención, aprenderán mucho.

2. _____ no es descortés, recibirá el respeto del grupo.

3. _____ se esfuerza, estará contento.

4. _____ participan en las actividades, se divertirán.

5. _____ sigue las reglas, no tendrá ningún problema.

6. _____ piden ayuda, deben dar las gracias.

7. _____ busca un problema, lo encontrará.

3.   Two Antecedents

If there are two antecedents, and there is need for clarification, _quien(-es)_ or _que_ is used to indicate the nearer of the two. The more distant antecedent is indicated by a form of _el (la, los, las) que_ or _el (la, los, las) cual(es)_.

La hermana de Lisa, _que (quien)_ vive en Toledo, tuvo un accidente.	_The sister of Lisa, who lives in Toledo, had an accident._ (Lisa lives in Toledo.)
La hermana de Lisa, _la cual (la que)_ vive en Toledo, llegará mañana.	_Lisa's sister, who lives in Toledo, will arrive tomorrow._

| EJERCICIO H | **Noticias** La señora Martínez acaba de hablar con su hermana en España. Exprese las noticias que recibió. Use la forma apropiada de _el (la, los, las) que_ o _el (la, los, las) cual(-es)_. |

EJEMPLO: La hija de Marisol, **la que (la cual)** estudia medicina, se gradúa en junio.

1. Los hijos de Beto, _____ ahora viven en Burgos, pasarán las vacaciones aquí.

2. La madre de mi esposo, _____ pasa mucho tiempo con nosotros, llegará mañana.

3. El hermano de Gregorio, _____ abrió su propio negocio, tiene mucho éxito.

4. La tía de Aniluz, _____ es muy grande, se cayó en la calle.

5. Todos los nietos de mi suegra, _____ la quieren muchísimo, le hablan a diario.

6. La novia de David, _____ nos fastidia mucho, dijo que se casará con él.

7. Los hijos de la señora Alcocer, _____ estudiaron en el extranjero, se quedarán allí.

4.   Relative Pronouns After Prepositions

a. *El (la, los, las) cual(-es)* and *el (la, los, las) que* are used after all prepositions, regardless of the position of the antecedent.

Abrió la ventana, *por la que (la cual)* entró el aire fresco de primavera.	*He opened the window, through which the fresh spring air entered.*
La oficina *en la que (la cual)* trabajamos es muy moderna.	*The office in which we work is very modern.*

b. *Que* and *quien(es)* may be used after *a, de, en,* and *con.*

Es la mujer *a la que (a quien)* me referí en mi mensaje.	*She is the woman to whom I referred in my message.*
Son los vecinos *con los que (con quienes)* peleo a menudo.	*They are the neighbors with whom I often fight.*
Es el amigo *del que (de quien)* hablo.	*He is the friend about whom I speak.*

EJERCICIO I   **Comentarios** Un grupo de amigos pasa el día en el centro de la ciudad. Exprese lo que ellos dicen usando una cláusula relativa. Sigan el ejemplo.

EJEMPLO: Hay muchos cafés buenos cerca del teatro.

Éste es el teatro cerca **del que (cual)** hay muchos cafés buenos.

1. Hay demasiadas tiendas dentro del centro comercial.

   Éste es el centro comercial _____ .

2. Se estrenan películas buenas en aquel cine.

   Aquél es el cine _____ .

3. Hay una parada de autobuses delante de esta entrada al centro comercial.

   Ésta es la entrada al centro comercial _____ .

4. Nunca salgo de esta tienda sin comprar algo.

   Ésta es la tienda _____ .

5. Mi amigo Rafael trabaja en ese edificio grande.

   Ése es el edificio grande _____ .

6. Hay un nuevo estacionamiento de carros grande al lado de la biblioteca.

   Ésta es la biblioteca _____ .

7. Había muchas tiendas pequeñas alrededor del parque.

   Éste es el parque _____ .

5.   *LO QUE*

a. *Lo que* is equivalent to the English relative pronoun *what* (*that which*).

   Le presté *lo que* me pidió.   *I loaned him (her) what he asked me for.*

b. *Lo que* and *lo cual* are equivalent to English *which* (*a fact that; something that*) if the antecedent is a clause or an idea.

   Juan no fue a la fiesta, *lo cual*   *Juan didn't go to the party, which*
   sorprendió a Luis.   *surprised Luis.*

EJERCICIO J   **Una lección**   Gerardo explica la reacción de sus compañeros de clase cuando el maestro se puso furioso con ellos. Exprese lo que dice.

EJEMPLO: yo / hacer caso de / decir el maestro
           Yo hice caso de **lo que** dijo el maestro.

1. Gloria / no comprender / decir el maestro

   _____

2. yo / escuchar atentamente / decir el maestro

   _____

3. Felipe / pedirme una explicación / decir el maestro

   _____

4. tú / repetir / decir el maestro

   _____

5. nadie / negar / decir el maestro

   _____

EJERCICIO K   **Ideas diferentes**   Exprese lo que cada amigo quiere hacer.

EJEMPLO: ver un partido de fútbol   **Lo que** quiero hacer es ver un partido de fútbol.

1. dormir la siesta _____

2. dar un paseo largo en la playa _____

3. ver una película _____

4. jugar a los naipes _____

5. comprar discos compactos _____

EJERCICIO L   **Observaciones**   A Daniel le gusta pasar el tiempo observando a las personas. Exprese sus comentarios en una sola frase, según el ejemplo.

EJEMPLO: El chofer enfrenó de repente. Esto asustó al peatón.
El chofer enfrenó de repente, **lo cual** asustó al peatón.

1. La niña tomó su primer paso. Esto le agradó a la madre.

   _____

2. Unos muchachos corrían por la calle. Esto les molestó a las personas.

   _____

3. Un niño cogió una hoja que caía del árbol. Esto le dio gusto al niño.

   _____

4. La señora perdió a su perro. Esto entristeció a la señora.

   _____

5. El niño dejó caer el helado. Esto le dio risa a su padre.

   _____

6.   *Cuyo*

Cuyo (-a, -os, -as), meaning *whose*, refers to both persons and things. *Cuyo* is a relative adjective and agrees in number and gender with the thing (or person) possessed, not with the possessor.

Conocí al periodista *cuyos* artículos leímos en la clase.	*I met the journalist whose articles we read in class.*
Éste es el señor *cuya* hija recibió la beca.	*This is the man whose daughter received the scholarship.*

EJERCICIO M   **Presentaciones**   Tomás invitó a varios estudiantes de intercambio a su casa y los presenta a su familia. Complete lo que dice de cada uno con la forma apropiada de *cuyo, cuya, cuyos* o *cuyas*.

1. Les presento a Iván, _____ familia vive en Moscú.

2. Ésta es Noriko, _____ hermanos participaron en los Juegos Olímpicos.

3. Éstos son Pierre y Jeanne, _____ abuelo tiene una granja en el sur de Francia.

4. Quiero que conozcan a Hans, _____ hermana vendrá el año próximo.

5. Linda es la chica _____ perro ganó muchos premios.

6. Luigi es el futbolista _____ equipo ganó en campeonato.

7. Les presento a Samuel, _____ pinturas decoran la escuela ahora.

8. Todavía no ha llegado Pedro _____ ausencia nos hace mucha falta.

CHAPTER 20
Negation; Interrogatives; Exclamations

1. Negation

a. The principal negatives and their opposite affirmatives are:

NEGATIVE	AFFIRMATIVE
no *no, not*	**sí** *yes*
nadie *no one, nobody, (not) anyone*	**alguien** *someone, somebody, anyone*
nada *nothing, (not) anything*	**algo** *something, anything*
nunca / **jamás** *never, (not) ever*	**siempre** *always*
nunca más *never again*	**otra vez** *again*
tampoco *neither, not either*	**también** *also*
ninguno(-a) *no, none, (not) any*	**alguno(-a)** *some, any*
ni, ni siquiera *not even*	**o** *or*
ni... ni *neither . . . nor, not . . . nor*	**o... o** *either . . . or*
sin *without*	**con** *with*
ya no *no longer*	**todavía** *still*

1. *No* is the most common negative. It always precedes the conjugated verb.

   Ella *no* trabaja aquí. *She doesn't work here.*
   ¿*No* trabaja Ud.? *Don't you work?*

2. If an object pronoun or reflexive pronoun precedes the verb, the negative precedes the pronoun.

   Ud. *no* lo ha comprado. *You haven't bought it.*
   Uds. *no* se levantaron temprano. *You didn't get up early.*

3. Spanish sentences may have two or more negatives. If one of the negatives is *no*, it precedes the verb. If *no* is omitted, another negative precedes the verb.

   Yo *no* visito a *nadie* nunca.
   Yo *nunca* visito a *nadie*. } *I never visit anyone.*

   No lo compré *tampoco*.
   Tampoco lo *compré*. } *I didn't buy it either. (Neither did I buy it.)*

   No como *ni* carne *ni* pollo.
   Ni carne *ni* pollo como. } *I eat neither meat nor chicken.*
   (I don't eat either meat or chicken.)

   NOTE: 1. A negative preceded by a preposition keeps that preposition when placed before the verb:

   A *nadie* visito.

2. The negatives *nadie, nada, ninguno, nunca,* and *jamás* are used after comparatives.

Declama la poesía mejor que *nadie*.	*He recites poetry better than anyone.*
Ahora la veo más que *nunca*.	*Now I see her more than ever.*
Quiero una «A» más que *nada*.	*I want an "A" more than anything.*

3. The negatives *nadie, nada, ninguno, nunca,* and *jamás* are used in questions expecting negative answers.

¿Has hablado *jamás* con alguien tan descortés?	*Have you ever spoken to someone so discourteous?*

4. The negatives *nadie, nada, ninguno, nunca,* and *jamás* are used in phrases beginning with *sin* and *antes* (*de* or *que*).

Entró *sin* saludar a *nadie*.	*He entered without greeting anyone.*
***Antes de* decir *nada*, debes escuchar lo que voy a decir.**	*Before saying anything, you should listen to what I am going to say.*
Contestó *antes* que *nadie*.	*She answered before anyone else.*

5. *Ninguno* as an adjective may be replaced by *alguno*. When so used, *alguno* follows the noun, and the negative is more emphatic.

***No* tengo *ningún* dinero.**	*I have no money.*
***No* tengo dinero *alguno*.**	*(I don't have any money.)*

EJERCICIO A   **Preguntas**   Conteste las preguntas que le hace un amigo. Use una expresión negativa en su respuesta.

EJEMPLO: ¿Hablas con alguien?   No, **no** hablo con **nadie**.

1. ¿Viste alguna película anoche?

   _____

2. ¿Le compraste algo a Nick?

   _____

3. ¿Van Uds. a esquiar siempre durante el invierno?

   _____

4. A mí no me gusta el tiempo frío. ¿Y a ti?

   _____

5. ¿Compraste una blusa o un suéter en el almacén?

   _____

6. ¿Todavía trabajas en la biblioteca?

_____

7. ¿Sirvieron algo rico en la fiesta?

_____

8. ¿Conoció Elena a alguien en la fiesta?

_____

9. ¿Alguien te ha llamado a tu nuevo teléfono celular?

_____

10. ¿Vas a salir con ese grupo otra vez?

_____

EJERCICIO B   **Un partido excepcional** Felipe le manda un mensaje electrónico a un amigo sobre un partido de fútbol al que asistió. Complete el mensaje con palabras o expresiones negativas.

_____ (1.) había _____ (2.) en el estadio cuando llegamos. _____ (3.) queríamos llegar tarde y queríamos conducir sin _____ (4.) de tráfico. _____ (5.) había _____ (6.) carros en el estacionamiento y pudimos estacionar el carro cerca de la entrada.

_____ (7.) Jorge _____ (8.) yo habíamos desayunado y buscamos un café, pero _____ (9.) uno estaba abierto en _____ (10.) parte. Jorge _____ (11.) aguanta el hambre y empezamos a caminar para encontrar algún café abierto. Las calles estaban llenas de gente, pero _____ (12.) pudimos pedirle ayuda _____ (13.) . Cuando volvimos al estadio, _____ (14.) había _____ (15.) lugar disponible en el estacionamiento. Me parece que _____ (16.) quería llegar tarde a este partido.

Buscamos nuestros asientos y me di cuenta de que no había _____ (17.) un asiento vacío en el estadio. ¡ _____ (18.) había visto una concurrencia tan grande! El partido fue muy emocionante y _____ (19.) había oído _____ (20.) tantos gritos _____ (21.) tanto apoyo por el equipo favorito. Al hacer un gol, _____ (22.) se quedó sentado. ¡ _____ (23.) los aficionados del otro equipo se quedaron sentados! El equipo favorito jugó mejor que _____ (24.) y ganó el partido. _____ (25.) menos que los jugadores del otro

equipo parecía triste. Durante el viaje de vuelta a la casa —————— pudimos hablar
                                                          26.

de —————— menos que el partido. Es todo por ahora. Hasta luego.
       27.

Tu amigo,

Felipe

| **EJERCICIO C** | **Quejas juveniles** Alicia cuenta las quejas que oye en la guardería de niños donde trabaja. Exprese lo que ella dice. |

EJEMPLO: Roberto / no / dejarme jugar con el camión
Roberto **no** me deja jugar con el camión.

1. yo / no / hacerlo tampoco

_____

2. yo / nunca / poder usar la computadora

_____

3. nadie / querer jugar conmigo

_____

4. yo / nada / tener en el bolsillo

_____

5. yo / nadie / pegarle

_____

6. yo / ya no / prestarles los bloques

_____

7. yo / nada / querer comer

_____

b. Negative Expressions

De nada. Por nada.	You're welcome.
Ellos no van. *Ni yo tampoco.*	They aren't going. Neither am I.
Ya no **viven aquí.**	They no longer live here.
No me queda *más que* **un dólar.**	I have no more than one dollar left.
No me queda *sino* **un dolár.**	I have only one dollar left.
¿Llamaste a Juan? — *Todavía no.*	Did you call Juan? — Not yet.
¿Puedo hablarte? — *Ahora no.*	Can I speak to you? — Not now.
Ni siquiera **me ha saludado.**	She hasn't even greeted me.
¿Cómo te va? — *Sin novedad.*	How's it going? — Nothing new.
¿Me prestas la tarea? — *De ninguna manera.* (**De ningún modo.**)	Will you lend me the assignment? — Certainly not.

Perdimos el último tren; *no hay remedio.*	*We missed the last train; it can't be.*
No cabe duda; **la salud es muy importante.**	*There's no doubt; health is very important.*
No obstante **mis gritos, nadie me ayudó.**	*In spite of my shouts, no one helped me.*
¡*No me digas*!	*You don't say!*

EJERCICIO D   ¿**Qué diría Ud.?**   Exprese lo que Ud. diría en varias circunstancias, usando las palabras a continuación.

de nada	todavía no	ya no
de ninguna manera	ni siquiera	ahora no
no hay remedio	sin novedad	no importa
ni ... tampoco	no ... más que	

EJEMPLO: Pensábamos salir pero unos primos llamaron y llegan en quince minutos.

Uds. responden: **No hay remedio.**

1. Unos compañeros le preguntan: — ¿Cómo te va?

   Ud. responde: _____

2. Su hermano le pide diez dólares prestados, pero Ud. no tiene tanto dinero.

   Ud. le dice: _____

3. Ud. trabaja en una oficina y alguien entra y pregunta por otro empleado, que acaba de salir de la oficina.

   Ud. le dice: _____

4. Ud. hace planes de ir al cine con un amigo, quien le dice que no le gustan las películas de ciencia-ficción.

   Ud. le dice: _____

5. Ud. le dio un regalo a una amiga. Ella le da las gracias.

   Ud. le dice: _____

6. Una amiga la espera a Ud. porque van a un concierto. Ella quiere saber si Ud. está lista.

   Ud. le dice: _____

7. El agua de la piscina está muy fría. Sus amigos quieren que Ud. se meta en la piscina con ellos.

   Ud. les dice: _____

8. Ud. se puso furioso cuando un amigo no le presentó a una amiga suya. Otro amigo quiere saber por qué Ud. está enojado.

   Ud. le dice: _____

9. Uds. perdieron el autobús. Su amigo le dice que ahora tendrán que esperar quince minutos.

   Ud. le dice: _____

10. Al salir de un restaurante, un amigo le pregunta si tiene ganas de ir a la heladería a comer un helado.

   Ud. le dice: _____

    c. *PERO* and *SINO*

Both *pero* and *sino* mean *but*. *Pero* is more general and may also mean *however*; *sino* is used only after a negative statement to express a contrast with the sense of *on the contrary* or *but rather*.

No están en casa ahora, *pero* **llegan pronto.**	*They are not at home now but they will arrive soon.*
Busca trabajo, *pero* **aún no lo encuentra.**	*He is looking for work but he hasn't found it yet.*
No es español, *sino* **portugués.**	*He's not Spanish but Portuguese.*
No compraron cerezas, *sino* **uvas.**	*They didn't buy cherries but grapes.*

NOTE: 1. The comparison is always between two equivalent parts of speech (noun-noun, adjective-adjective, infinitive-infinitive).

No me gusta *correr,* **sino** *patinar.*	*I don't like to run, but (on the contrary) to skate.*
No habló *chino,* **sino** *japonés.*	*She didn't speak Chinese, but Japanese.*

    2. If the contrasting verbs are not infinitives, *sino que* is used.

No compró el reloj, *sino que* **devolvió los aretes.**	*She didn't buy the watch but (on the contrary) returned the earrings.*

EJERCICIO E **De mal en peor** Por alguna razón, no les ha ido bien a unos amigos. Exprese lo que ellos dicen en una sola oración.

EJEMPLO: Víctor prometió llamarme por teléfono. Yo no le di el número.

Víctor prometió llamarme por teléfono, **pero** no le di el número.

1. Me ofrecieron el trabajo. No lo acepté.

   _____

2. Perdí la cartera y me la devolvieron. No contenía el dinero.

   _____

3. Sabía el horario del tren. No fui a la estación correcta.

   _____

4. Les mandé el cheque. No lo recibieron.

   _____

5. Llovió a cántaros. No cerré las ventanas antes de salir.

_____

EJERCICIO F **Definiciones** Claudia trata de mostrar cuánto ha aprendido en la clase de español. Exprese lo que su amiga le dice al oír lo que Claudia dice.

EJEMPLO: Un clavel es un postre.   (_una flor_)   Un clavel no es un postre, **sino** una flor.

1. Una bodega es una clase de barco.   (_una tienda_)

_____

2. Abril es un nombre de un hombre.   (_un mes_)

_____

3. Un bolígrafo es un videojuego.   (_instrumento para escribir_)

_____

4. Un éxito es una salida.   (_un logro_)

_____

5. Una beca es un animal.   (_un premio_)

_____

6. Una carpeta es una alfombra.   (_un portapapeles_)

_____

EJERCICIO G **Una cosa sí, otra no** Exprese lo que la señora Sierra dice que su familia hizo o no hizo.

EJEMPLO: papá / no limpiar el garaje / ver el partido de fútbol
        Papá **no** limpió el garaje **sino que** vio el partido de fútbol.

1. Miguel / no hacer la tarea / ir al cine con los amigos

_____

2. Trini / no pasar la aspiradora / arreglarse las uñas

_____

3. los muchachos / no arreglar el jardín / montar en bicicleta

_____

4. tú / no lavar los platos / sacar todos los juguetes

_____

5. yo / no quedarse en casa / salir con una amiga

_____

6. Uds. / regar las flores / cortarlas

_____

2. Interrogatives

a. Common Interrogative Expressions

¿qué? *what?*

¿quién?, ¿quiénes? *who?*

¿a quiénes?, ¿a quiénes? *whom?, to whom?*

¿de quién?, ¿de quiénes? *whose?, of whom?*

¿con quién?, ¿con quiénes? *with whom?*

¿cuál?, ¿cuáles? *which one(s)?*

¿cuándo? *when?*

¿cuánto (-a)? *how much?*

¿cuántos (-as)? *how many?*

¿cómo? *how*

¿dónde? *where?*

¿adónde? *(to) where?*

¿de dónde? *(from) where?*

¿para qué? *why? (for what purpose?)*

¿por qué? *why? (for what reason?)*

NOTE: All interrogative words have a written accent.

b. In Spanish, questions have an inverted question mark (¿) at the beginning and a standard one (?) at the end.

c. When interrogative words such as *¿qué?*, *¿cuándo?*, and *¿dónde?* are used in a question, the subject–verb order is reversed from the order in statements.

¿Qué **leen ellos?**	*What are they reading?*
Ellos leen revistas.	*They are reading magazines.*
¿Cuándo **sale ella?**	*When does she leave?*
Ella sale a las cinco.	*She leaves at five o'clock.*

d. Both *¿qué?* and *¿cuál?* are equivalent to English *what?* and *which?*, but the two words are not usually interchangeable in Spanish.

1. *¿Qué?* seeks a description, definition, or explanation. It is used instead of *¿cuál?* before a noun.

¿Qué **es esto?**	*What is this?*
¿Qué **sabor te gusta?**	*What flavor do you like?*

2. *¿Cuál?* implies a choice or selection.

¿Cuál **es la fecha de hoy?**	*What is today's date?*
¿Cuáles **son los días de la semana?**	*What are the days of the week?*
¿Cuál **de los sabores te gusta?**	*Which of the flavors do you like?*

e. *¿Adónde?* is used instead of *¿dónde?* to indicate direction with verbs of motion.

¿Adónde van Uds.?   *Where are you going?*

f. *¿Por qué?* and *¿para qué?* are equivalent to English *why? ¿Por qué?* asks about a reason; *¿para qué?* asks about a purpose.

¿Por qué llevas anteojos?   *Why are you wearing eyeglasses?*
Porque los necesito para ver bien.   *Because I need them to see well.*

¿Para qué deseas ir al museo?   *Why do you want to go to the museum?*
Para ver las pinturas de Goya.   *To see Goya's paintings.*

NOTE: 1. *¿Por qué?* is logically used in questions calling for a response with *porque* (because); *¿para qué?* calls for a response with *para*.

2. Interrogative words, whether in direct or indirect questions, have written accents. Indirect questions, however, do not have question marks.

¿Dónde está Andrés?   *Where is Andres?*
No sé *dónde* está.   *I don't know where he is.*

EJERCICIO H   **El entrenamiento** Justino acaba de conseguir trabajo en el departamento de crédito de un banco. Usando las respuestas dadas exprese las preguntas que él debe hacer para establecer la identidad de la persona con quien habla por teléfono.

> ## PARA EXPRESARSE MEJOR
>
> **el apellido de soltera** *maiden name*   **el número de cuenta** *account number*
> **la fecha de nacimiento** *date of birth*   **el seguro social** *Social Security*

1. 8787–265901–0001
   __seguro social__

2. Luis Vega Solera
   __El apeido de soltera__

3. Calle Monterey, 234, Chicago, Illinois
   __Fecha de nacimiento__

4. (630) 561–2384
   _____

5. el 8 de junio de 1978
   __Fecha de nacimiento__

6. 098–27–7342
   __Acount number__

7. Celia Solera Abreu

Apeido de soltera

8. Quiero saber el límite de crédito que tengo en esta cuenta.

_____

| EJERCICIO I | **Preguntas** El alcalde de su ciudad visitó su escuela y Ud. lo entrevistó para el periódico estudiantil. Lea lo que Ud. escribió en el artículo y exprese doce preguntas que Ud. le hizo para obtener esta información.

El señor Antonio Mora es el alcalde de nuestra ciudad. Él nació en esta ciudad hace cuarenta y cinco años. Sus padres nacieron en Puerto Rico, pero se mudaron a esta ciudad cuando eran jóvenes. Asistió a una de las universidades del estado y recibió un doctorado en planificación urbana. Enseñó por varios años en la universidad y llegó a ser el director de la Escuela de Planificación.

Hace tres años se lanzó a la vida política y los ciudadanos lo eligieron alcalde. Su meta principal como alcalde es mejorar el sistema educativo de esta ciudad. El señor Mora vive con su esposa y sus tres hijos en el mismo barrio en que nació. Le interesan la política, la música clásica y el fútbol.

1. _____
2. _____
3. _____
4. _____
5. _____
6. _____
7. _____
8. _____
9. _____
10. _____
11. _____
12. _____

| EJERCICIO J | **Una devolución** Kati trabaja en un almacén y atiende a los clientes que desean devolver algo. Cuando el cliente no presenta el recibo, ella debe hacerle varias preguntas al cliente. Usando las respuestas indicadas, exprese las preguntas que ella hizo.

1. Quiero devolver esta blusa.

_____

2. No tengo el recibo, se me perdió.

_____

3. La compré el sábado pasado.

_____

4. Pagué veinticinco dólares.

_____

5. Es talla mediana.

_____

6. Encontré una mancha en la manga.

_____

7. No quiero un recibo de crédito, prefiero dinero en efectivo.

_____

EJERCICIO K   **Una memoria corta** Jenny nunca recuerda lo que sus amigas le dicen. Exprese las palabras interrogativas que ella usó para obtener la información que no recordaba.

EJEMPLO: **¿Adónde** vas el domingo? ¿Al cine?

1. ¿ _Adónde_ vas? ¿Con Lucy y María?
2. ¿ _Cuándo_ salen Uds. de la casa? ¿A la una?
3. ¿ _Adónde_ van a llegar? ¿En carro?
4. ¿ _Cuál_ es el carro? ¿De tu hermano?
5. ¿ _quién_ va a conducir? ¿Tú o María?
6. ¿ _____ veces has visto esa película? ¿Dos?
7. ¿ _Cómo_ se llama la película?
8. ¿ _El_ cine se estrena? ¿En el del centro comercial?
9. ¿ _Cuánto_ cuestan las entradas?
10. ¿ _Cuándo_ van a cenar? ¿En un restaurante del centro comercial?
11. ¿ _Cuál_ de los restaurantes te gusta más? ¿El mexicano?
12. ¿ _Qué_ hora llegarás a casa? ¿A las ocho?
13. ¿ _Qué_ piensas hacer al llegar a casa? ¿Descansar?
14. ¿ _Qué_ exámenes tienes el lunes? ¿Tres?
15. ¿ _Qué_ estás nerviosa? ¿No tendrás tiempo para estudiar?

EJERCICIO L ¿**Qué o cuál?** Una vez a la semana Emilio ayuda a la maestra del primer año cuando ella les enseña español a los alumnos. Complete las preguntas que él prepara para la clase con *qué, cuál* o *cuáles*.

1. ¿ __Que__ es el primer mes del año?

2. ¿ __Que__ día es hoy?

3. ¿ __cuales__ son las estaciones del año?

4. ¿ __cual__ de las estaciones es la más templada?

5. ¿ __Que__ significa «templada»?

6. ¿ __Que__ haces cuando hace mal tiempo y no puedes salir?

7. ¿ __cual__ es tu videojuego favorito?

8. ¿ __Que__ sueles comer en la cafetería de la escuela?

9. ¿ __cuales__ son los días de la semana más divertidos para Uds.?

10. ¿ __Que__ piensan Uds. hacer después de las clases hoy?

EJERCICIO M **Una invitación** Jaime invitó a Frida a acompañarlo a una fiesta. Exprese las preguntas que Frida le hizo sobre los siguientes detalles:

(a) la fecha de la fiesta
(b) el lugar
(c) la hora
(d) el propósito de la fiesta
(e) la manera de llegar a la fiesta
(f) la clase de ropa que debe llevar
(g) el anfitrión
(h) lo que deben llevar a la fiesta
(i) los otros invitados
(j) la hora a que debe estar lista.

1. _____
2. _____
3. _____
4. _____
5. _____
6. _____
7. _____
8. _____
9. _____
10. _____

EJERCICIO N **Una reservación** Fernando piensa hacer el viaje a Lima, Perú. Llama a la aerolínea para hacer su reservación. Según las respuestas que da Fernando, exprese las preguntas que le hace el agente.

1. Quiero hacer una reservación para viajar.

   _____

2. Es de ida y vuelta. Saldré de Miami con destino a Lima, Perú y regreso a Miami.

   _____

3. Quiero salir para el 1° de julio y regresar para el 25.

   _____

4. Viajan dos personas.

   _____

5. Viajaremos en clase de turista.

   _____

6. Los pasajeros son Fernando Acevedo y Lupe Acevedo.

   _____

7. Es el 305-421-0865.

   _____

8. Le daré el número de mi tarjeta de crédito.

   _____

9. El nombre en la tarjeta es el mío, Fernando Acevedo.

   _____

10. Es todo por ahora. Gracias.

   _____

3. Exclamations

a. Common Exclamatory Words

¡Qué... ! *What . . . !, What a . . . !, How . . . !*
¡*Qué* bonita es!   *How pretty she is!*
¡*Qué* viaje!   *What a trip!*
¡*Qué* cortés es el niño! *How polite the boy is!*

¡Cuánto, -a ...! *How much ...!*
¡*Cuánta* lluvia!   *How much rain!*

¡Cuántos, as ...! *How many ...!*
¡*Cuántos* perros tienen! *How many dogs they have!*

b. Exclamatory words, like interrogative words, have written accents.

¡*Qué* día!	*What a day!*
¡*Cuántos* niños hay aquí!	*How many children are here!*

c. In Spanish, exclamations have an inverted exclamation mark (¡) at the beginning and a standard one (!) at the end.

d. If there is an adjective next to a noun, the exclamation is made more intense by placing *tan* or *más* before the adjective.

¡Qué comida *más* (*tan*) sabrosa!	*What a delicious meal!*

EJERCICIO O **El circo** Al salir del circo, un grupo de niños hablan de lo que vieron allí. Exprese lo que ellos dicen, usando ¡qué…!, ¡cuánto…!, o ¡cuántos…!

> ## PARA EXPRESARSE MEJOR
>
> | | | | |
> |---|---|---|---|
> | **el entrenador** | *trainer* | **el mago** | *magician* |
> | **la foca** | *seal* | **el malabarista** | *juggler* |

EJEMPLO: grande / ser / los elefantes   ¡**Qué grandes son** los elefantes!

1. payasos / cómico _____

2. hábilmente / trabajar / los malabaristas _____

3. valiente / ser / el entrenador _____

4. feroz / parecer / los leones _____

5. foca / inteligente _____

6. fácilmente / brincar / los caballos _____

7. mago / divertido _____

8. agilidad / tener / los tigres _____

EJERCICIO P **Una crítica seria** Los estudiantes de la clase de inglés acaban de leer una novela y ofrecen su crítica personal de ella. Exprese lo que varios estudiantes dicen.

EJEMPLO: La novela tenía muchos personajes.   ¡**Cuántos** personajes!

1. El argumento era exagerado. _____

2. El vocabulario era muy difícil. _____

3. El fin era inesperado. _____

4. Los personajes eran muy auténticos. _____

5. Había demasiadas referencias históricas. _____

6. La acción se desarrollaba muy lentamente. _____

7. Había ideas geniales. _____

EJERCICIO Q   **De acuerdo**   La señora Pérez recibió muchos regalos en la fiesta de cumpleaños. Exprese lo que ella exclama al oír los comentarios de los invitados.

EJEMPLO: Las rosas son muy fragantes.   ¡Sí, **qué** fragantes son las rosas!

1. El sombrero es muy elegante.   _____

2. El abrigo es de un color muy bello.   _____

3. La pulsera es muy delicada.   _____

4. Los dulces son muy deliciosos.   _____

5. Ud. recibió muchos regalos.   _____

6. Esta tarjeta es muy chistosa.   _____

7. La fiesta fue muy alegre.   _____

EJERCICIO R   **Actividad oral**   Trabajando con un compañero, prepare las preguntas que Ud. le hará sobre su experiencia de estudiante de intercambio en Costa Rica el año pasado. Use tantas expresiones interrogativas y palabras negativas como pueda.

EJERCICIO S   **Lectura**   Lea el siguiente anuncio y conteste las preguntas.

QUIERES HACER UN VIAJE QUE DURE CIEN AÑOS?
¿HAS PENSADO ALGUNA VEZ EN CÓMO ERA
LA VIDA DIARIA HACE CIEN AÑOS?

¿Qué estaba de moda?   *¿Cómo se comunicaban?*

¿Qué comía la gente?   *¿Cuáles eran las invenciones más futuristas?*

¿Cómo se vestían las personas?   *¿Dónde pasaban el tiempo libre?*

¿Cuáles eran las diversiones predilectas?

Visita el Museo Nacional para contestar estas preguntas.

Busca las respuestas en la nueva exposición «*Retrospectiva a través de 100 años*»,

que tendrá lugar del 1º de marzo al 30 de noviembre.

El Museo Nacional... dónde puedes comprobar
si cualquier tiempo pasado fue mejor.
Avenida de los Leones, 800

Tel.: 55 98 87 00

Cerrado los lunes

1. ¿Qué se anuncia?

    (a) Una serie de conferencias

    (b) Un festival de películas

    (c) Un estreno de un nuevo salón

    (d) Una exhibición especial

2. ¿Qué esperan lograr por medio del anuncio?

    (a) Aclarar unas dudas históricas

    (b) Mostrar un uso práctico del museo

    (c) Honrar a varios pintores célebres

    (d) Limitar el número de participantes

Appendix

1. Regular Verbs

INFINITIVE	trabajar	comer	subir
PRESENT	trabajo	como	subo
	trabajas	comes	subes
	trabaja	come	sube
	trabajamos	comemos	subimos
	trabajáis	coméis	subís
	trabajan	comen	suben
PRETERIT	trabajé	comí	subí
	trabajaste	comiste	subiste
	trabajó	comió	subió
	trabajamos	comimos	subimos
	trabajasteis	comisteis	subisteis
	trabajaron	comieron	subieron
IMPERFECT	trabajaba	comía	subía
	trabajabas	comías	subías
	trabajaba	comía	subía
	trabajábamos	comíamos	subíamos
	trabajábais	comíais	subíais
	trabajaban	comían	subían
FUTURE	trabajaré	comeré	subiré
	trabajarás	comerás	subirás
	trabajará	comerá	subirá
	trabajaremos	comeremos	subiremos
	trabajaréis	comeréis	subiréis
	trabajarán	comerán	subirán
CONDITIONAL	trabajaría	comería	subiría
	trabajarías	comerías	subirías
	trabajaría	comería	subiría
	trabajaríamos	comeríamos	subiríamos
	trabajaríais	comeríais	subiríais
	trabajarían	comerían	subirían

COMMANDS (IMPERATIVE)	trabaja / no trabajes } (tú)	come / no comas } (tú)	sube / no subas } (tú)
	trabajad / no trabajéis } (vosotros)	comed / no comáis } (vosotros)	subid / no subáis } (vosotros)
	trabaje (Ud.)	corra (Ud.)	suba (Ud.)
	trabajemos (nosotros)	corramos (nosotros)	subamos (nosotros)
	trabajen (Uds.)	corran (Uds.)	suban (Uds.)
PRESENT SUBJUNCTIVE	trabaje	coma	suba
	trabajes	comas	subas
	trabaje	coma	suba
	trabajemos	comamos	subamos
	trabajéis	comáis	subáis
	trabajen	coman	suban
IMPERFECT SUBJUNCTIVE			
(-RA FORM)	trabajara	comiera	subiera
	trabajaras	comieras	subieras
	trabajara	comiera	subiera
	trabajáramos	comiéramos	subiéramos
	trabajarais	comierais	subierais
	trabajaran	comieran	subieran
(-SE FORM)	trabajase	comiese	subiese
	trabajases	comieses	subieses
	trabajase	comiese	subiese
	trabajásemos	comiésemos	subiésemos
	trabajaseis	comieseis	subieseis
	trabajasen	comiesen	subiesen
PRESENT PERFECT INDICATIVE	he / has / ha / hemos / habéis / han } trabajado / comido / subido		
PLUPERFECT INDICATIVE	había / habías / había / habíamos / habíais / habían } trabajado / comido / subido		

FUTURE PERFECT	habré habrás habrá habremos habreís habrán	trabajado / comido / subido
CONDITIONAL PERFECT	habría habrías habría habríamos habríais habrían	trabajado / comido / subido
PRESENT PERFECT SUBJUNCTIVE	haya hayas haya hayamos hayáis hayan	trabajado / comido / subido
PLUPERFECT SUBJUNCTIVE		
(-RA FORM)	hubiera hubieras hubiera hubiéramos hubierais hubieran	trabajado / comido / subido
(-SE FORM)	hubiese hubieses hubiese hubiésemos hubieseis hubiesen	trabajado / comido / subido

2. Stem-Changing Verbs

a. -AR Verbs

INFINITIVE	pensar (e to ie)	mostrar (o to ue)	jugar (u to ue)

PRESENT	pienso	muestro	juego
	piensas	muestras	juegas
	piensa	muestra	juega
	pensamos	mostramos	jugamos
	pensáis	mostráis	jugáis
	piensan	muestran	juegan
PRESENT SUBJUNCTIVE	piense	muestre	juegue
	pienses	muestres	juegues
	piense	muestre	juegue
	pensemos	mostremos	juguemos
	penséis	mostréis	juguéis
	piensen	muestren	jueguen

b. *-ER* Verbs

INFINITIVE	perd**er** (**e** to **ie**)	volv**er** (**o** to **ue**)
PRESENT	pierdo	vuelvo
	pierdes	vuelves
	pierde	vuelve
	perdemos	volvemos
	perdéis	volvéis
	pierden	vuelven
PRESENT SUBJUNCTIVE	pierda	vuelva
	pierdas	vuelvas
	pierda	vuelva
	perdamos	volvamos
	perdáis	volváis
	pierdan	vuelvan

c. *-IR* Verbs

INFINITIVE	ped**ir** (**e** to **i, i**)	sent**ir** (**e** to **ie, i**)	dorm**ir** (**o** to **ue, u**)
PRESENT	pido	siento	duermo
	pides	sientes	duermes
	pide	siente	duerme
	pedimos	sentimos	dormimos
	pedís	sentís	dormís
	piden	sienten	duermen

PRETERIT	pedí	sentí	dormí
	pediste	sentiste	dormiste
	pidió	sintió	durmió
	pedimos	sentimos	dormimos
	pedisteis	sentisteis	dormisteis
	pidieron	sintieron	durmieron
PRESENT SUBJUNCTIVE	pida	sienta	duerma
	pidas	sientas	duermas
	pida	sienta	duerma
	pidamos	sintamos	durmamos
	pidáis	sintáis	durmáis
	pidan	sientan	duerman
IMPERFECT SUBJUNCTIVE			
(-*RA* FORM)	pidiera	sintiera	durmiera
	pidieras	sintieras	durmieras
	pidiera	sintiera	durmiera
	pidiéramos	sintiéramos	durmiéramos
	pidierais	sintierais	durmierais
	pidieran	sintieran	durmieran
(-*SE* FORM)	pidiese	sintiese	durmiese
	pidieses	sintieses	durmieses
	pidiese	sintiese	durmiese
	pidiésemos	sintiésemos	durmiésemos
	pidieseis	sintieseis	durmieseis
	pidiesen	sintiesen	durmiesen
COMMANDS	pide / no pidas } (tú)	siente / no sientas } (tú)	duerme / no duermas } (tú)
	pida (Ud.)	sienta (Ud.)	duerma (Ud.)
	pidamos (nosotros)	sintamos (nosotros)	durmamos (nosotros)
	pedid / no pidáis } (vosotros)	sentid / no sintáis } (vosotros)	dormid / no durmáis } (vosotros)
	pidan (Uds.)	sientan (Uds.)	duerman (Uds.)

3. Spelling-Changing Verbs

a. Verbs Ending in -*CER* and -*CIR*

INFINITIVE	ofrecer (c to zc)	conducir (c to zc)	convencer (c to z)

PRESENT	ofrezco	conduzco	convenzo
	ofreces	conduces	convences
	ofrece	conduce	convence
	ofrecemos	conducimos	convencemos
	ofrecéis	conducís	convencéis
	ofrecen	conducen	convencen
PRESENT SUBJUNC- TIVE	ofrezca	conduzca	convenza
	ofrezcas	conduzcas	convenzas
	ofrezca	conduzca	convenza
	ofrezcamos	conduzcamos	convenzamos
	ofrezcáis	conduzcáis	convenzáis
	ofrezcan	conduzcan	convenzan
COMMANDS	ofrece / no ofrezcas } (tú)	conduce / no conduzcas } (tú)	convence / no convenzas } (tú)
	ofrezca (Ud.)	conduzca (Ud.)	convenza (Ud.)
	ofrezcamos (nosotros)	conduzcamos (nosotros)	convenzamos (nosotros)
	ofreced / no ofrezcáis } (vosotros)	conducid / no conduzcáis } (vosotros)	convenced / no convenzáis } (vosotros)
	ofrezcan (Uds.)	conduzcan (Uds.)	convenzan (Uds.)

b. Verbs That Change *í* to *Y*

INFINITIVE	**leer**	**caer**	**oír**	**incluir**
PRETERIT	leí	caí	oí	incluí
	leíste	caíste	oíste	incluíste
	leyó	cayó	oyó	incluyó
	leímos	caímos	oímos	incluímos
	leísteis	caísteis	oísteis	incluísteis
	leyeron	cayeron	oyeron	incluyeron
IMPERFECT SUBJUNCTIVE				
(-*RA* FORM)	leyera	cayera	oyera	incluyera
	leyeras	cayeras	oyeras	incluyeras
	leyera	cayera	oyera	incluyera
	leyéramos	cayéramos	oyéramos	incluyéramos
	leyerais	cayerais	oyerais	incluyerais
	leyeran	cayeran	oyeran	incluyeran

(*-SE* FORM)	leyese	cayese	oyese	incluyese
	leyeses	cayeses	oyeses	incluyeses
	leyese	cayese	oyese	incluyese
	leyésemos	cayésemos	oyésemos	incluyésemos
	leyeseis	cayeseis	oyeseis	incluyeseis
	leyesen	cayesen	oyesen	incluyesen
PAST PARTICIPLE	leído	caído	oído	incluído
GERUNDIO	leyendo	cayendo	oyendo	incluyendo

c. Verbs Ending in *-GER* or *-GIR*

INFINITIVE	cog**er**	dirig**ir**	
PRESENT INDICATIVE	cojo	dirijo	
	coges	diriges	
	coge	dirige	
	cogemos	dirigimos	
	cogéis	dirigís	
	cogen	dirigen	
PRESENT SUBJUNCTIVE	coja	dirija	
	cojas	dirijas	
	coja	dirija	
	cojamos	dirijamos	
	cojáis	dirijáis	
	cojan	dirijan	

d. Verbs Ending in *-GUIR*

INFINITIVE	distin**guir**	
PRESENT INDICATIVE	distingo	
	distingues	
	distingue	
	distinguimos	
	distinguís	
	distinguen	

PRESENT SUBJUNCTIVE	distinga distingas distinga distingamos distingáis distingan	

e. Verbs Ending in -*CAR*, -*GAR*, and -*ZAR*

INFINITIVE	sacar (c to qu)		pagar (g to gu)		gozar (z to c)
PRETERIT	saqué		pagué		gocé
	sacaste	pagaste		gozaste	
	sacó pagó	gozó			
	sacamos	pagamos		gozamos	
	sacasteis	pagasteis		gozasteis	
	sacaron	pagaron		gozaron	
SUBJUNCTIVE	saque		pague		goce
	saques	pagues goces			
	saque pague	goce			
	saquemos	paguemos		gocemos	
	saquéis	paguéis		gocéis	
	saquen	paguen		gocen	

4. Irregular Verbs

NOTE: Only the tenses containing irregular forms are given.

INFINITIVE	andar
PRETERIT	anduve, anduviste, anduvo, anduvimos, anduvisteis, anduvieron
IMPERFECT SUBJUNCTIVE	
(-*RA* FORM)	anduviera, anduvieras, anduviera, anduviéramos, anduvierais, anduvieran
(-*SE* FORM)	anduviese, anduvieses, anduviese, anduviésemos, anduvieseis, anduviesen

INFINITIVE	caber
PRESENT	**quep**o, cabes, cabe, cabemos, cabéis, caben
PRETERIT	**cupe**, **cup**iste, **cup**o, **cup**imos, **cup**isteis, **cup**ieron
FUTURE	cabré, cabrás, cabrá, cabremos, cabréis, cabrán
CONDITIONAL	cabría, cabrías, cabría, cabríamos, cabríais, cabrán
PRESENT SUBJUNCTIVE	**quep**a, **quep**as, **quep**a, **quep**amos, **quep**áis, **quep**an
IMPERFECT SUBJUNCTIVE	
(-RA FORM)	**cup**iera, **cup**ieras, **cup**iera, **cup**iéramos, **cup**ierais, **cup**ieran
(-SE FORM)	**cup**iese, **cup**ieses, **cup**iese, **cup**iésemos, **cup**ieseis, **cup**iesen

INFINITIVE	caer
PRESENT	caigo, caes, cae, caemos, caéis, caen
PRETERIT	caí, caíste, cayó, caímos, caísteis, cayeron
PRESENT SUBJUNCTIVE	caiga, caigas, caiga, caigamos, caigáis, caigan
IMPERFECT SUBJUNCTIVE	
(-RA FORM)	cayera, cayeras, cayera, cayéramos, cayerais, cayera
(-SE FORM)	cayese, cayeses, cayese. cayésemos, cayeseis, cayesen
PAST PARTICIPLE	caído
GERUND	cayendo

INFINITIVE	dar
PRESENT	doy, das, da, damos, dais, dan
PRETERIT	di, diste, dio, dimos, disteis, dieron
PRESENT SUBJUNCTIVE	dé, des, dé, demos, deis, den
IMPERFECT SUBJUNCTIVE	
(-RA FORM)	diera, dieras, diera, diéramos, dierais, dieran
(-SE FORM)	diese, dieses, diese, diésemos, dieseis, diesen

INFINITIVE	decir
PRESENT	digo, dices, dice, decimos, decís, dicen
PRETERIT	dije, dijiste, dijo, dijimos, dijisteis, dijeron
FUTURE	diré, dirás, dirá, diremos, diréis, dirán
CONDITIONAL	diría, dirías, diría, diríamos, diríais, dirían
PRESENT SUBJUNCTIVE	diga, digas, diga. digamos, digáis, digan
IMPERFECT SUBJUNCTIVE	
(-RA FORM)	dijera, dijeras, dijera, dijéramos, dijerais, dijeran
(-SE FORM)	dijese, dijeses, dijese, dijésemos, dijeseis, dijesen
COMMAND	di (tú), diga (Ud.), digan (Uds.), digamos (nosotros)
PAST PARTICIPLE	dicho
GERUND	diciendo

INFINITIVE	estar
PRESENT	estoy, estás, está, estamos, estáis, están
PRETERIT	estuve, estuviste, estuvo, estuvimos, estuvisteis, estuvieron
PRESENT SUBJUNCTIVE	esté, estés, esté, estemos, estéis, estén
IMPERFECT SUBJUNCTIVE	
(-RA FORM)	estuviera, estuvieras, estuviera, estuviéramos, estuvierais, estuvieran
(-SE FORM)	estuviese, estuvieses, estuviese, estuviésemos, estuvieseis, estuviesen

INFINITIVE	haber
PRESENT	he, has, ha, hemos, habéis, han
PRETERIT	hube, hubiste, hubo, hubimos, hubisteis, hubieron
FUTURE	habré, habrás, habrá, habremos, habréis, habrán
CONDITIONAL	habría, habrías, habría, habríamos, habríais, habrían
PRESENT SUBJUNCTIVE	haya, hayas, haya, hayamos, hayáis, hayan
IMPERFECT SUBJUNCTIVE	
(-RA FORM)	hubiera, hubieras, hubiera, hubiéramos, hubierais, hubieran
(-SE FORM)	hubiese, hubieses, hubiese, hubiésemos, hubieseis, hubiesen

INFINITIVE	hac**er**
PRESENT	ha**go**, haces, hace, hacemos, hacéis, hacen
PRETERIT	hice, hiciste, hizo, hicimos, hicisteis, hicieron
FUTURE	haré, harás, hará, haremos, haréis, harán
CONDITIONAL	haría, harías, haría, haríamos, haríais, harían
PRESENT SUBJUNCTIVE	ha**ga**, ha**ga**s, ha**ga**, ha**ga**mos, ha**gá**is, ha**ga**n
IMPERFECT SUBJUNCTIVE	
(-*RA* FORM)	hic**ie**ra, hic**ie**ras, hic**ie**ra, hic**ié**ramos, hic**ie**rais, hic**ie**ran
(-*SE* FORM)	hic**ie**se, hic**ie**ses, hic**ie**se, hic**ié**semos, hic**ie**seis, hic**ie**sen
COMMAND	haz (tú), ha**ga** (Ud.), ha**ga**n (Uds.), ha**ga**mos (nosotros)
GERUND	he**cho**

INFINITIVE	**ir**
PRESENT	**voy, vas, va, vamos, vais, van**
IMPERFECT	**ib**a, **ib**as, **ib**a, **íb**amos, **ib**ais, **ib**an
PRETERIT	**fui, fuiste, fue, fuimos, fuisteis, fueron**
PRESENT SUBJUNCTIVE	**vay**a, **vay**as, **vay**a, **vay**amos, **vay**áis, **vay**an
IMPERFECT SUBJUNCTIVE	
(-*RA* FORM)	**fue**ra, **fue**ras, **fue**ra, **fué**ramos, **fue**rais, **fue**ran
(-*SE* FORM)	**fue**se, **fue**ses, **fue**se, **fué**semos, **fue**seis, **fue**sen
COMMAND	**ve** (tú), **vay**a (Ud.), **vay**an (Uds.), **vay**amos (nosotros)
GERUND	**y**endo

INFINITIVE	o**í**r
PRESENT	oi**go**, oyes, oye, oímos, oís, oyen
PRETERIT	oí, oíste, oyó, oímos, oísteis, oyeron
PRESENT SUBJUNCTIVE	oi**ga**, oi**ga**s, oi**ga**, oi**ga**mos, oi**gá**is, oi**ga**n
IMPERFECT SUBJUNCTIVE	
(-*RA* FORM)	oyera, oyeras, oyera, oyéramos, oyerais, oyera
(-*SE* FORM)	oyese, oyeses, oyese. oyésemos, oyeseis, oyesen
COMMAND	oye (tú), oi**ga** Ud., oi**ga**n Uds., oi**ga**mos (nosotros)
PAST PARTICIPLE	oído
GERUND	oyendo

INFINITIVE	poder
PRESENT	puedo, puedes, puede, podemos, podéis, pueden
PRETERIT	pude, pudiste, pudo, pudimos, pudisteis, pudieron
FUTURE	podré, podrás, podrá, podremos, podréis, podrán
CONDITIONAL	podría, podrías, podría, podríamos, podríais, podrían
IMPERFECT SUBJUNCTIVE	
(-RA FORM)	pudiera, pudieras, pudiera, pudiéramos, pudierais, pudieran
(-SE FORM)	pudiese, pudieses, pudiese, pudiésemos, pudieseis, pudiesen
GERUND	pudiendo

INFINITIVE	poner
PRESENT	pongo, pones, pone, ponemos, ponéis, ponen
PRETERIT	puse, pusiste, puso, pusimos, pusisteis, pusieron
FUTURE	pondré, pondrás, pondrá, pondremos, pondréis, pondrán
CONDITIONAL	pondría, pondrías, pondría, pondríamos, pondríais, pondrían
PRESENT SUBJUNCTIVE	ponga, pongas, ponga, pongamos, pongáis, pongan
IMPERFECT SUBJUNCTIVE	
(-RA FORM)	pusiera, pusieras, pusiera, pusiéramos, pusierais, pusieran
(-SE FORM)	pusiese, pusieses, pusiese, pusiésemos, pusieseis, pusiesen
COMMAND	pon (tú), ponga (Ud.), pongan (Uds.), pongamos (nosotros)
PAST PARTICIPLE	puesto

INFINITIVE	querer
PRESENT	quiero, quieres, quiere, queremos, queréis, quieren
PRETERIT	quise, quisiste, quiso, quisimos, quisisteis, quisieron
FUTURE	querré, querrás, querré, querremos, querréis, querrán
CONDITIONAL	querría, querrías, querría, querríamos, querríais, querrían
PRESENT SUBJUNCTIVE	quiera, quieras, quiera, queramos, queráis, quieran
IMPERFECT SUBJUNCTIVE	
(-RA FORM)	quisiera, quisieras, quisiera, quisiéramos, quisierais, quisieran
(-SE FORM)	quisiese, quisieses, quisiese, quisiésemos, quisieseis, quisiesen

INFINITIVE	saber
PRESENT	**sé**, sabes, sabe, sabemos, sabéis, saben
PRETERIT	**supe**, **supiste**, **supo**, **supimos**, **supisteis**, **supieron**
FUTURE	sa**bré**, sa**brás**, sa**brá**, sa**bremos**, sa**bréis**, sa**brán**
CONDITIONAL	sa**bría**, sa**brías**, sa**bría**, sa**bríamos**, sa**bríais**, sa**brían**
PRESENT SUBJUNCTIVE	**sepa**, **sepas**, **sepa**, **sepamos**, **sepáis**, **sepan**
IMPERFECT SUBJUNCTIVE	
(-*RA* FORM)	**supiera**, **supieras**, **supiera**, **supiéramos**, **supierais**, **supieran**
(-*SE* FORM)	**supiese**, **supieses**, **supiese**, **supiésemos**, **supieseis**, **supiesen**
COMMAND	sabe (tú), **sepa** (Ud.), **sepan** (Uds.), **sepamos** (nosotros)

INFINITIVE	sal**ir**
PRESENT	sal**go**, sales, sale, salimos, salís, salen
FUTURE	sal**dré**, sal**drás**, sal**drá**, sal**dremos**, sal**dréis**, sal**drán**
CONDITIONAL	sal**dría**, sal**drías**, sal**dría**, sal**dríamos**, sal**dríais**, sal**drían**
PRESENT SUBJUNCTIVE	sal**ga**, sal**gas**, sal**ga**, sal**gamos**, sal**gáis**, sal**gan**
COMMAND	**sal** (tú), sal**ga** (Ud.), sal**gan** (Uds.), sal**gamos** (nosotros)

INFINITIVE	se**r**
PRESENT	**soy**, **eres**, **es**, **somos**, **sois**, **son**
IMPERFECT	**era**, **eras**, **era**, **éramos**, **erais**, **eran**
PRETERIT	**fui**, **fuiste**, **fue**, **fuimos**, **fuisteis**, **fueron**
PRESENT SUBJUNCTIVE	sea, seas, sea, seamos, seáis, sean
IMPERFECT SUBJUNCTIVE	
(-*RA* FORM)	**fuera**, **fueras**, **fuera**, **fuéramos**, **fuerais**, **fuera**
(-*SE* FORM)	**fuese**, **fueses**, **fuese**. **fuésemos**, **fueseis**, **fuesen**
COMMAND	**sé** (tú), **sea** (Ud.), **sean** (Uds.), **seamos** (nosotros)

INFINITIVE	tener
PRESENT	tengo, tienes, tiene, tenemos, tenéis, tienen
PRETERIT	tuve, tuviste, tuvo, tuvimos, tuvisteis, tuvieron
FUTURE	tendré, tendrás, tendrá, tendremos, tendréis, tendrán
CONDITIONAL	tendría, tendrías, tendría, tendríamos, tendríais, tendrían
PRESENT SUBJUNCTIVE	tenga, tengas, tenga, tengamos, tengáis, tengan
IMPERFECT SUBJUNCTIVE	
(-RA FORM)	tuviera, tuvieras, tuviera, tuviéramos, tuvierais, tuvieran
(-SE FORM)	tuviese, tuvieses, tuviese, tuviésemos, tuvieseis, tuviesen
COMMAND	ten (tú), tenga (Ud.), tengan (Uds.), tengamos (nosotros)

INFINITIVE	traer
PRESENT	traigo, traes, trae, traemos, traéis, traen
PRETERIT	traje, trajiste, trajo, trajimos, trajisteis, trajeron
PRESENT SUBJUNCTIVE	traiga, traigas, traiga, traigamos, traigáis, traigan
IMPERFECT SUBJUNCTIVE	
(-RA FORM)	trajera, trajeras, trajera, trajéramos, trajerais, trajeran
(-SE FORM)	trajese, trajeses, trajese, trajésemos, trajeseis, trajesen
PAST PARTICIPLE	traído
COMMAND	trae (tú), traiga (Ud.), traigan (Uds.), traigamos (nosotros)
GERUND	trayendo

INFINITIVE	valer
PRESENT	valgo, vales, vale, valemos, valéis, valen
FUTURE	valdré, valdrás, valdrá, valdremos, valdréis, valdrán
CONDITIONAL	valdría, valdrías, valdría, valdríamos, valdríais, valdrían
PRESENT SUBJUNCTIVE	valga, valgas, valga, valgamos, valgáis, valgan

INFINITIVE	venir
PRESENT	vengo, vienes, viene, venimos, venís, vienen

PRETERIT	vine, viniste, vino, vinimos, vinisteis, vinieron
FUTURE	vendré, vendrás, vendrá, vendremos, vendréis, vendrán
CONDITIONAL	vendría, vendrías, vendría, vendríamos, vendríais, vendrían
PRESENT SUBJUNCTIVE	venga, vengas, venga, vengamos, vengáis, vengan
IMPERFECT SUBJUNCTIVE	
(-RA FORM)	viniera, vinieras, viniera, viniéramos, vinierais, vinieran
(-SE FORM)	viniese, vinieses, viniese, viniésemos, vinieseis, viniesen
COMMAND	ven (tú), venga (Ud.), vengan (Uds.), vengamos (nosotros)
GERUND	viniendo

INFINITIVE	ver
PRESENT	veo, ves, ve, vemos, veis, ven
IMPERFECT	veía, veías, veía, veíamos, veíais, veían
PRESENT SUBJUNCTIVE	vea, veas, vea, veamos, veáis, vean
PAST PARTICIPLE	visto
COMMAND	ve (tú), vea (Ud.), vean (Uds.), veamos (nosotros)

5.   Punctuation

Although Spanish punctuation is similar to English, it has the following major differences:

a. In Spanish, questions have an inverted question mark (¿) at the beginning and a normal one at the end.

¿Quién es?　　*Who is it?*

b. In Spanish, exclamatory sentences have an inverted exclamation point (¡) at the beginning and a normal one at the end.

¡Qué día!　　*What a day!*

c. The comma is not used before *y, e, o, u,* or *ni* in a series.

El lunes, el martes y el miércoles　　*There are classes on Monday,*
**　hay clases.**　　*Tuesday, and Wednesday.*

d. In Spanish, decimals uses a comma where English uses a period.

3,5 (tres coma cinco)　　*3.5 (three point five)*

e. In Spanish, quotation marks precede the comma or period.

Cervantes escribió «El Quijote».   *Cervantes wrote "The Quijote."*
«No me dejes aquí», dijo Pedro.   *"Don't leave me here," said Pedro.*

6. Syllabication

In Spanish, words are generally divided according to units of sound.

a. A syllable normally begins with a consonant. The division is made before the consonant.

va / **l**er   ca / **mi** / sa   a / **me** / **ri** / **ca** / **no**   re / **fe** / **rir**

b. *Ch, ll,* and *rr* are never divided.

pe / **rr**o   ha / **ll**a / do   di / **ch**o

c. If two or more consonants are combined, the division is made before the last consonant, except in the combinations *bl, br, cl, cr, pl, pr,* and *tr.*

trans / por / te   des / cu / bier / to   con / ti / nuar   al / ber / ca
But:

ha/**bl**ar   cu/**br**ir   es/**cr**i/bir   a/**pr**en/der   dis/**tr**i/buir

d. Compound words, including words with prefixes and suffixes, may be divided by components or by syllables.

sur / a / me / ri / ca / no   *OR*   su / ra / me / ri / ca / no
mal / es / tar   *OR*   ma / les / tar

7. Pronunciation

Word stress follows three general rules:

a. If the word ends in a vowel or *n* or *s,* the next-to-last syllable is stressed.

es / **cue** / la   de/**sas**/tre   **jo**/ven   se/**ño**/res

b. If the word ends in a consonant, except *n* or *s,* the final syllable is stressed.

com/pren/**der**   a/la/**bar**   re/ci/**bir**   se/**ñor**

c. All exceptions to the above have a written accent mark.

sá/ba/do   **jó**/ve/nes   A/**dán**   **Cé**/sar   fran/**cés**

Spanish-English Vocabulary

The Spanish-English Vocabulary is intended to be complete for the context of this book.

Nouns are listed in the singular. Regular feminine forms of nouns are indicated by **(-a)** or the ending that replaces the masculine ending: **amigo(-a)** or **consejero(-era)**. Irregular feminine forms of nouns are given in full: **héroe** *m.* hero (*f.* **heroína** heroine). Regular feminine forms of adjectives are indicated by **-a**.

ABBREVIATIONS

adj.	adjective	*irr.*	irregular
aux.	auxiliary verb	*m.*	masculine
f.	feminine	*pl.*	plural
inf.	infinitive	*sing.*	singular

a to, at; **a eso de** about (time); **a menudo** often
abogado(-a) lawyer
abordar to board
abrazar (c) to embrace, to hug
abrelatas *m. sing & pl.* can opener
abrir to open
abrocharse to fasten
abuela *f.* grandmother
abuelo *m.* grandfather; *pl.* grandfathers, grandparents
aburrir to bore; **aburrirse** to become bored
acabar to finish, to end; **acabar de** to have just
acampar to camp
acceder to agree
acerca de about
acercarse (qu) to approach
acertar (ie) to be on target, to guess right
aclarar to clear, to explain
acomodar to place
acompañar to accompany
aconsejar to advise
acontecimiento *m.* event

acordarse (ue) (de) to remember
acostar(se) (ue) to put to bed; to go to bed
actividad *f.* activity
actuar (ú) to act
acudir to go to
acuerdo *m.* agreement; **estar de acuerdo** to agree
además besides
adivinanza *f.* riddle
admirar to admire
adorno *m.* decoration
adquirir to acquire
aduana *f.* customs
advertencia *f.* warning
advertir (ie, i) to notify, warn
aerolínea *f.* airline
aeropuerto *m.* airport
afán *m.* eagerness
afectar to affect
afeitarse to shave
aficionado, -a fan
afligir (j) to afflict, grieve
agenda *f.* calendar, appointment book
agilidad *f.* agility

agotar to exhaust, use up
agradar to please, to like
agradecer (zc) to thank
agradecimiento *m.* appreciation
agregar (gu) to add
agrícola agricultural
aguacate *m.* avocado
aguacero *m.* downpour
aguantar to endure, bear, tolerate
águila *f.* eagle
ahogar(se) (gu) to drown
ahora now; **ahora mismo** right now
ahorrar to save
aire *m.* air; **al aire libre** out-of-doors
ajedrez *m.* chess
ajeno, -a foreign; of or belonging to another
albaricoque *m.* apricot
alborotado, -a excited
alcalde(-esa) mayor
alcance *m.* reach
alcanzar (c) to reach, to overtake
alegrarse (de) to be glad

alejar to separate; **alejarse (de)** to move away from

alergia *f.* allergy

alfombra *f.* rug, carpet

algo something, anything

algodón *m.* cotton

alguien someone, somebody, anyone

alguno, -a some, any

alimenticio, -a nourishing, nutritious

allá there

allí there

alma *f.* soul

almohada *f.* pillow

almorzar (ue, c) to eat lunch

alojamiento *m.* lodging

alpinismo *m.* mountain climbing

alquilar to rent

alto, -a tall

alzar (c) to lift

amabilidad *f.* kindness

amanecer (zc) to dawn; **al amanecer** at dawn

ambiente *m.* atmosphere, environment

ambulancia *f.* ambulance

amenazar (c) to threaten

amigable *m. & f. adj.* friendly

amigo(-a) friend

amistad *f.* friendship

amo(-a) master, mistress, owner, boss

amplio, -a ample, large

analfabetismo *m.* illiteracy

ancho, -a wide

anciano, -a aged, old; *m.* old man, *f.* old woman

andar *irr.* to walk

anexar to annex

anfitrión(-ona) host(ess)

angosto, -a narrow

anillo *m.* ring

animado, -a animated, lively

animar to animate; to encourage

año *m.* year; **el año escolar** school year

anoche last night

añoranza *f.* nostalgia

añorar to recall with nostalgia

anotar to make notes on

antemano: de antemano previously; beforehand

anteojos *m. pl.* eyeglasses

antes (de) before

antigüedad *f.* antique, antiquity

antiguo, -a old, ancient

antipático, -a unpleasant, disagreeable

antojo *m.* whim

anuncio *m.* announcement

apagar (gu) to put out; **apagarse** to shut off

aparato *m.* ride (amusement park), apparatus

apellido *m.* last name; **apellido de soltera** maiden name

aplauso *m.* applause

aplicado, -a studious, smart

aplicar (qu) to apply

apoderarse (de) to take possession of

apoyo *m.* support

aprender to learn; **aprender de memoria** to memorize

aprendizaje *m.* learning

apresurarse (a) to hurry

apretar (ie) to tighten, to squeeze

aprovecharse (de) to avail oneself (of); to profit (by); to take unfair advantage (of)

apuntar to note, to write down

aquí here

árbol *m.* tree

arbusto *m.* shrub

arena *f.* sand

argentino(-a) Argentine person; also *adj.* **argentino, -a** Argentine

argumento *m.* plot

armar to assemble, put together

armario *m.* closet

arpa *f.* harp

arquitecto(-a) architect

arquitectura *f.* architecture

arrancar (qu) to root out, to pull out

arreglar to arrange, fix

arrepentirse (ie) (de) to repent, to regret

arte *f.* **(el arte)** art

artista *m. & f.* artist

ascendencia *f.* ancestry

ascender (ie) to promote

ascensor *m.* elevator

asegurar to assure

así so; thus

asiento *m.* seat

asistencia *f.* attendance

asistir (a) to attend

asomarse to lean out

aspiradora *f.* vaccum cleaner

astronauta *m. & f.* astronaut

astuto, -a astute, clever

asunto *m.* subject matter; affair

asustarse to be frightened

atacar (qu) to attack

aterrizar to land

atracciones *f. pl.* attractions; **parque de atracciones** amusement park

atraer *irr.* to attract

atraso *m.* delay, lag

atravesar (ie) to cross

atreverse (a) to dare (to)

auditorio *m.* auditorium

aula *f.* classroom

aumentar to increase

aumento *m.* raise, increase

aún still

aunque although, even though, even if

ausente *m. & f. adj.* absent

auténtico, -a authentic

autobús *m.* bus

autógrafo *m.* autograph

auxilio *m.* help, aid

avanzar (c) to advance

ave *f.* bird
avión *m.* airplane
aviso *m.* notice
ayer yesterday
ayudante *m. & f.* helper
azar *m.* chance; **al azar** at random
azotar to beat; to lash; to whip
azúcar *m. & f* sugar
azucarero *m.* sugar bowl

bajar to go down, descend; to lower; **bajar(se) de** to get off (the bus, train, etc.)
bañarse to take a bath, to bathe
banco *m.* bank; bench
bandera *f.* flag
barato, -a cheap, inexpensive
barco *m.* boat; **barco de vela** sailboat
barrer to sweep
barrera *f.* barrier, fence
barrio *m.* neighborhood
bastar to be enough, to suffice
basura *f.* garbage
bata *f.* robe
baúl *m.* trunk
bebé *m. & f.* baby
beca *f.* scholarship
belleza *f.* beauty; **salón de belleza** beauty parlor
bello, -a beautiful; **bellas artes** *f.* fine arts
beneficiado(-a) beneficiary
beneficio *m.* benefit
bienvenida *f.* welcome
bilingüe *m & f. adj.* bilingual
billete *m.* ticket
bloque *m.* block
bloqueo *m.* blockade
boda *f.* wedding
bodega *f.* grocery
boleto *m.* ticket
bolsa *f.* bag; **la Bolsa** *f.* stock market
bolsillo *m.* pocket
bombero(-era) firefighter

bondadoso, -a kind
borrador *m.* eraser; draft
bosque *m.* woods
bostezar (c) to yawn
bota *f.* boot
breve brief
brincar (qu) to jump
brindis *m.* toast
broma *f.* joke
bronce *m.* bronze
broncear to tan
brújula *f.* compass
bucear to snorkel; to dive
bueno, -a good
burlarse (de) to make fun (of)
buscar (qu) to look for, seek
búsqueda *f.* search
buzón *m.* mailbox

caballo *m.* horse
caber *irr.* to fit, to be room for
cada each, every
cadena *f.* chain
caer(se) *irr.* to fall
cafetera *f.* coffee maker
caja *f.* box; cashier, cash register; safe
cajón *m.* drawer
calculadora *f.* calculator
calentamiento *m.* heating
caliente *m. & f. adj.* warm
calificación *f.* grade
callar(se) to be silent, to be quiet
calor *m.* heat
camarón *m.* shrimp
cambiar to change
cambio *m.* change
caminar to walk
camino *m.* road, path
camión *m.* truck
campamento *m.* camp
campana *f.* bell
campaña *f.* campaign
campeonato *m.* championship
campesino(-a) farmer
campo *m.* country, field

canadiense *m. & f.* Canadian person; *also m. & f. adj.* Canadian
canal *m.* channel (television)
canasta *f.* basket
candelero *m.* candlestick
candidato(-a) candidate
canela *f.* cinnamon
canoa *f.* canoe
cansado, -a tired
cantante *m. & f.* singer
cántaro *m.* earthen jug; **llover a cántaros** to rain cats and dogs
cantidad *f.* quantity
cantimplora *f.* canteen, thermos
canto *m.* song; singing
capa *f.* cape
cara *f.* face
carácter *m.* character, personality
característica *f.* characteristic
carecer (zc) (de) to lack
cargar (gu) to charge; to load
caridad *f.* charity
cariñoso, -a loving
carne *f.* meat
carpeta *f.* file folder
carpintero(-a) carpenter
carretera *f.* highway, road
carril *m.* lane
carrito *m.* cart
carro *m.* car
carrusel *m.* merry-go-round
carta *f.* setter
cartel *m.* poster
cartera *f.* wallet
cartero(-a) mail carrier
casa *f.* house
casarse (con) to marry
caseta *f.* small house, cottage
castigar (gu) to punish
castillo *m.* castle
catalán *m.* Catalonian language; *also adj.*
catalán, -ana Catalonian
cavar to dig

cazar (c) to hunt

centro *m.* center, downtown; **centro comercial** mall

cepillarse to brush (one's hair, teeth, clothes)

cerca (de) near; close to

cerdo *m.* pork

ceremonia *f.* ceremony

cereza *f.* cherry

cerradura *f.* lock

cerrar (ie) to close

certamen *m.* contest

césped *m.* lawn, grass

champú *m.* shampoo

chaqueta *f.* jacket

charla *f.* chat

charlar to chat

chicle *m.* gum

chisme *m.* rumor, gossip

chiste *m.* joke

chistoso, -a funny, humorous

chocar (qu) to crash

chofer *m. & f.* driver

ciclo *m.* cycle

cielo *m.* sky

cien (ciento) one hundred; **por ciento** percent

ciencia *f.* science

cine *m.* movies (movie theater)

cinturón *m.* belt

circular to circulate

cita *f.* appointment

ciudad *f.* city

ciudadano(-a) citizen

clavel *m.* carnation

clima *m.* climate

clínica *f.* clinic

cobrar to charge

cocer (ue, z) to cook

cocinero (-era) cook

código *m.* code

coger (j) to seize, to grasp, to catch

cohete *m.* rocket

cojear to limp

cola *f.* line (of people); **hacer cola** to get on line

colchón *m.* mattress

coleccionar to collect

colega *m. & f.* colleague

colegiatura *f.* tuition

colegio *m.* school

colgar (gu) to hang

collar *m.* necklace

colocar (qu) to place, to put

comedor *m.* dining room

comenzar (ie, c) to begin

comerciante *m. & f.* business person

cometer to commit; **cometer un error** to make a mistake

comida *f.* meal, food

como as; **¿cómo?** how?

cómoda *f.* dresser

cómodo, -a comfortable

compañero(-a) companion

compañía *f.* company

compartir to share

competencia *f.* competition

competidor(-ora) contestant

componer *irr.* to compose

compra *f.* purchase

comprador(-ora) buyer

comprar to buy

comprender to understand

comprobar (ue) to prove

comprometido(-a) fiancé, fiancée

compromiso *m.* appointment; engagement

computadora *f.* computer

comunicar to communicate

con with; **con tal que** provided that

concertar (ie) to arrange

concluir (y) to conclude, to end

concurrencia *f.* attendance; gathering

concurso *m.* contest

conde *m.* count (*f.* **condesa** countess)

condominio *m.* condominium

conducir (zc) (j) to drive

confección *f.* confection, preparation

confeccionar to prepare; to make

conferencia *f.* conference

confesar (ie) to confess

confiar (en) (í) to rely (on), to confide (in)

conforme a according to, in accordance with

confundir to confuse

congelar to freeze

conmover (ue) to move (emotionally)

conocer (zc) to know (a person)

conseguir (i, g) to get, to obtain, to succeed in

consejo *m.* advice; **consejo de estudiantes** student council

consentido, -a pampered, spoiled

consentir (ie, i) to consent; to pamper

conserva *f.* conserve; preserve

conservador, -ora conservative

conservar to keep

consolar to console

construir (y) to construct

consulta *f.* consultation

consultorio *m.* office (medical)

contado: al contado cash

contador(-ora) accountant

contar (ue) to count; to tell; **contar con (ue)** to count on

contener *irr.* to contain

contestación *f.* response, answer

contestar to answer, to respond

continuar (ú) to continue

contraer *irr.* to catch, get

contraseña *f.* password

contribuir (y) to contribute

convencer (z) to convince

convenir(se) *irr.* to convene, to agree; to fit, to suit someone, to be good for someone

convertir (ie, i) to convert

corazón *m.* heart

corbata *f.* tie

coreano, -a Korean

coro *m.* chorus

corregir (i) (j) to correct

correo, *m.* mail; post office

correr to run

correspondencia *f.* correspondence

corte *f.* court

corte *m.* cutting (garment)

cortesía *f.* courtesy

cortina *f.* curtain

corto, -a short

coser to sew

costar (ue) to cost

costarricense *m. & f. adj.* Costa Rican

costumbre *f.* custom

costura *f.* sewing; **alta costura** high fashion

crear to create

crecer (zc) to grow

creer to believe

creíble credible, believable

crimen *m.* crime

crítico, -a critical

cronómetro *m.* stop watch

crucero *m.* cruise

cuadra *f.* (street) block

¿cuál(-es)? which one(s)?

cualidad *f.* quality

cualquier(-a) any; whatever

cuando when; **¿cuándo?** when?; **cuandoquiera** whenever

cuanto, -a as much; **¿cuánto (-a)?** how much?; **¡cuánto, -a!** how much ...!; **¿cuántos (-as)?** how many?; **¡cuántos (-as)** ...! How many ...!

cuarto *m.* room

cubiertos *m. pl.* cutlery, utensils

cubrir to cover

cucharada *f.* tablespoon

cucharadita *f.* teaspoon

cuenta *f.* bill, (restaurant) check

cuento *m.* story

cuidado *m.* care

cuidadoso, -a careful

cuidar to take care of;

cuidarse to take care of oneself

culinario, -a culinary

culpa *f.* guilt; blame; **tener la culpa** to be guilty; to be to blame

cumpleaños *m. sing. & pl.* birthday

cumplir to fulfill, to accomplish; **cumplir con la palabra** to keep one's word

cupo *m.* quota

cura *m.* priest; *also f.* cure

curar to cure

curso *m.* course

cuyo, -a whose

dañar to damage

danza *f.* dance

dar to give; **dar con** to meet; **dar vuelta** to turn

datar to date

dato *m.* datum, fact

de of, from; **de hecho** in fact; **de repente** suddenly; **de manera (de modo) que** so that

debajo (de) under, beneath

debate *m.* debate

deber to have to (should, ought), to owe

débito *m.* debit

decena *f.* a quantity of ten

decir *irr.* to say, to tell

decisión *f.* decision; **tomar una decisión** to make a decision

declamación *f.* declamation, recitation

declamar to recite

declaración *f.* declaration, statement

defender (ie) to defend

dejar to let, allow, leave (behind)

delante (de) in front of, ahead of

delantero, -a foremost; first

delicado, -a delicate

demandado(-a) defendant; accused

demandar to sue

demasiado too much, too many

demora *f.* delay

dentista *m. & f.* dentist

dependiente *m. & f.* clerk, salesperson

deportista *m. & f.* sportsperson

deportivo, -a pertaining to sports, sporty

depósito *m.* deposit; depository

deprimido, -a depressed

derecho, -a right; **derecho** straight ahead; **derecho** *m.* right; **derechos humanos** human rights

derrota *f.* defeat

desafío *m.* challenge

desaparecer (zc) to disappear

desarraigar (gu) to uproot

desarrollar to develop

desarrollo *m.* development

desastroso, -a disastrous

desayunar(se) to have breakfast

descansar to rest

descender (ie) to descend, to decline

descortés *m. & f. adj.* discourteous

desde from; since

desechable *m. & f. adj.* disposable

desfile *m.* parade

deshacer to melt, to mash

desilusionar to disillusion, to disappoint

deslizarse (c) to slip, to glide

desmayarse to faint

despacio slowly

despedida *f.* farewell

despedir (i) to fire;
despedirse (de) to take leave
(of), **to say goodbye (to)**

despegar (gu) to take off
(airplane)

despertar(se) (ie) to awaken,
wake up

después later; **después de**
after; **después de que** after

destacado, -a outstanding

destreza *f.* skill

destruir (y) to destroy

desván *m.* attic

detallado, -a detailed

detalle *m.* detail

detener *irr.* to detain

detrás de behind

devolución *f.* return

devolver (ue) to return
(something); to give back

día *m.* day

diálogo *m.* dialog

diario *m.* diary; newspaper;
a diaro daily

dibujo *m.* drawing; **dibujos
animados** cartoons

dificultad *f.* difficulty

diligencia *f.* errand

dineral *m.* a large sum of
money

dinero *m.* money

dirección *f.* address

dirigir (j) to direct; **dirigirse
(j)** to make one's way
toward; to address

disco *m.* record, disk;
disco compacto CD

disculpa *f.* excuse, apology

discutir to discuss, to argue

diseñador(-ora) designer

diseñar to design

disfraz *m.* disguise

disfrutar to enjoy

disponer *irr.* to dispose;

disponerse (a) to get ready (to)

disponible available

distinguir (g) to distinguish

distraer *irr.* to distract

distraído, -a distracted

distribuir (y) to distribute

divertido, -a amusing

divertirse (ie) (i) to enjoy
oneself

doblar to turn; to fold.

docena *f.* dozen

documental *m.* documentary

dólar *m.* dollar

doler (ue) to ache, to pain

dolor *m.* pain, ache; **tener
dolor de muelas** to have
a toothache

domingo *m.* Sunday

donativo *m.* donation

donde where; **¿dónde?**
**where?; ¿adónde? (to)
where?; ¿de dónde?** (from)
where?; **dondequiera**
wherever

dormir (ue) (u) to sleep;

dormirse to fall asleep

dosis *f.* dosage

ducharse to take a shower

duda *f.* doubt

dudar to doubt

dudoso doubtful

dueño(-a) owner

dulce *m.* candy; *also m. & f.
adj.* sweet

durante during

durar to last

duro, -a hard

echar to throw; **echar al
correo** to mail

edificio *m.* building

editorial *f.* publishing house

educar (qu) to educate

efectivo *m.* cash

eficaz *m. &. f. adj.* efficient

ejercer (z) to exert, to exercise
or practice (profession)

ejercicio *m.* exercise

elaborador(-ora) *m.*
manufacturer

elección *f.* election

electrónico, -a electronic

elegir (i, j) to elect

elogiado, -a praised

embarcar(se) (qu) to embark

emisora *f.* broadcasting station

emocionante *m. & f. adj.*
exciting

empanada *f.* meat pie

empapelado *m.* wallpaper

empeñarse (en) to be
determined (to); to insist on

empezar (ie) (c) to begin

empleado(-a) employee

empresa *f.* enterprise; business

en in, on; **en seguida**
immediately; **en cuanto**
as soon as

encaje *m.* lace

encantado, -a enchanted;
haunted

encargado(-a) person in charge

encargar (gu) to put in
charge; to entrust; to order

encender (ie) to light; to ignite

encerrar (ie) to lock in, to
contain; **encerrarse** to lock
oneself; to seclude oneself

enchufar to plug in, to connect

encima (de) on top of

encontrar (ue) to find, to meet

encuesta *f.* survey, poll

enfadarse to get angry

enfermero(-a) nurse

enfermo(-a) sick person,
patient; *also adj.* sick, ill

enfrenar to brake

engañar to deceive

engañoso, -a deceitful

engrasar to grease

enjuagar to rinse

enojarse to get angry
ensayar to rehearse
ensayo *m.* essay; rehearsal
enseñar to teach; to show
entablar to start; **entablar amistad** to start a friendship
entender (ie) to understand
enterado, -a informed; aware
enterarse (de) to find out about
entero, -a entire
entrada *f.* entrance, entry; ticket
entre among
entregar (gu) to deliver, to hand over
entrenador(-ora) trainer
entrenamiento *m.* training
entretener *irr.* to entertain
entrevista *f.* interview
entristecer (z) to become sad, to sadden
entusiasmado, -a enthusiastic
enviar (í) to send
envidioso, -a envious
envolver (ue) to wrap
época *f.* epoch, era
equipo *m.* team; equipment
equitación *f.* horsemanship
equivocación *f.* error, mistake
equivocarse (qu) to be mistaken
escaparse (de) to escape (from)
escasez *f.* scarcity
escenario *m.* scenery
escocés(-esa) Scotch; *also adj.* Scottish
escoger (j) to choose, to select
esconder to hide; **esconderse** to hide oneself
escribir to write
escritorio *m.* desk
escuchar to listen
esforzarse (ue, c) to exert oneself
esfuerzo *m.* effort; **coordinación de esfuerzo** team work

esmeralda *f.* emerald
eso that
espacio *m.* space
español(-ola) Spaniard; *also adj.* Spanish
espantar to frighten
especie *f.* species, kind
espejo *m.* mirror
esperanza *f.* hope
esperar to wait for, to await, to hope, to expect
espiar (í) to spy
espíritu *m.* spirit
esposo(-a) spouse
esquiar (í) to ski
establecer (zc) to establish
estación *f.* season; station
estacionamiento *m.* parking
estadio *m.* stadium
estado *m.* state
estampilla *f.* stamp
estancia *f.* stay
estanco *m.* (tobacco) store
estar *irr.* to be; **estar conforme (con)** to be in agreement (with), to agree
estelar *m. & f. adj.* stellar
estilo *m.* style
estirar to stretch
estornudar to sneeze
estrechar la mano to shake hands
estrella *f.* star
estrenar to open (a film, play)
estreno *m.* opening (movie)
estuche *m.* case
etapa *f.* stage, phase
exigencia *f.* demand
exigir (j) to demand, to require
existencia *f.* stock
éxito *m.* success; **tener éxito** to be successful
exitoso, -a successful
experiencia *f.* experience
explicar (qu) to explain
explorador *m.* boy scout

exploradora *f.* girl scout
exponer *irr.* to expose
extinguir (g) to extinguish
extrañar to miss
extranjero, -a foreign

fábrica *f.* factory
fabricar (qu) to make, to manufacture
factibilidad *f.* feasibility
factible *m. & f. adj.* feasible
falda *f.* skirt
fallar to miss; to fail
falta *f.* lack; error, mistake
faltar to lack
fanático(-a) fan
farmacia *f.* pharmacy
faro *m.* lighthouse
farol *m.* (street) lamp
fecha *f.* date; **fecha de nacimiento** date of birth
fécula de maíz corn starch
felicidad *f.* happiness
felicitar to congratulate
feliz *m. & f. adj.* happy
feria *f.* fair
feroz *m. & f. adj.* ferocious
ferrocarril railroad
fiarse (í) (de) to trust
fibra *f.* fiber
fiel *m. & f. adj.* faithful
figurarse to imagine
fijarse (en) to stare (at), to notice
fijo, -a fixed
fin *m.* end; **fin de semana** weekend; **a fin (de) que** in order that, so that
fingir (j) to pretend
físico, -a physical
flor *f.* flower
foca *f.* seal
folleto *m.* pamphlet
fórmula *f.* formula
foro *m.* stage
fotografía *f.* photograph

francés *m.* French language,
   Frenchman (*f.* **francesa**
   Frenchwoman)
frase *f.* sentence
frente *f.* forehead;   **de frente**
   straight ahead;   **frente a**
   facing, in front of
fresa *f.* strawberry
fresco, -a fresh
frío *m.* cold;   **hacer frío**
   to be cold (*weather*);
   tener frío to be cold
frito, -a fried
fuego *m.* fire
fuente *f.* fountain
fuera de outside of
fuerte *m. & f. adj.* strong; loud
fuerza *f.* force; strength
función *f.* function, showing
funcionamiento *m.*
   performance, operation
funcionar to function, to work
funcionario(-a) public official,
   civil servant

galería *f.* gallery
galleta *f.* cookie, cracker
gana *f.* desire;   **tener ganas**
   de to feel like
ganar to win; to earn
garaje *m.* garage
gastronomía *f.* gastronomy
gemelo(-a) twin
gemir (i) to groan, to moan
genial *m. & f. adj.* brillant
gente *f.* people
gerente *m. & f.* manager
gimnasio *m.* gym
globo *m.* balloon
gobernar (ie) to govern
gol *m.* goal
golosina *f.* sweet
goma *f.* rubber
gorra *f.* cap
gozar (c) to enjoy
grabado *m.* engraving, print
gracioso, -a cute, adorable

graduarse (ú) to graduate
gramática *f.* grammar
granja *f.* farm
gratuito, -a free, free of charge
griego m. Greek language;
   griego(-a) Greek
   (nationality); *also adj.* Greek
grito *m.* shout
gruñir to growl
guardar to keep; to store
gubernativo, -a governmental
guía *m.* guide; *also f.* guidebook
guiar (í) to guide; to drive
guión *m.* script
gustar to please

haba *f.* fava bean
haber to have (*aux. verb*)
hábil *m. & f. adj.* skillful; clever
hablar to speak
hacer *irr.* to make, to do;
hacer caso to heed, to listen to
hacia toward
hasta until;   **hasta que** until
hazaña *f.* deed
hebilla *f.* buckle
heladera *f.* refrigerator
heladería *f.* ice cream shop
helado *m.* ice cream
helar (ie) to freeze
helicóptero *m.* helicopter
herencia *f.* heredity; inheritance
herido, -a injured
hermana *f.* sister
hermano *m.* brother; *pl.*
   brothers, brothers and sisters
hervido, -a boiled
hervir (ie, i) to boil
hijo *m.* son; *pl.* sons, children
hogar *m.* home
hoguera *f.* bonfire
hoja *f.* leaf
hombre *m.* man
hora *f.* tour;   **hora punta**
   rush hour
horario *m.* schedule
horno *m.* oven

hoyo *m.* hole
huelga *f.* strike
hueso *m.* bone
huésped *m. & f.* guest
huevo *m.* egg
huir (y) to flee
humor *m.* humor; disposition,
   mood

idioma *m.* language
iglesia *f.* church
imaginarse to imagine
impedir (i) to prevent
impermeable *m.* raincoat
imponer *irr.* to impose
impuesto *m.* tax
inasistencia *f.* lack of
   attendance, absence
inauguración *f.* inauguration,
   opening
incertidumbre *f.* uncertainty
incluir (y) to include
indeciso, -a undecided;
   indecisive
indicar (qu) to indicate
indígena *m. & f. adj.*
   indigenous, native
índole *f.* nature; kind; class
inesperado, -a unexpected
inestablidad *f.* instability
inflar to inflate
influir (y) to influence,
   to have influence
ingeniería *f.* engineering
ingeniero(-a) engineer
inglés *m.* English language,
   Englishman; (*f.* **inglesa**
   Englishwoman); *also adj.*
   inglés, inglesa English
inolvidable unforgettable
inquilino(-a) tenant
inscribirse to register
insistir (en) to insist on
insoportable unbearable
intercambio *m.* exchange
interés *m.* interest
intérprete *m. & f.* interpreter

interrumpir to interrupt
interruptor *m.* electric switch
inundar to flood
invento *m.* invention
investigación *f.* research
invierno *m.* winter
invitación *f.* invitation
ir to go; **irse** to leave, to go away
isla *f.* island
italiano *m.* Italian language, Italian man; **italiana** *f.* Italian woman; *also adj.* **italiano, -a** Italian
izquierdo, -a left

jabón *m.* soap
jacatarse (de) to boast; to brag
jamás never, (not) ever
japonés Japanese language, Japanese man (*f.* **japonesa** Japanese woman); *also adj.* **japonés, -esa** Japanese
jardín *m.* garden
jardinero(-a) gardener
jarra *f.* pitcher, carafe
jefe(-a) chief, head
jornada *f.* day's work
joven *m. & f.* young person; *also m. & f. adj.* young
joyería *f.* jewelry
jubilarse to retire
juego *m.* game; **juego de mesa** table game
juez *m. & f.* judge
jugada *f.* play
jugador(-ora) player
jugar (ue) to play (games, sports)
jugo *m.* juice
juguete *m.* toy
juguetería *f.* toy store
juntar to join; to gather
junto together
juvenil *m. & f. adj.* juvenile

labio *m.* lip
laboratorio *m.* laboratory

lácteo, -a lacteal; milky
lado *m.* side; **por todos lados** everywhere
lago *m.* lake
lámpara *f.* lamp
lana *f.* wool
lanzar (c) to hurl, throw; to launch; **lanzarse** to throw oneself, to enter
largo, -a long
lástima *f.* pity, compassion
lastimar to hurt; **lastimarse** to hurt oneself
lata *f.* can
lavacoches *m. sing. & pl.* car wash
lavandería *f.* laundry
lavar to wash; **lavarse** to wash oneself
leal *m. & f. adj.* loyal
lección *f.* lesson
lector(-ora) reader
leer to read
legumbre *m.* vegetable
lento, -a slow
letra *f.* letter
levantarse to get up
ley *f.* law
libertad *f.* liberty
libra *f.* pound
librería *f.* book store
librero *m.* bookcase
libro *m.* book
licencia *f.* license
licuadora *f.* blender
limitar to limit
limonada *f.* lemonade
limpiar to clean
limpio, -a clean
listo, -a ready; **estar listo, -a** to be ready; **ser listo, -a** to be clever
liviano, -a lightweight
llamada *f.* call
llamarse to be named, to be called
llamativo, -a gaudy

llanta *f.* tire
llave *f.* key
llavero *m.* key ring
llegada *f.* arrival
llegar (gu) to arrive; **llegar a ser** to become
llenar to fill
lleno, -a full
llevar to carry, to wear; **llevar a cabo** to carry out
llorar to cry
llover (ue) to rain
loción *f.* lotion
locutor(-ora) announcer
lograr to achieve, to attain; to succeed in
logro *m.* achievement
loro *m.* parrot
luego then; **luego que** as soon as
lugar *m.* place; **tener lugar** to take place; **en lugar de** instead of
lujoso, -a luxurious
luna *f.* moon
lunes *m.* Monday

madre *f.* mother
madrugar (gu) to rise early
mago *m.* magician
malabarista *m. & f.* juggler
malcriado, -a illbred; spoiled; pampered
maleta *f.* suitcase
malla *f.* sweater
malo, -a evil, bad
mañana tomorrow; *m.* future; *f.* morning; **de la mañana** A.M.
mancha *f.* stain
mandar to send, to order
mandato *m.* command
manejar to drive
manga *f.* sleeve
maniquí *m.* mannequin
mano *f.* hand
manteca *f.* lard, fat; grease

mantener *irr.* to maintain
mantenido, -a maintained
manzana *f.* apple
mapa *m.* map
maquillarse to put on makeup
máquina *f.* machine
mar *m.* sea
maratón *m.* marathon
marcar (qu) to designate,
   to mark; to dial
marcharse to leave, to go away
marco *m.* (picture) frame
mareado, -a dizzy
marginar to marginalize;
   to exclude
marido *m.* husband
marinar to marinade
martes *m.* Tuesday
mascar (qu) to chew
mascota *f.* mascot, pet
masticar (qu) to chew
material *f.* subject
matrícula *f.* enrollment,
   registration
mayor older, greater
mayoría *f.* majority
mecánico, -a mechanical
medalla *f.* medal
mediano, -a medium
medianoche *f.* midnight
médico(-a) doctor
medio, -a half
medioambiente *m.*
   environment
mediodía *m.* noon
medir (i) to measure
mejor better; best
mejorar to improve
melocotón *m.* peach
melón *m.* melon
menester *m.* need;
   es menester it is necessary
menor lesser, younger
menos less; **a menos**
   que unless
mensaje *m.* message

mentira *f.* lie
merecer (zc) to deserve
merecido, -a deserved
merienda *f.* snack
mes *m.* month
mesa *f.* table
mesera *f.* waitress
mesero *m.* waiter
meta *f.* goal
metro *m.* subway
mezcla *f.* mix, mixture, blend
miedo *m.* fear; **tener miedo**
   (de) to fear, to be afraid
miel *f.* honey
mientras while
miércoles *m.* Wednesday
miga *f.* crumb
mismo, -a same; **sí mismo, -a**
   himself, herself
mochila *f.* backpack, book
   bag, knapsack
moda *f.* fashion
modista *f.* seamstress
modo *m.* way; **de todos**
   modos anyway
mojar to wet
molde *m.* baking dish
molestar to bother, to annoy
molido, -a ground
monopatín *m.* skateboard
montaña *f.* mountain;
   montaña rusa rollercoaster
montar to ride; **montar**
   a caballo to go horseback
   riding; **montar en bicicleta**
   to ride a bicycle
morder (ue) to bite
morir (ue) to die
mostrador *m.* showcase
mostrar (ue) to show
mover (ue) to move
muchedumbre *f.* crowd
mucho, -a a lot, many
mudarse to move
mueble *m.* piece of furniture
mugido *m.* moo (*sound*)

mujer *f.* woman
muleta *f.* crutch
mundial *m. & f. adj.* world
mundo *m.* world; **todo el**
   mundo everyone
muñeca *f.* doll
mutuo, -a mutual

nacer (zc) to be born
nacionalidad *f.* nationality
nada nothing, (not) anything;
   de nada (por nada) you're
   welcome
nadador(-ora) swimmer
nadar to swim
nadie no one, nobody, (not)
   anyone
natación *f.* swimming
natal *m. & f. adj.* native,
   birth place
Navidad *f.* Christmas
necesitar to need
negar (gu) (ie) to deny;
   negarse (a) to refuse (to)
negocio *m.* business
nervio *m.* nerve
nevada *f.* snowfall
nevar (ie) to snow
ni... ni neither . . . nor, not . . .
   nor; **ni siquiera** not even;
   ni yo tampoco me neither
nido *m.* nest
nieta *f.* granddaughter
nieto *m.* grandson; *pl.*
   grandsons, grandchildren
niñez *f.* childhood
ninguno, -a no, none, (not) any
niña *f.* girl
niño *m.* boy; *pl.* boys, children
nivel *m.* level
noche *f.* night; **esta noche**
   tonight
nocivo, -a hazardous,
   dangerous
noticia *f.* news
noticiero *m.* news show

novedad *f.* bit of news
novela *f.* novel
novia *f.* girlfriend
novio *m.* boyfriend
nube *f.* cloud
nuestro, -a our
nuevo, -a new
número *m.* number; **número de cuenta** account number
numeroso, -a numerous
nunca never, (not) ever; **nunca más** never again

o or; **o... o** either . . . or
obedecer (zc) to obey
obligar (gu) to obligate, to compel
obra *f.* work; **obra de teatro, obra teatral** play
obstante: no obstante in spite of
obtener *irr.* to obtain
ocupado, -a busy, occupied
odiar to hate
oeste *m.* west
oferta *f.* offer
ofrecer (zc) to offer
oír *irr.* to hear
¡ojalá! God grant that . . !, Would that . . !
ola *f.* wave
oler (hue) to smell
oloroso, -a fragrant
olvidar to forget; **olvidarse (de)** to forget
oponer(se) *irr.* to oppose
optimista *m. & f.* optimist; *also m. & f. adj.*
orden *f.* order, command
ordenador *m.* computer
ordenar to order
organizar (c) to organize
orgulloso, -a proud
oro *m.* gold
orquesta *f.* orchestra
oscilar to oscillate, to vary

oscuro, -a dark
oso *m.* bear
otoño *m.* autumn
otro, -a other, another; **otra vez** again

paciencia *f.* patience
padecer (zc) to suffer
padre *m.* father
pagar (gu) to pay (for)
país *m.* country
pálido, -a pale
palo *m.* stick, club; **palos de golf** golf clubs
pan *m.* bread
pantalla *f.* screen
pantufla *f.* slipper
pañuelo *m.* handkerchief
papa *f.* potato
papel *m.* paper; role; **papel de celofán** waxed paper
papelería *f.* stationery store
para for, (in order) to; **para que** so that, in order that; **¿para qué?** why (for what purpose?)
parabrisas *m.* windshield
paracaídas *m. sing. & pl.* parachute
parada *f.* stop
paraguas *m. sing. & pl.* umbrella
parar to stop
parecer (zc) to seem; **parecerse (a)** to resemble
parecido, -a similar
pared *f.* wall
parque *m.* park
párrafo *m.* paragraph
parrilla *f.* grill
participar to participate
participio *m.* participle
partidario(-a) follower; supporter
partido *m.* game
pasado, -a past; **pasado**

mañana day after tomorrow
pasajero(-a) passenger
pasar to pass, spend (time)
pasearse to take a walk
paso *m.* step; **paso a paso** step by step
pastel *m.* cake
pastilla *f.* lozenge, tablet
patín *m.* skate
patinar to skate
patria *f.* native country; fatherland, mother country
patrocinador(-ora) sponsor
patrocinar to sponsor
pavo *m.* turkey
payaso, -a clown
paz *f.* peace
peatón(-ona) pedestrian
pegar (gu) to stick, to glue; to hit, to strike (a blow)
peinarse to comb one's hair
pelear to fight
peligroso, -a dangerous
pelo *m.* hair
pelota *f.* ball
peluche: animal de peluche stuffed animal
pensar (ie) to think; to intend
peor worse
pequeño, -a small
perder (ie) to lose
perezoso, -a lazy
perfumería *f.* perfumery
periódico *m.* newspaper
periodismo *m.* journalism
periodista *m. & f.* reporter, journalist
permanecer (zc) to remain
permiso *m.* permission; **pedir permiso** to ask for permission
perro *m.* dog
perseguir (i, g) to pursue, to persecute
personalidad *f.* personality
pertenecer (zc) to belong

peruano(-a) Peruvian people;
also adj. Peruvian
pesadilla *f.* nightmare
pesado, -a heavy; tedious
pesar *m.* regret, sorrow;
a pesar de in spite of;
notwithstanding
pesa *f.* weight
(*exercise equipment*)
pescado *m.* fish
pescar (qu) to fish
picante *m. & f.* spicy
paciencia *f.* patience
pico, -a peak; **la hora pico**
rush hour
pie *m.* foot; **a pie** on foot
pieza *f.* piece
pijama *m.* pajama
piloto *m. & f.* pilot
pimienta *f.* pepper
pintar to paint
pintor(-ora) painter
pintura *f.* paint; painting
pirámide *f.* pyramid
pisar to step on
piscina *f.* swimming pool
piso *m.* floor
placa *f.* plate
placentero, -a pleasant
planear to plan
planificación *f.* planning;
planificación urbana urban
planning
plátano *m.* plantain
(similar to banana)
plática *f.* chat
plato *m.* dish, plate
playa *f.* beach
plomero, -a plumber
pobre *m. & f.* poor
podar to prune
poder (ue) to be able, can
policía *m. & f.* police officer;
f. police force
policial *m. & f. adj.* police
pollo *m.* chicken

polvo *m.* dust, powder
ponchado, -a punctured,
flattened
poner *irr.* to put; **poner la
mesa** to set the table;
ponerse to put on; to become
por qué why?
(for what reason?)
porcelana *f.* porcelain
porcentaje *m.* percentage
porque because; **¿por qué?**
why?
portapapeles *m. sing. & pl.*
folder
portarse to behave
porteño, -a from Buenos Aires,
Argentina
portero *m.* doorman
poseer (y) to possess
postre *m.* dessert
potable potable, drinkable
practicar (qu) to practice
práctico, -a practical
precio *m.* price
precoz *m. & f. adj.* precocious
predilecto, -a favorite
preferir (ie, i) to prefer
preguntar to ask
premio *m.* prize
prendedor *m.* pin
preocupado, -a worried
preparativo *m.* preparation
presentar to present,
introduce; **presentarse**
to introduce oneself
prestar to loan; **prestar
atención** to pay attention
prevenir *irr.* to prevent
prever to foresee
primaria *f.* elementary school
primavera *f.* spring
primo(-a) cousin
príncipe *m.* prince
(*f.* **princesa** princess)
principio *m.* beginning;
a principios in the beginning

prisa *f.* haste, promptness;
tener prisa to be in a hurry
privilegiar to favor
probarse (ue) to try on
proceso *m.* process
procurar to procure; to secure;
to try to
producir (zc) to produce
promesa *f.* promise
prometer to promise
pronto soon; **tan pronto
como** as soon as
propina *f.* tip
pronóstico *m.* forecast
proponer (*irr.*) to propose
proseguir (i, g) to continue,
to proceed
protagonista *m. & f.* main
character
proteger (j) to protect
proveedor(-ora) provider
prueba *f.* proof; test
psicólogo(-a) psychologist
publicar (qu) to publish
público, -a public; *also m.
noun* audience
pueblo *m.* town
puente *m.* bridge
puerta *f.* door
puertorriqueño(-a) Puerto
Rican person; *also adj.*
Puerto Rican
puesto *m.* position, post
pulsar to push
pulsera *f.* bracelet
puño *m.* fist

que that, which; **¡qué...!** what
...!, what a ...!, how ...!;
¿qué? what
quebrar (ie) to break
quedar to remain; **quedarle
bien** to look (fit) well;
quedarle a uno to have left;
quedarse to stay
quehacer *m.* chore, task, errand

quejarse (de) to complain
querer (ie) to want; to wish;
  to love
querido, -a dear
queso *m.* cheese
quien (*pl.* **quienes**) who;
  ¿quién,(-es)? who?;
  ¿a quién(-es)? whom?, to
  whom?; **¿con quién(-es)?**
  with whom?; **¿de quién(-es)?**
  whose? of whom?
quienquiera
  (*pl.* **quienesquiera**) whoever
químico(-a) chemist
quinceañera *f.* fifteen year old
quiosco *m.* kiosk
quitar to take away; **quitarse**
  to take off (clothing)
quizá(s) perhaps

radio *m.* radio (*appliance*); *f.*
  radio (*broadcasting system*)
radiolocutor(-ora) disk jockey
rascacielos *m. sing. & pl.*
  skyscraper
raspadilla *f.* snow cone
rato *m.* time
realizar to realize; to fulfill
rebajado, -a reduced
recado *m.* message
recaudar to collect
receta *f.* recipe, prescription
recetario *m.* recipe book
rechazar to reject
recibir to receive
recibo *m.* receipt
reciclaje *m.* recycling
recoger (j) to gather, to pick up
recompensa *f.* reward
reconocer (zc) to recognize
recordar (ue) to remember
recorrer to pass through
recreo *m.* recreation, recess
recuerdo *m.* souvenir
recurrir to resort, to have
  recourse

recurso *m.* resource
red *f.* net; network
reducir (zc) to reduce
referir (ie, i) to recount; to refer
reflexión *f.* reflection
refresco *m.* refreshment, soda
refugiarse to take refuge
regalar to give a gift
regalo *m.* gift, present
regaño *m.* scolding
regar (ie, gu) to water,
  to irrigate
regla *f.* rule; ruler
reglamento *m.* regulation
regresar to return
reina *f.* queen
reír (i) to laugh; **reír a
  carcajadas** to laugh
  hysterically; **reírse (de)** to
  laugh (at), to make fun (of)
relámpago *m.* lightening
reloj *m.* watch; clock
remedio *m.* remedy; **no hay
  remedio** it can't be helped
remendar (ie) to patch, to mend
remitir to refer
reñir (i) to quarrel, to scold
renovar (ue) to remodel,
  to renew
reparar to repair
repetir (i) to repeat
replicar (qu) to reply;
  to contradict (argue)
requisito *m.* requirement
reseña *f.* review; description
resfriarse (í) to catch cold
resolver (ue) to solve;
  to resolve
respaldo *m.* backing, support
respetar to respect
responder to respond, answer
resultado *m.* result
resumen *m.* summary
retirar to remove
retrospectiva *f.* retrospective
reunión *f.* meeting

reunirse to meet
revisar to review
revista *f.* magazine
rezar (c) to pray
rico, -a rich; delicious
rifa *f.* raffle
rociar to sprinkle
rodear to surround
rogar (gu) to ask for, to beg
romper to break
roncar (qu) to snore
ronquido *m.* snore
ropa *f.* clothing
roto, -a broken
rotular to label
ruido *m.* noise
ruso, -a Russian
ruta *f.* route
rutinario, -a routine

sábado *m.* Saturday
saber *irr.* to know
sabor *m.* flavor
saborear to savor
sacapuntas *m. sing. & pl.*
  pencil sharpener
sacar (qu) to take out; **sacar
  fotografías** to take pictures
sacarina *f.* saccharin
sacrificar (qu) to sacrifice
sacrificio *m.* sacrifice
sacudir to dust
sal *f.* salt
salir *irr.* to go out; to leave
salón *m.* room; **salón de
  espejos** hall of mirrors
salpullido *m.* (skin) rash
salsa *f.* sauce
salud *f.* health
saludar to greet
salvar to save
salvavidas *m. & f.* lifeguard;
  m. life preserver
sandía *f.* watermelon
sano, -a healthy
santo, -a saint

sazonar to season

secar (qu) to dry; **secarse** to dry oneself

sed *f.* thirst; **tener sed** to be thirsty

seda *f.* silk

seguir (i, g) to follow, to continue

según according to

seguridad *f.* security, safety

seguro, -a sure, safe; **seguro social** *m.* Social Security

semáforo *m.* traffic light

semana *f.* week

semanal *m. & f. adj.* weekly

semejante *m. & f.* similar

senador(-ora) senator

señal *f.* signal

sencillo, -a simple

sensitivo, -a sensitive

sentar(se) (ie) to seat, to sit down

sentir (ie, i) to regret, to feel sorry; **sentirse (ie, i)** to feel (well, ill)

sequía *f.* drought

ser *irr.* to be

serie *f.* series

serio, -a serious

serpiente *f.* snake

servidor *m.* server

servir (i) to serve

siempre always

siesta *f.* nap: **dormir la siesta** to take a nap

significar (qu) to mean

silbido *m.* whistle

silla *f.* chair; **sillas voladoras** flying swings

simbolizar to symbolize

simpatico, -a nice, pleasant

sin without; **sin embargo** nevertheless

sindicato *m.* union

sino but; only

síntesis *f.* synthesis

sirena *f.* siren

sitio *m.* place, site

smoking *m.* tuxedo

sobrar to be left over, to have too much

sobre on top of; *also m.* envelope

sobrina *f.* niece

sobrino *m.* nephew

socio(-a) member; **hacerse socio** to become a member

sol *m.* sun

soler (ue) to be in the habit of, to be accustomed to

solicitar to solicit, request

solicitud *f.* request

solo, -a alone

soltar to let out, to release

soltero, -a single (unmarried)

someterse to submit

soñar (ue) to dream

sonar (ue) to sound

sonido *m.* sound

sonreír(se) to smile

sopa *f.* soup

soporte *m.* support

sorprendente *m. & f. adj.* surprising

sorprenderse (de) to be surprised

sorpresa *f.* surprise

sorteo *m.* drawing (for a raffle)

sospechar to suspect

sostener *irr.* to sustain

sótano *m.* basement, cellar

subir to go up, to climb

subvencionado, -a subsidized

suceder to happen, occur

sucio, -a dirty

suegra f. mother-in-law

suegro *m.* father-in-law; **suegros** in-laws

sueldo *m.* salary

suelo *m.* ground

sueño *m.* dream; sleep; **tener sueño** to be sleepy

suerte *f.* luck; **tener suerte** to be lucky

suéter *m.* sweater

sugerencia *f.* suggestion

sujeto *m.* subject

superficie *f.* surface

suplicar (qu) to beg, to implore

surgir (j) to spurt up, to spring up

suscripción *f.* subscription

suscrito, -a subscribed

suspendido suspended; **salir suspendido** to fail

sustituir (y) to substitute

suyo, -a his, her, your, their

tabla *f.* table

tablao *m.* stage; **tablao flamenco** Flamenco show

tablero *m.* bulletin board

talentoso, -a talented

talla *f.* size

tamaño *m.* size

también also

tampoco neither, not either

tanto, -a so much, so many

tapar to cover

taquilla *f.* box office

tarde late; *also f.* afternoon

tarea *f.* homework, assignment

tarifa *f.* tariff, fare

tarjeta *f.* card; **tarjeta postal** postcard

taza *f.* cup

telefónico, -a telephonic

teléfono *m.* telephone; **teléfono celular** cellular telephone

televisor *m.* TV set

tema *m.* theme

temblar to shake

temblor *m.* earthquake

temer to fear

templado, -a temperate

temporada *f.* time; period of time; season

temprano early

tenedor *m.* fork
tener *irr.* to have; **tener que** to have to
tenis *m.* tennis; *m. pl.* sneakers
terminar to finish, end
testigo *m. & f.* witness
tía *f.* aunt
tiempo *m.* time; weather; **a tiempo** on time
tienda *f.* store; **tienda de campaña** tent
tigre *m.* tiger
tímido, -a shy
tintorería *f.* dry cleaner
tío *m.* uncle
tirar to throw
títere *m.* puppet
toalla *f.* towel
tobillo *m.* ankle
tocadiscos *m. sing. & pl.* record player
tocar (qu) to play (instrument); to touch; **tocarle a uno** to be someone's turn
todavía still, yet
todo, -a all, every
tomar to take
tómbola *f.* raffle
tonto, -a foolish
torcer (ue, z) to twist
tormenta *f.* storm
torneo *m.* tournament
toro *m.* bull
torpe *m. & f. adj.* clumsy
torre *f.* tower
tostadora *f.* toaster
trabajador(-ora) worker
trabajar to work
trabajo *m.* work
traducir (zc) to translate
traer *irr.* to bring
tráfico *m.* traffic
trago *m.* swallow, gulp
tramitar to process, to expedite
transmisión *f.* transmission, broadcast

transmitir to transmit, to broadcast
transporte *m.* transportation
trapo *m.* cloth
tras after
trasero, -a rear; back
tratamiento *m.* treatment
tratar de to try to; **tratarse (de)** to concern, to be a question (of)
través: a través de through, across
tren *m.* train
trigo *m.* wheat
tripulación *f.* crew
triste *m. & f. adj.* sad
tristeza *f.* sadness
tronar (ue) to thunder
tropezar (ie) (c) to stumble
trueno *m.* thunder
turno *m.* turn; **tomar turnos** to taken turns

último, -a last
uña *f.* nail; fingernail; toenail
único, -a only
unido, -a united, close
unos, -as some
usuario(-a) user
útil *m. & f. adj.* useful; **útiles** *m. pl.* school supplies
uva *f.* grape

vaca *f.* cow
vacante *f.* vacancy
vacío, -a empty
valer *irr.* to be worth
valiente *m. & f.* valient, courageous
valioso, -a valuable
valor *m.* value
vapor *m.* steamship
variar (í) to vary
varios, -as various
vaso *m.* drinking glass
vecindario *m.* neighborhood

vecino(-a) neighbor; *also adj.* **vecino, -a** neighboring
vela *f.* candle
velocidad *f.* speed
vencer (z) to conquer, to overcome
vendedor(-ora) salesperson
vender to sell
venir *irr.* to come
venta *f.* sale
ventaja *f.* advantage
ventilador *m.* fan
ver to see, to watch
verano *m.* summer
verdad *f.* truth
verdura *f.* greens, vegetable
verter (ie) to pour
vestido *m.* dress
vestirse (i) to get dressed
vez *f.* (*pl.* **veces**) time; **en vez de** instead of; **otra vez** again
vía *f.* track
viajar to travel
viaje *m.* trip
videocasete *m.* videocassette
videojuego *m.* video game
vidrio *m.* glass
viento *m.* wind
vitamina *f.* vitamin
vivo, -a alive
volantín *m.* kite
volar (ue) to fly
voluntario(-a) volunteer: *also adj.* voluntary
volver (ue) to return
vuelo *m.* flight; **vuelo de ida y vuelta** roundtrip flight

ya already; **ya no** no longer

zapatería *f.* shoe store
zoológico, -a zoological